Education and Social Justice

Education and Social Justice

Edited by

J. Zajda,
Australian Catholic University (Melbourne Campus), Australia

S. Majhanovich,
University of Western Ontario, Canada

V. Rust,
UCLA, USA

Springer

A C.I.P. Catalogue record for this book is available from the Library of Congress.

ISBN-10 1-4020-4721-5 (PB)
ISBN-13 978-1-4020-4721-3 (PB)
ISBN-10 1-4020-4722-3 (e-book)
ISBN-13 978-1-4020-4722-0 (e-book)

Published by Springer,
P.O. Box 17, 3300 AA Dordrecht, The Netherlands.

www.springer.com

Printed on acid-free paper

Printed in the Netherlands

CONTENTS

PREFACE

Education and Social Justice presents up-to-date scholarly research on *global* and comparative trends in education, social justice and policy research. It provides an easily accessible, practical yet scholarly source of information about the international concern in the field of social justice, globalisation, and policy research. Above all, the book offers the latest findings to the critical issues in education and social justice.

Education and Social Justice is a sourcebook of ideas for researchers, practitioners and policy makers in education, and social justice. It offers a timely overview of current changes in and social justice. It provides directions in education, social justice, and policy research, relevant to transformational educational reforms in the 21st century. The book explores the problematic relationship between education, social justice and the State, against the background of comparative education research. Social justice is an attempt to answer the following pressing question: How can we contribute to the creation of a more equitable, respectful, and just society for everyone? The creation of a more equitable, respectful, and just society for everyone is a dream for all concerned citizens on spaceship Earth, be they democratic policy makers, empowering and egalitarian pedagogues, and others, who believe in much needed reform. In an inaugural address given by the Minister of Education of the Republic of Cuba, at the 12th World Congress of the Comparative and International Education Society, on the theme Education and Social Justice, Luis Gómez Gutiérrez stressed the appalling conditions that disadvantaged people around the world live in today. He focused on illiteracy and the plight of children:

> Despite the commitments made by many nations to provide education for all, illiteracy continues to rise, forcing over 860 million adults to live in utter ignorance, while 120 million children –that is to say one in every five school-age children – do not attend primary school…Over 200 million girls and boys work and millions more are sexually exploited (Gómez Gutiérrez 2004: 3).

Equality of educational opportunity is difficult to achieve in highly stratified societies and economic systems. In 1975, Coleman (1975), and other have argued that education alone was not sufficient to overcome significant SES differences in the society divided along dimensions of class, power, income, wealth, and privilege. The difficulty of attaining social justice in the global economy is explained by Rikowski (2000), who argues that sustainable social justice is impossible on the basis of capitalist social forms. Globalisation, in most developing countries (the majority of humanity) is articulated in the form of finance-driven policy reforms concerning efficiency and effectiveness. Their effect on education systems is likely to 'increase' educational inequalities and access (Carnoy, 1999).

Furthermore, a lack of emphasis on the relationship between policy, poverty and schooling, and the 'withdrawal of the state as a major provider in the field of education in many parts of the world' raise serious human rights and ethical questions (Soudien, 1999). The growth of global education policy hegemony defining accountability, standards, quality assurance, and assessment fails to respond to the changing relationships between the state, education and social justice in the global economy.

The prospect of widening inequalities in education, due to market-oriented schooling, and substantial tolerance of inequalities and exclusion, are more than real. Access and equity continue to be "enduring concerns" in education (OECD, 2001, *Education Policy Analysis,* p. 26). The policy shift away from the progressive and egalitarian vision of education that characterised the 1960s and the 1970s has serious implications for human rights, social justice and democracy.

The chapters in the book explore the following themes:

1. Globalisation, social justice and education
2. The rhetoric of 'education for all'
3. The social, economic and educational problems experienced by the Black American children and implications for social justice
4. Gender relations and implications for democracy and social justice
5. Cultural diversity as resistance to neoliberal globalisation
6. Decentralisation, public spending, and social justice
7. Global currents of colonialism, decolonisation and postcolonialism and implications for social justice

The general intention is to make *Education and Social Justice* available to a broad spectrum of users among policy-makers, academics, graduate students, education policy researchers, administrators, and practitioners in the education and related professions. *Education and Social Justice* is unique in that it

- provides an easily accessible, practical yet scholarly source of information about the changing nature of cultural capital, social justice and schooling globally
- presents issues confronting policy makers and educators on current education reforms concerning social justice and equality of educational opportunities globally
- provides strategic education policy analysis on recent shifts in education, social justice and policy research
- gives suggestions for directions in education and social justice policy changes, relevant to democratic and empowering pedagogy in the 21st century.

We hope that you will find *Education and Social Justice* useful in your teaching, future research and discourses concerning schooling, social justice and policy reforms in the global culture.

References

Carnoy, Martin. 1999. *Globalization and Educational Reform: What Planners Need to Know*. Paris: UNESCO, International Institute for Education Planning.

Coleman, J. (1975). What is Meant by 'an Equal Educational Opportunity'? *Oxford Review of Education*, 1: 27.

Gomez Gutiérrez, Luis I. 2004 Inaugural Address to the Twelfth World Congress.: The profound educational revolution. Presented at the World Congress of the Comparative and International Education Society (CIES), Havana, Cuba, 25-29 October.

OECD 2001. *Education Policy Analysis*: *Education and Skills*. Paris: OECD.

Rikowski, Glenn. (2000**).** Education and Social Justice within the Social Universe of Capital. Paper presented at the BERA day seminar on "Approaching Social Justice in Education: Theoretical Frameworks for Practical Purposes", Faculty of Education, Nottingham Trent University, 10th April.

Soudien, Crain, and Peter Kallaway. 1999. *Education, Equity and Transformation*. Dordrecht: Kluwer Academic Publishers.

ACKNOWLEDGEMENTS

We wish to thank the following individuals who have provided invaluable help, advice and support with this major research project:

Bernadette Deelen, Springer
Harmen van Paradijs, Publishing Editor, Springer
Mark Bray, University of Hong Kong
Dorothy Murphy, Assistant Editor, *Educational Practice and Theory*, James Nicholas Publishers
Heidi Ross, Indiana University
Elvira Martín Sabina, Universidad de La Habana
Orrin F. Summerell, Head of Publications and Information, UNESCO Institute for Education

We also want to thank numerous reviewers who were prepared to review various drafts of the chapters. These include:

Helena Allahwerdi, University of Finland
Ari Antikainen, University of Helsinki
Alberto Arenas, University of Arizona
Nigel Bagnall, University of Sydney
Karen Biraimah, University Of Central Florida
Jill Blackmore, Deakin University
Malcolm Campbell, Bowling Green State University
Paul Carlin, Australian Catholic University (Melbourne Campus)
David Gamage, University of Newcastle
Mark Hanson, University of California (Riversdale)
Yaacov Iram, Bar Ilan University
Erwin Epstein, Loyola University Chicago
Irving Epstein, Illinois Wesleyan University
Andreas Kazamias, University of Wisconsin-Madison
Kyu Hwan Lee, Ewha Womans University (South Korea)
Sheryl Lutjens, Northern Arizona University
Ljubo Majhanovich, Windsor University
Kas Mazurek, University of Lethbridge
Marie-Laure Mimoun-Sorel (Australian Catholic University)
Wolfgang Mitter, German Institute for International Educational Research
Adam Nir, Hebrew University of Jerusalem
Carlos Ornelas, Universidad Autonoma Metropolitana
Mary Nutall, Australian Catholic University (Melbourne Campus)
Jerzy Smolicz, University of Adelaide
Noah Sobe, Loyola University Chicago
Sandra L Stacki, Hofstra University
Nelly Stromquist, University of Southern California

Margaret Secombe, University of Adelaide
Margaret Sutherland, University of Leeds
David Wilson, OISE, University of Toronto

We are particularly grateful to Harmen van Paradijs, Publishing Editor, Springer who supported this project, and who took the responsibility for the book production process, and whose energy and enthusiasm ensured that the book was published on time.

The final preparation of the camera-ready manuscript for publication was facilitated by the outstanding and creative work of Nikolai Zajda, BA, B.Com., MIB (University of Melbourne).

CONTRIBUTORS

Madeleine Arnot (MA (Hons) from Edinburgh University and Ph.D (Open University). She is Professor in Sociology of Education and is Professorial Fellow at Jesus College at Cambridge University, England. She is a Fellow of the Academy of Social Sciences (AcSS) and of the Royal Society for the Encouragement of the Arts, Manufactures and Commerce (RSA). She has acted as gender expert for the Council of Europe, an international consultant for the UNESCO *Education for All: Gender Monitoring Project* and has advised on equal opportunities policies in Portugal, Greece, Argentina and Spain.. She directed major EC funded projects on *Women as Citizens: promoting equality awareness* and on *Broadening Adolescent Masculinity* and projects on pupil consultation, gender education policy and refugee and asylum seeker children's education. She has written and edited 17 books and over 80 book chapters and articles in the sociology of education, educational policy and citizenship education. Her recent book publications include *"Challenging Democracy" gender, education and citizenship* (with J. Dillabough, RoutledgeFalmer, 2000) and *Reproducing Gender? Essays on educational theory and feminist politics,* (RoutledgeFalmer, 2002*), Consultation in the Classroom: developing dialogue about teaching and learning* (with D. Reay et al., Pearson 2004). *Contact address*: Professor Madeleine Arnot, Faculty of Education, University of Cambridge, 184 Hills Road, Cambridge CB2 2PQ, UK. E-mail: mma1000@cam.ac.uk

Jennifer Chan-Tiberghien is Assistant Professor in the Department of Educational Studies, Faculty of Education, as well as a faculty associate in the Center for Research in Women's Studies and Gender Relations and in the Centre for Japanese Research at the University of British Columbia, Canada. She is also a Visiting Scholar in the Reischauer Institute for Japanese Studies at Harvard University.
Contact Address: Reischauer Institute for Japanese Studies, Harvard University, 1737 Cambridge Street, Cambridge, MA 02138, USA. E-mail: chan7@fas.harvard.edu and jentiber@interchange.ubc.ca.

Kassie Freeman (Bowdoin College) is Professor of Education, and Dean, Dean for Academic Advancement. She has published extensively in major comparative education journals. In 2002 she received $138,000 grant from the Board of Regents, State of Louisiana, to conduct research on Teacher Education and African American Males (TEAM). Her recent publications include The Underutilization of the Human Potential of Individuals Who Are Different: Costs to Societies and Individuals (*Society and Economy*, 24:2, 2002), and Reconceptualizing the Transition of Higher Education Students to the Labor Market (*Education and Society*, 19:2, 2001). Her latest book is *African Americans and College Choice:*

The Influence of Family and School (2004, State University of New York Press). *Contact address*: Bowdoin College, 5700 College Station, Brunswick, ME 04011-8448, USA. E-mail: kfreeman@ bowdoin.edu

Macleans A. Geo-JaJa (Brigham Young University, Utah) is Professor and holds the Chair of the Comparative and International Development Education Program at Brigham Young University. He is Professor of Economics of Education. He previously taught at the University of Port Harcourt in Nigeria, and at the University of Utah. He has a PhD in Labor Economics. His main research areas are: education regeneration and nation-building, structural adjustment policies and globalisation, and social and economic aspects of education markets. He has been involved in numerous national and international projects, including the first ever Human Development Index of American Cities. In 2003 he guest-edited a special issue of *World Studies in Education*. He has served as consultant to UNDP, USAID, IFAD, IDRC, and the World Bank, on topics dealing with educational planning and finance, decentralization, human resource development and education reforms in Africa. He has published widely.
Contact Address: Dr. Macleans Geo-JaJa, 306P, David McKay School of Education, Brigham Young University, Provo, Utah 84602, USA. E-mail: geo-jaja@byu.edu

Dominique Groux est professeur des universités à l'IUFM de Versailles. Elle est actuellement détachée comme attachée de coopération universitaire à l'Ambassade de France en Allemagne et elle travaille à l'université de Potsdam (Allemagne). Ses champs de recherche sont l'éducation comparée, l'apprentissage précoce des langues, les échanges internationaux et l'éducation à l'altérité.
Contact Address: 5, cite de Phalsbourg, 75011, Paris, France. E-mail: dgroux@noos.fr

Anne Hickling-Hudson teaches international and inter-cultural studies in education at the Queensland University of Technology, Brisbane. Jamaican born and raised, she has worked as a teacher in the UK, as a teacher, teacher educator and education planner in the Caribbean, and has continued her career in teacher education in Australia since 1987. As the immediate past President of the World Council of Comparative Education (2001-2004), she coordinated the council representing comparative education societies from over thirty countries and led the organization of the 12th World Congress of Comparative Education, held in Havana, Cuba, in October 2004. Her research interests focus on race relations and policy analyses of education, and on intercultural and postcolonial approaches in comparative and international pedagogy.
Contact Address: School of Cultural and Language Studies in Education, Queensland University of Technology, Kelvin Grove, Q. 4059, Australia. E-mail: a.hudson@qut.edu.au

W. James Jacob is Assistant Director at the Center for International and Development Education (CIDE) at the University of California, Los Angeles where he also received his Ph.D. in Comparative and International Education. His

current research focuses on program evaluation, social change and development, and higher education organizational analysis in developing countries with geographic emphases in China and East Africa. He has worked as a policy analyst and evaluator of HIV/AIDS education programs in Uganda from 2001 to 2005, where he was simultaneously the principal investigator of a Sub-Saharan African HIV/AIDS literacy education research program. He is currently co-directing a Global Higher Education Trends Analysis (GHETA) study on the influences of the market economy on higher education.
Contact Address: Center for International & Development Education, Graduate School of Education & Information Studies, Box 951521, Moore Hall, Los Angeles, CA 90095-152, USA. . E-mail: wjacob@gseis.ucla.edu.

Karen Mundy is Associate Professor and Canada Research Chair in Global Governance and Educational Change at the Ontario Institute for Studies in Education of the University of Toronto, where she also directs the Comparative, International and Development Education Programme. Her research focuses on three themes: educational change in sub-Saharan Africa, the evolution of international governmental and non-governmental organizations in education, and the politics of foreign aid to education.
Contact Address: Canada Research Chair in Global Governance and Comparative Education, OISE-University of Toronto, 252 Bloor Street West, Toronto, Ontario, Canada M5S 1V6. E-mail: kmundy@oise.utoronto.ca

Clara Lig Long Rangel has a Masters of Education from the Pedagogical University of Enrique José Varona. She holds a chair in adult education at the Medical University of the Isla de la Juventud. She is a qualified teacher and has worked in numerous community projects on public health education. She was an assistant professor in student health at the National Centre of Hygiene and Epidemiology. She is the President of the Isla de la Juventud Branch of the Association of Cuban Educators (APC), a non-profit NGO. She has given courses on international issues and has studied in depth areas of guidance, and links between education and work, didactics and pedagogy. Her current research focuses on adult education.
Contact Address: The Universidad Pedagógica y Facultad de Ciencias Médica, Isla de la Juventud, República de Cuba. E-mail: clara@ahao.ijv.sld.cu

Suzanne Majhanovich PhD, is Professor of Languages in the Faculty of Education, the University of Western Ontario, where she teaches courses in theories of education as well as in issues in language acquisition and second language teaching and learning. Her current research interests include educational restructuring, decentralisation, and privatisation. She is also involved in a major study on the history of women teachers in 20th Century Ontario. She is Editor of *The Canadian and International Education Review*.
Contact Address: Faculty of Education, University of Western Ontario, 1137 Western Road, London, Ontario, N6G 1G7 Canada. E-mail: smajhano@uwo.ca.

Regina Moromizato Izu is an educator who holds a Masters in Social Management from the Pontificia Universidad Catolica of Peru and is pursuing doctoral studies in childhood, youth, and social sciences at the Universidad Manizales — CINDE (Colombia). She is currently teaching on alternative early childhood programs in the Department of Education at the Pontificia Universidad Catolica of Peru. She has conducted various research projects and consulting work for government agencies concerning programs hearing on early childhood, the family, and the community.
Contact Address: Professor for Alternative Programs for Early childhood at the Facultad de Education of the Pontilicia Universidad Catolica de Peru, Lima, Peru. E-mail: rmoromi(a pucp.edu.pe

Val D. Rust (University of California, Los Angeles) is Professor of Education at the University of California, Los Angeles. He received his PhD from the University of Michigan He is the UCLA Education Abroad Program Director and was the Associate Editor of the *Comparative Education Review* (1998-2003). His recent works include *Alternatives in Education*, *The Democratic Tradition and the Evolution of Schooling in Norway*, *The Unification of German Education*, *Education and the Values Crisis in Central and Eastern Europe*, *Toward Schooling for the Twenty-first Century* and Theory in Comparative Education (*World Studies in Education*, 4, 1, 2003).
Contact Address: Social Sciences and Comparative Education, University of California - Los Angeles, Los Angeles, CA 90095 USA. *Contact address*: vrust@gseis.ucla.edu, or vrust@cox.net.

Zenaida Sánchez Proenza holds a Masters of Education from the Pedagogical University of Enrique José Varona. She is adjunct professor and deputy director of research and postgraduate studies at the Pedagogical University of Carlos Manuel de Céspedes, the Isla de la Juventud. She is a member of the Executive Board of the Association of Cuban Educators (APC) and is in charge of the Secretariat of Continuing Education. She has lectured in postgraduate courses covering international issues. Her research interests cover the nexus between education and work, didactics and biology. She is currently conducting research on teacher education and higher education reforms.
Contact Address: The Universidad Pedagógica y Facultad de Ciencias Médica, Isla de la Juventud, República de Cuba. E-mail: fcmij@infomed.sld.cu

Joseph Zajda holds BA (Hons), MA, MEd and PhD from Monash University. He coordinates and teaches Research Methods in Education (M.Ed), Learning, and Education and Society courses. He was awarded *'Excellence in Teaching'* Award in 2004. He edits *World Studies in Education, Education and Society*, and *Curriculum and Teaching*. His many publications include works in the areas of comparative education, curriculum reforms, education policy, lifelong learning, education reforms in Russia, and decentralisation and privatisation in education. His latest work is *The International Handbook of Globalisation, Education and*

Policy Research (Springer, 2005). He is also the editor of the 12-volume book series *Globalisation, and Comparative Education* (Springer, 2006/2007).
Contact Address: School of Education, St Patrick's Campus, Australian Catholic University, 115 Victoria Parade, Fitzroy, Vic., Australia, 3065. Tel: (613) 9 953-3268; Fax: (613) 9 699 2040. E-mail: j.zajda@patrick.acu.edu.au.

Education and Social Justice: Issues of Liberty and Equality in the Global Culture

The Epistemology of Social Justice

Social justice has fascinated many thinkers around the world, including Plato (427 BC-347 BC). In *The Republic* he argued that an ideal state would rest on the following four virtues: wisdom, justice, courage, and moderation. When Thomas Aquinas (1225-74), influenced by Aristotle, wrote that "Justice is a certain rectitude of mind whereby a man does what he ought to do in the circumstances confronting him" (quoted in Kirk 1993), he believed that justice was a form of natural duty owed by one person to another. Similarly, Immanuel Kant (1724-1804) maintained that actions are morally right if they are motivated by duty without regard to any personal motive, or self-interest. Kant's theory of social justice is based on the concept of selflessness and moral duty. His moral theory based on duty is also known as deontology. In his view, the only relevant feature of moral law is its universalisability, and any rational being understands the categorical imperative, namely "Act only on that maxim which you can at the same time will to become a universal law." (Flew 1979: 191).

The term "social justice" was first used in 1840 by a Sicilian priest, Luigi Taparelli d'Azeglio, and given exposure by Antonio Rosmini-Serbati (1848) in *La Costitutione Civile Secondo la Giustizia Sociale*. Subsequently, John Stuart Mill (1960: 57-8) gave this anthropomorphic approach to social justice almost omnipotent status in his book *Utilitarianism, Liberty and Representative Government*:

> …we should treat all equally well…who have deserved equally well of *us*, and that society should treat all equally well who have deserved equally well of it, that is, who have deserved equally well absolutely. This is the highest abstract standard of social and distributive justice; towards which all institutions, and the efforts of all virtuous citizens, should be made in the utmost degree to converge.

At the end of the nineteenth century, the term "social justice" was used by social reformers as an appeal to the ruling classes to attend to the needs of the new masses of uprooted peasants who had become urban workers, or dispossessed.

The meaning of social justice may vary according to different definitions, perspectives and social theories. Most conceptions of social justice refer to an egalitarian society that is based on the principles of equality and solidarity, that understands and values human rights, and that recognises the dignity of every human being. In this sense, it reflects the three values and symbols of the French Revolution (1789–1799) – liberty, equality and fraternity. Globally, the most frequently quoted expression of the founding principles of social justice is the Universal Declaration of Human Rights, which was endorsed by the international community in 1948. Most social contract theories, from Rousseau and Mill

J. Zajda (ed.), Education and Social Justice, 1-12.

onwards stress the importance of the State that gives priority to the "welfare of its citizens and that ensures that some basic inalienable rights are protected" (Schugurensky 2004: 2). A social justice-oriented government, if it is to reflect its ideology of egalitarianism and move beyond the level of policy rhetoric, has to ensure a more equitable and fair access to resources, and socially valued commodities. As White and Talbert (2005: 59) explain, education for social justice needs to move beyond functionalist and vocationalist-oriented perspectives on schooling (which stresses education for jobs), to one where the traditional model of schooling becomes a transformational pedagogy:

> . . . we must prepare children for active participation as global citizens; this means that we have a responsibility to teach for social justice . . . Social justice education moves beyond traditionalist essentialist practice by suggestion that student and teachers are active and equal participants in all schooling . . . Advocates for social justice education suggest that our schools are often demeaning and disempowering places where children and their teachers are either bored into submission or where the transmission and socialization techniques destroy any hope for critical-thinking . . .

Traditionally when wrestling with the questions of inequality and social injustice, scholars and social reformers have turned to the works of such philosophers as Jeremy Bentham, John Locke, Thomas Hobbes and John Stuart Mill. Notions of social justice typically find their derivation in Plato and Kant's Moral Philosophy and in particular the latter's concern that actions must be connected to moral considerations. Jeremy Bentham (1748-1832) and John Stuart Mill (1806-1873) judged the morality of an act solely on the basis of its results. He also argued passionately that "All persons are deemed to have a *right* to equality of treatment" (Mill 1960: 59). Justice was achieved in any situation where the greatest happiness was achieved by the greatest number of people. Bentham advocated socially-imposed external sanctions of punishment and blame to make the consequences of improper action more obviously painful. Social Justice was achieved through *deterrence* which is based on the rational calculation of "equal punishment for equal crime". Mill took the view that human beings are also motivated by such internal sanctions as self-esteem, guilt, and conscience. He also argued, from a Kantian categorical imperative, that "we ought to shape our conduct by a rule which all rational beings might adopt *with benefit to their collective interest.*" (Mill 1960: 49).

One needs to remember, however, that justice is, by definition, social. The shift in meaning occurs when the term "social" no longer describes the *product* of the virtuous actions of many individuals, but rather the *utopian goal* toward which all institutions and all individuals are "made in the utmost degree to converge" by coercion. In that case, the "social" in "social justice" refers to something that emerges not organically and spontaneously from the rule-abiding behaviour of free individuals, but rather from an abstract ideal of legal justice, imposed from above (see Novak 2000). One of key factor in achieving social justice is the emergence of a consensus that the society is working in a *fair* way, where individuals are allowed as much freedom as possible given the role they have within the society. Hence, true social justice is attained only through the harmonious cooperative effort of the citizens who, in their own self-interest, accept the current norms of morality as the price of membership in the community.

In recent years the concept of social justice has been associated with the moral and political philosopher, John Rawls, particularly in his works *A Theory of Social Justice* (1971) and *Political Liberalism* (1993). He draws on the utilitarian principles of Bentham and Mill, the social contract ideas of Locke, and the categorical imperative ideas of Kant. His reference to social justice was made in *A Theory of Justice* (1971), where he proposed that "Each person possesses an inviolability founded on justice that even the welfare of society as a whole cannot override. For this reason justice denies that the loss of freedom for some is made right by a greater good shared by others" (Rawls 1971: 3). Social justice, as defined by Rawls, is an abstraction, which is humanistic in essence.

As Maxine Greene (1998) has noted regarding Rawls' conception of social justice, although he follows in the Kantian tradition of moral reason, his view of justice is "not necessarily universal, nor does it reflect some higher order" (Greene 1998: xxxv). While Greene finds Rawls' theory of "justice providing a regulative framework for what individuals think and do in a free society" laudable (Greene 1998: xxxvi), she cautions that Rawls has in mind a self-determining citizen as an individual not necessarily as a participant member of society (Greene 1998: xxxvi). For Greene, community and its responsible interactions is the key. For this reason she finds that Jürgen Habermas (1979) has provided a more promising alternative for educating for justice in his theory of "communicative democracy", whereby members of a community come together voluntarily to discuss matters of significance and must justify their preferences through arguments, explanations, and different modes of persuasion (Greene 1998: xxxvii). Greene also reminds us that when the requirements for justice are addressed that distinctions have to be made: "Equitable or fair treatment . . . does not mean equal treatment – certainly when that means treating people with widely disparate needs in the same way" (Greene 1998: xxxviii). When Maxine Greene speaks about social justice, and more specifically about ways we can teach for social justice, she embraces that interpretation of social justice that is concerned with basic human rights that all people are entitled to, regardless of conditions of economic disparity or of class, gender, race, ethnicity, citizenship, religion, age, sexual orientation, disability or health. She advocates that teachers become activists in raising their students' consciousness (à la Freirean 'conscientisation' of 1970), to conditions of oppression and to ways to work for the eradication of injustices and disparities in society. She exhorts teachers of conscience to take up the challenge:

> To teach for social justice is to teach for enhanced perception and imaginative explorations, for the recognition of social wrongs, of sufferings, of pestilences wherever and whenever they arise. It is to find models in literature and in history of the indignant ones who have taken the side of the victims of pestilences, whatever their names or places of origin. It is to teach so that the young may be awakened to the joy of working for transformation in the

> smallest places, so that they may become healers and change their worlds. (Greene 1998: xlv).

In presenting this notion of social justice and recommending ways to teach to bring about positive social change, Greene is clearly endorsing an articulation of the concept as it is understood by those who stand on the left of the political spectrum. Her understanding of the concept parallels the work of such critical theorists of Bowles and Gintis, Levin, Carnoy, Torres, Giroux, Apple, Shapiro, and McLaren among others. Of course, people of other political persuasions have also claimed social justice as an ideal to be sought after, but in their interpretation, social justice will be realized by the individual efforts of free citizens to "exercise self-government by doing for themselves, and without turning to government, what needs to be done" (see Novak 2000.) Such interpretations reject any notions of a social safety net to assist the disadvantaged, or social contracts where those privileged with power and means voluntarily support those in need, or government regulations to bring about a gradual end to inequalities and disparities. For people of this political standpoint such actions would be considered as misguided efforts in social engineering. Naturally, this group would support the free market economy, deregulation and privatization.

On the surface the need for social justice in the world is self-evident. But we must explore the questions that John Rawls asked: "What makes a society just? How is social justice connected to an individual's pursuit of the good life?" (Nussbaum 2001). Is social justice simply achieved through the moral acts of autonomous citizens in a free society who of their own volition and with good will and by consensus meet the ethical obligations of their community? But what if the moral norms of the society include reprehensible practices? What then are the responsibilities of citizens with regard to norms of morality of their community when the norms contravene basic human rights? In a just society the citizens understand that results of their acts are incumbent not only on themselves but are universally applicable.

Social Justice as an Ideal Construct

The word *social* distinguishes *social justice* from the concept of justice as applied in the law, and from more informal concepts of justice embedded in systems of public policy and morality, which differ from culture to culture and therefore lack a global dimension. *Social justice* refers to the overall fairness of a society in its divisions and distributions of rewards and burdens. Hayek points out a major defect of twentieth century theories of social justice. Most authors assert that they use it to designate a *virtue* (a moral virtue). But most of their descriptions ascribed to social justice refer to impersonal states of affairs – "high unemployment" or "inequality of incomes" or "lack of a living wage" are cited as instances of "social injustice." Hayek argues that social justice is either a virtue or it is not. If it is, it can properly be ascribed only to the reflective and deliberate acts of individual persons. Some scholars who use the term, however, ascribe it not to individuals but to social systems. They use "social justice" to denote a regulative principle of order, especially the redistribution of wealth, income and power. Their focus is not virtue but political economy and power (see Novak 2000).

The nexus between social justice and education indicates the problematic relationship between society and the State, against the background of comparative education research. Social justice as a construct is an attempt to answer the following question: How can we contribute to the creation of a more equitable, respectful, and just society for everyone? There are at least three conceptual and methodological issues that are relevant to current discourses of education and social justice.

Firstly, there exists an assumption that the term "social justice" has a monocultural and linear definition. However, the term "social justice" is a multi-layered ideal construct and refers to a contested and contentious concept (Troyna andVincent 1995). Sharon Gewirtz (1998: 469), for instance, found "very little *explicit* discussion of what social justice means or ought to mean". Similarly, Fazal Rizvi (1998: 47) has noted a semantic ambiguity concerning social justice:

> . . . the immediate difficulty one confronts when examining the idea of social justice is the fact that it does not have a single essential meaning – it is embedded within discourses that are historically constituted and that are sites of conflicting and divergent political endeavours.

Others have expressed concerns that that some terms commonly used as synonyms for the term social justice are in fact "dangerous" (Dunkwu and Griffiths 2001: 11) because they could denote a monocultural or other limiting position, rather than connotate the contested and competing interpretations of the term in a culturally and ideologically diverse world.

Secondly, it is assumed, as one of the many taken-for-granted assumptions, that social justice is attainable in any society, and at any time. Glenn Rikowski (2000) in his paper "Education and Social Justice within the Social Universe of Capital" argues that social justice cannot exist in a capitalist society:

> Social justice is a latent social form within capitalist society that cannot attain real existence. As sustainable social justice is impossible on the basis of capitalist social forms, the drive to *create* social justice in capitalist society – fired by the anger of shocking social inequality – pushes at the boundaries of capitalist social relations, and against the limits of capital itself. The struggle for social justice in capitalist society is, therefore, an aspect of a struggle for a form of life where social justice is possible.

Thirdly, there is an ambivalent nexus between the State, social stratification and social justice. The greater the social inequality, the less one finds social justice. The unequal distribution of economic, social, and political capital is likely to make it difficult for pedagogues to address differences and oppressions in schools and society globally.

Social Justice and Inequality

Despite the seemingly egalitarian spirit of the reformers and policy makers promoting social justice, and in view of the market forces dictating privatisation, and marketisation in education and society, ambivalent legacies of the past, and unresolved critical education and policy issues continue, by and large, to remain the same, and are "still on the policy agenda" (Zajda 2002: 87). They include, among other things, the "stubborn issue of inequality" (Coombs 1982: 153), first examined in a comparative context in 1957 by (Kandel 1957: 2) with reference to schooling in the West. Similarly Carnoy (1999) argues that while decentralisation and school autonomy may result in some educational improvement, decentralisation reforms tended to *increase inequality* in educational performance between "the poorer states (municipalities) and the richer ones" (Carnoy 1999: 55-56). Privatisation, decentralisation and marketisation in education and society have a direct impact on the implementation of the principles of social justice in schools. However, as I have argued elsewhere:

> …the principle of providing quality education for all, in view of the presently widening gap of wealth, power, income, SES disadvantage and inequity between the rich and the poor locally and globally continues to remain a myth. To solve the inequalities requires an ideological and radical policy shift in current models of governance, and an authentic and equal partnership between the state, multi-national corporations, policy-makers and educators, all working together towards the eradication of inequality and poverty locally and globally – for the common good of humanity. (Zajda 2005: 18).

Some critics argue (Weiler and Maher 2002) that social justice is difficult to achieve in a society where social inequality debate is dormant:

> …examples of transformative pedagogy, the need to respect and encourage the voices of students, curriculum which critiques popular culture and analyzes social inequality are invaluable to prospective teachers. Moreover, progressive programs educating prospective teachers need to include both models of progressive pedagogy and curriculum and courses exploring the historical and contemporary politics of education, to give prospective teachers tools of analysis and action. On the other hand, calls for liberatory teaching can appear to ring hollow notes in underfunded and inequitable public schools, where knowledge and teaching practices are increasingly standardized and monitored through high stakes testing…

The creation of an egalitarian and just society for everyone is a dream for all empowering and egalitarian pedagogues. But it will remain a dream, and mere hollow rhetoric, or magic words in policy, unless we debate more vigorously social inequality in the global culture. We also need to act, not just talk. We need to critique vigorously the existing status quo of stratified school systems. We need to focus our debate on the "dialectic of the global and the local and the unequal distribution of socially valued commodities." (Zajda 2005: 18).

Weiler and Maher (2002) argue that inequalities in education, together with privatisation and marketisation have a profound effect on social justice:

> As numerous educational researchers have documented, existing schools are profoundly unequal, stratified by race and class, and increasingly driven by the standardized testing of students and teachers and the deskilling of teachers through the introduction of packaged curricula geared to standardized tests. The "marketization" of education is dominant at both the federal and state levels, with free-market educators calling for the privatization of schooling through a variety of means – vouchers, for-profit charter schools, the commercialization of school spaces and forced dependence on advertising.

Social justice as a social policy is the natural aspiration of all democratic societies and remains the only long-term guarantee for developing and sustaining peace, tolerance and harmony in the world.

The structure of this volume

The book chapters in this volume are revised versions of scholarly papers presented at the 12th World Congress of Comparative Education on the theme "Education and Social Justice". In his inaugural address, the Minister of Education of the Republic of Cuba, Dr. Luis Gómez Gutiérrez reminding delegates of the appalling conditions that disadvantaged people around the world live in today. He focused on illiteracy and the plight of children:

> Despite the commitments made by many nations to provide education for all, illiteracy continues to rise, forcing over 860 million adults to live in ignorance, while 120 million children –that is to say one in every five school-age children – do not attend primary school. According to UNICEF this problem, which should shame a society living in the 21st century, will not be resolved until 2100 . . . This, however, isn't the only problem that affects our youngsters. Every year 11 million children die from diseases that could have been prevented or cured. Over 200 million girls and boys work and millions more are sexually exploited (Gómez Gutiérrez 2004: 3).

The papers selected for this volume, reflect the on-going dynamics of comparative education, and offering some of the insights on policy shifts in educational systems that reflect an equitable and just society. Some of these paradigmatic shifts have been evident in the policy work of the World Council of Comparative Education Societies (WCCES), an umbrella body which currently includes 34 comparative education societies. The most visible activities of the WCCES since its creation in 1970 have been a series of high-profile world Congresses of Comparative Education. WCCES also promotes research programmes involving scholars in various countries. Currently, joint research programmes focus on: theory and methods in comparative education, education of women and girls, teacher education, education for peace and justice, and other topics.

At an international congress with close to one thousand delegates presenting in fourteen thematic groups, three special symposia, along with invited keynote addresses, there were numerous worthy scholarly papers and studies to choose from when compiling this collection. Indeed, those book chapters that are finally included represent but a small fragment of the scholarly papers presented during the conference.

This volume analyses and critiques the overall interplay between education, social justice and the State. The book chapters draw upon recent studies in the areas of education and social justice. By referring to Bourdieu's call for critical policy analysts to engage in a 'critical sociology' of their own contexts of practice, and postmodernist/poststructuralist pedagogy, this collection of book chapters examines the way central discourses surrounding the debate of education and social justice are formed in the contexts of dominant ideology, power, and culturally and historically derived perceptions and practices.

The book chapters that follow in this volume critically evaluate some of these issues and their future implications for both policy makers and educators. They suggest policy solutions in resolving some of the paradoxes and dilemmas of the problematic and ambivalent relationship between the State, democracy, social justice and the market forces of globalization.

Karen Mundy (Ontario Institute for Studies in Education, University of Toronto) in "Education for All and the New Development Compact", in attempting to explain the somewhat misleading rhetoric of 'education for all', looks critically at the evolution of an 'education for all' consensus within the international community, redistributive forms of multilateralism, and a global public good. Kassie Freeman (Dillard University) explores the formation of social identity in the USA, the social, economic and educational problems experienced by the Black American children, social inequality, and implications for social justice. She also discusses the under-utilization of the Black American children's educational/human potential and provides the rationale for rethinking social justice and the assimilation paradigm is suggested. In "Freedom's Children: a Gender Perspective on the Education of the Learner Citizen", Madeleine Arnot (University of Cambridge) focuses on the *Learner as Citizen* who, through citizenship education courses, is prepared often for a gender divided world – even though the processes of individualisation have significantly reshaped contemporary gender relations. She discusses its implications for democracy and social justice. Jennifer Chan-Tibergien (University of British Columbia) in "Cultural Diversity as Resistance to Neoliberal Globalization: The Emergence of a Global Movement and Convention" considers the globalising processes of commodification to argue that the neo-liberal policy discourses in education define and shape dominant patterns in cultural diversity. She argues that cultural diversity in the global culture merely serves to re-assert the cultural hegemony of the North.

Dominique Groux (IUFM de Versailles, Université de Paris) in "L'apprentissage Précoce des Langues: des Pratiques Sociologiquement et Politiquement Marquées", contrasts the various forms of language training of certain countries and within countries. She evaluates the correlation between bilingual training and private schools, and the choice of bilingual education as a political and economic goal and suggests that curricula may be culturally discriminatory. The latter has implications for social justice in education and society.

Macleans A. Geo-JaJa (Brigham Young University) in "Educational Decentralization, Public Spending, and Social Justice in Nigeria" critiques the process of decentralisation and privatisation in Nigeria. By reviewing the impact of decentralisation and privatisation on education, the author shows that they have not led to desired outcomes, such as equity and social justice. W. James Jacob (University of California, Los Angeles) in "Social Justice, and Gender in Chinese Higher Education: Regional Issues of Equity and Access", provides an analysis of the contemporary history of the gender gap in education generally and higher education specifically. He examines issues related to the ethnic boundaries that exist in higher education and suggests that social justice issues of equity and access need to be resolved.

Clara Lig Long Rangel and Antonia Zenaida Sánchez Proenza (Universidad Pedagógica y Facultad de Ciencias Médica, Isla de la Juventud) in "La Universidad del Adulto Mayor una Mirada Desde la Universalización de la Universidad" focus on the new program of university studies for adults, looking specifically at the Special Municipality of the Isle of Youth against the backdrop of the larger policy of "universalization of higher education." The authors provide useful information about Cuban perspectives of adult education (*andragogia*), and discusses the "workshop" as an important mode of educational work. The authors comment on students' evaluations of the program. Regina Moromizato Izu (Peru) in "Calidad y Equidad en la Atención a la Infancia Temprana" discusses policy documents and programs of the early childhood education in Peru. She presents various conceptual models and data and concludes that most programs are successful.

Finally, in her WCCES Presidential Address, "Integrating Cultural Complexity, Postcolonial Perspectives, and Educational Change: challenges for Comparative Educators", Anne Hickling-Hudson (Queensland University of Technology), in examining global currents of colonialism, decolonisation and postcolonialism affecting education and society, uses some of her personal insights into the postcolonial condition to reflect on comparative education. She argues that socialisation in neo-colonial ideas of race is still hegemonic, and that understanding how this works will help comparative educators to carry critical studies of how education can be changed to provide social justice.

By focusing on social justice globally, there is an attempt to answer one of the most pressing global questions: Are social, economic and cultural divisions between the nations, between school sectors, between schools and between student numbers growing or declining? The authors consider and examine current discourses surrounding social justice, education and social stratification. There is a lack of emphasis in comparative education research on the relationship between poverty and education and the "withdrawal of the state as a major provider in the field of education in many parts of the world" (Soudien and Kallaway 1999: 378). This has serious implications for global discourses surrounding democracy, human rights and social justice. What are the implications for democracy, and social justice of the policy shift away from 'the social democratic vision of education that was characteristic of the 1960s and 1970s?" (Soudien and Kallaway 1999: 378). By examining the competing discourses of education and social justice the authors attempt to evaluate critically both the reasons and outcomes of education reforms, policy change, with respect to social justice, thus providing a more informed critique on the Western-driven models of social justice, democracy and equality in education.

JOSEPH ZAJDA
SUZANNE MAJHANOVICH
and
VAL RUST

References

Bourdieu, Pierre and Jean-Claude Passeron. 1990. *Reproduction in Education, Society and Culture*, 2nd ed. London: Sage Books.

Carnoy, Martin. 1999. *Globalization and Educational Reform: What Planners Need to Know*. Paris: UNESCO, International Institute for Education Planning.

Coombs, Philip. 1982. Critical World Educational Issues of the Next Two Decades. *International Review of Education* 28 (1): 143-158.

Dunkwu, K. and M. Griffiths. 2001. *Social Justice in Education: Approaches and Processes* (review). British Educational Research Association. http://www.bera.ac.uk. accessed 15 March, 2004.

Flew, Antony. 1979. *A Dictionary of Philosophy*. London: Pan Books/Macmillan.

Freire, Paolo.1970. *Pedagogy of the Oppressed.* New York: Herder & Herder.

Gaus, Gerald, Courtland, Shane D. 2003. Liberalism, in *The Stanford Encyclopedia of Philosophy* (Winter 2003 Edition) Edward N. Zalta (ed.) URL http://plato.stanford.edu/archives/win2003/entries/liberalism/ accessed 2 August, 2005.

Gewirtz, Sharon. 1998. Conceptualizing social justice in education: Mapping the territory. *Journal of Education Policy* 13(4): 469-484.

Gomez Gutiérrez, Luis I. 2004 Inaugural Address to the Twelfth World Congress.: The profound educational revolution. Presented at the World Congress of the Comparative and International Education Society (CIES), Havana, Cuba, 25-29 October.

Greene, Maxine. 1998. Introduction: Teaching for Social Justice, in Ayers, William, Hunt, Jean Ann and Quinn, Therese (eds.) *Teaching for Social Justice,* pp. xxvii-xlvi. New York: Teachers College Press.

Habermas, Jürgen. 1979. *Communication and the Evolution of Society.* Boston: Beacon Press.

Johnson, Robert. 2004. Kant's Moral Philosophy, in *The Stanford Encyclopedia of Philosophy* (Spring 2004 Edition) Edward N. Zalta (ed.) URL http://plato.stanford.edu/archives/spr2004/entries/kant-moral/ accessed 2 August, 2005.

Kandel, Issac. 1957. Equalizing Educational Opportunities and its Problems. *International Review of Education* 3(1): 1-10.
Kirk, Russell. 1993. The Meaning of Justice. Heritage Lecture #457. http://www.heritage.org/Research/PoliticalPhilosophy/HL457.cfm, accessed 2 June, 2005.
Mill, John Stuart. 1960. *Utilitarianism, Liberty and Representative Government.* London: Dent and Sons.
Novak, Michael. 2000. Defining Social Justice. http://www.firstthings.com/ftissues/ft0012/opinion/novak/html, accessed 2 August, 2005
Nussbaum, Marth. 2001. The Enduring Significance of John Rawls. In *The Chronicle of Higher Education. The Chronicle Review.* 20 July, 2001, http://chronicle.com/free/v47/i45/45b00701.htm, accessed 1 August, 2005.
Rawls, John. 1971. *A Theory of Justice.* Cambridge MA: Harvard University Press.
Rawls, John. 1993. *Political Liberalism.* New York: Columbia Univ. Press.
Rikowski, Glenn. 2000. Education and Social Justice within the Social Universe of Capital. http://www.leeds.ac.uk/educol/documents/00001618.htm, accessed 15 March, 2004.
Rizvi, Fazal. 1998. Some Thoughts on Contemporary Theories of Social Justice. In *Action Research In Practice: Partnerships for Social Justice In Education*, ed. by Bill Atweh, Stephen Kemmis, and Patricia Weeks, 47-56. London: Routledge.
Sandretto, Susan et al., (2003) A Collaborative Self-Study Into Teacher Education And Social Justice. http://www.aare.edu.au/03pap/san03373.pdf, accessed 12 March, 2005.
Social Justice. 2005. Wikipedia, the Free Encyclopedia,http://en.wikipedia.org/wiki/Social_justice, accessed 10 June 2005.
Schugurensky, Daniel. 2004. The Heteronomous University and the Question of Social Justice:in Search of a New Social Contract. Paper presented at the World Congress of the Comparative and International Education Society (CIES), Havana, Cuba, 25-29 October.
Soudien, Crain, and Peter Kallaway. 1999. *Education, Equity and Transformation.* Dordrecht: Kluwer Academic Publishers.
Troyna, Barry, and C. Vincent. 1995. The Discourses of Social Justice in Education. *Discourse: Studies in the Cultural Politics of Education* 16(2): 149-166.
White, Cameron, and Tony Talbert. 2005. Comfortably Numb? Rethinking social Studies for Social Justice. In: *Current Issues in School Leadership*, ed. by Larry Hughes, 57-71. Mahwah: Lawrence Erlbaum.
Weiler, Kathleen and Frinde Maher. 2002. Teacher Education and Social Justice. *Radical Teacher* Winter 2002. http://www.findarticles.com/p/articles/mi_m0JVP/is_2002_Winter/ai_97483138, accessed 10 June 2005.
Zajda, Joseph. 2002. Education Policy: Changing Paradigms and Issues. *International Review of Education* 48(1-2): 67-91.
Zajda, Joseph. 2005. *The International Handbook of Globalisation, Education and Policy Research*. Dordrecht: Springer.

The Editors

Joseph Zajda holds BA (Hons), MA, MEd and PhD from Monash University. He coordinates and teaches Research Methods in Education (M.Ed), Learning, and Education and Society courses. He was awarded *'Excellence in Teaching'* Award in 2004. He edits *World Studies in Education, Education and Society*, and *Curriculum and Teaching*. His many publications include works in the areas of comparative education, curriculum reforms, education policy, lifelong learning, education reforms in Russia, and decentralisation and privatisation in education. His latest work is *The International Handbook of Globalisation, Education and Policy Research* (Springer, 2005). He is also the editor of the 12-volume book series *Globalisation, and Comparative Education* (Springer, 2006/2007).

Contact address: School of Education, St Patrick's Campus, Australian Catholic University, 115 Victoria Parade, Fitzroy, Vic., Australia, 3065. Tel: (613) 9 953-3268; Fax: (613) 9 699 2040. E-mail: j.zajda@patrick.acu.edu.au.

Suzanne Majhanovich, PhD, is Professor of Languages in the Faculty of Education, the University of Western Ontario, where she teaches courses in theories of education as well as in issues in language acquisition and second language teaching and learning. Her current research interests include educational restructuring, decentralisation, and privatisation. She is also involved in a major study on the history of women teachers in 20th Century Ontario. She is Editor of *The Canadian and International Education Review.*

Contact address: Faculty of Education, University of Western Ontario, 1137 Western Road, London, Ontario, N6G 1G7 Canada. E-mail: smajhano@uwo.ca.

Val D. Rust (University of California, Los Angeles) is Professor of Education at the University of California, Los Angeles. He received his PhD from the University of Michigan He is the UCLA Education Abroad Program Director and was the Associate Editor of the *Comparative Education Review* (1998-2003). His recent works include *Alternatives in Education*, *The Democratic Tradition and the Evolution of Schooling in Norway*, *The Unification of German Education*, *Education and the Values Crisis in Central and Eastern Europe*, *Toward Schooling for the Twenty-first Century* and Theory in Comparative Education (*World Studies in Education*, 4, 1, 2003).

Contact address: Social Sciences and Comparative Education, University of California - Los Angeles, Los Angeles, CA 90095 USA. E-mail address: vrust@gseis.ucla.edu, or vrust@cox.net.

EDUCATION FOR ALL AND THE NEW DEVELOPMENT COMPACT

KAREN MUNDY

Abstract – Over the past decade, the achievement of universal primary education, under the somewhat misleading rubric of 'Education for All' (EFA), has steadily built momentum in international forums as a focus for discussion and action. The present study looks critically at the evolution of consensus about EFA within the international community. The first section of this contribution provides an overview of 'education for development' in the form in which it has been inherited from the 20th century. The second describes what has changed in the context, rhetoric and practice of such 'education for development'. The final section reflects on two questions: 'Why has EFA now moved beyond international rhetoric to action?'; and 'What can our experience with EFA tell us about the prospects for multilateralism and global governance in the 21st century?'

Zusammenfassung – BILDUNG FÜR ALLE UND DER NEUE VERTRAG ZUR ENTWICKLUNG – Über die letzten zehn Jahre hat die Errungenschaft allgemeiner Primärbildung unter der ein wenig irreführenden Überschrift ‚Bildung für alle' (Education for All/EFA) in internationalen Foren als ein Zentrum für Diskussionen und Aktionen stetig mehr Beachtung gefunden. Die vorliegende Untersuchung wirft einen kritischen Blick auf die Entwicklung von Einigkeit in Bezug auf EFA innerhalb der internationalen Gemeinschaft. Der erste Abschnitt dieses Beitrages bietet einen Überblick über, Bildung für Entwicklung' in der Form, in der das Konzept aus dem 20. Jahrhundert ererbt ist. Der zweite Abschnitt beschreibt, was sich im Kontext der Rhetorik und der Praxis einer solchen, Bildung für Entwicklung' verändert hat. Der letzte Abschnitt stellt Reflexionen über zwei Fragen an: Warum ist EFA nun über internationale Rhetorik hinaus zur Umsetzung fortgeschritten, und was kann uns unsere Erfahrung mit EFA über die Aussichten für multilaterale Verhältnisse und globale Lenkung im 21. Jahrhundert sagen?

Résumé – L'ÉDUCATION POUR TOUS ET LE NOUVEL ACCORD DE DÉVELOPPEMENT – Durant la dernière décennie, la réalisation d'une éducation primaire universelle, sous la rubrique quelque peu trompeuse de l'« Éducation pour Tous » (EPT) a continuellement donné une impulsion aux forums internationaux en étant au centre de la discussion et de l'action. La présente étude jette un regard critique sur l'évolution du consensus à propos de l'EPT au sein de la communauté internationale. La première section de cette contribution offre une vue d'ensemble de « l'éducation pour le développement » selon la forme qui nous a été léguée par le XXe siècle. La seconde décrit ce qui a changé dans le contexte, la rhétorique et la pratique d'une telle 'éducation pour le développement'. La dernière section est une réflexion sur deux questions : 'Pourquoi l'EPT a-t-elle maintenant dépassé la rhétorique internationale pour favoriser l'action' ; et 'Que peut nous apprendre notre expérience de l'EPT à propos des perspectives du multilatéralisme et du gouvernement global au XXIe siècle ?'

J. Zajda (ed.), Education and Social Justice, 13-38.

Resumen – EDUCACIÓN PARA TODOS Y EL NUEVO PACTO PARA EL DESARROLLO – A lo largo de la última década, el objetivo de lograr una educación primaria universal bajo el título un poco equívoco de "Educación para Todos" (EPT) ha impulsado permanentemente los foros internacionales como foco de debates y de acción. El presente estudio echa una mirada crítica a la evolución de un consenso en cuanto a la EPT dentro de la comunidad internacional. La primera parte de esta contribución provee una visión sinóptica de la 'educación para el desarrollo' en la forma en la que este objetivo se ha heredado del siglo XX. La segunda, describe qué es lo que ha cambiado en el contexto, la retórica y la práctica de esa 'educación para el desarrollo'. La parte final reflexiona sobre dos interrogantes: ¿Por qué la EPT no ha pasado de la retórica internacional a la acción?; y ¿Qué nos puede decir nuestra experiencia con la EPT sobre las perspectivas de multilateralidad y gobernabilidad global en el siglo XXI?

Резюме – ОБРАЗОВАНИЕ ДЛЯ ВСЕХ И СОГЛАШЕНИЕ О ДАЛЬНЕЙШЕМ РАЗВИТИИ – На протяжении последнего десятилетия успехи, достигнутые во всеобщем начальном образовании, провозглашенном под лозунгом «Образование для всех» (EFA), сообщают непрерывный импульс и находятся в центре дискуссий и решений международных форумов. Данное исследование критически рассматривает эволюцию единого взгляда на EFA внутри международного сообщества. В первой части данной статьи предлагается обзор «образования для развития» в той форме, в которой оно было заимствовано из 20 века. Во второй части статьи рассматривается, что именно изменилось в контексте, дискуссиях и на практике такого «образования для развития». В заключительной части обсуждаются два вопроса: «почему в настоящее время EFA вышло за рамки обсуждений на международном уровне и перешло к принятию конкретных решений?» и «что наш опыт по EFA говорит нам о перспективах многосторонности и глобального управления в 21 веке?»

Over the past decade the achievement of universal primary education (UPE), under the somewhat misleading rubric of 'education for all', has steadily built momentum as a focus for discussion and action within the international community. The idea of UPE is not, of course, a new one. Rich countries have long made support for education a part of their international development efforts, and multilateral organizations have been active in the educational development of poorer countries since at least the end of World War II. However, the focus on education for development by the international community today is both strikingly different from that in past decades, and profoundly paradoxical. The idea of 'education for all' has become part of a broadly based consensus about 'what works' among bilateral and multilateral development agencies. It is also a rallying call for heads of state and international financial institutions, a focus for transnational advocacy, and an arena of expanding development practice characterized by widespread experimentation with new modes of aid delivery, new kinds of donor–recipient relationships and relatively high volumes of aid spending.

The last 5 years are in sharp contrast to the 1990s, post-World Declaration on Education for All (EFA) decade – which saw funds decline and little collective momentum behind education for all commitments. The paradox lies primarily in the fact that universal basic education has become a prominent concern of the international community in a period characterized by the fracturing of post-World War II multilateralism, and following a decade of decline in rich country support for foreign aid.

Then and Now: Changes in Context, Actors, Rhetoric, and Practices

Writing in 1998, I described the evolution of a highly contradictory multilateral regime for international cooperation in education after World War II. The foundations of that regime were laid in the establishment of systems of mass public education in Western countries in the period between the late 19th and mid-20th century when many features of the social welfare state were institutionalized and accepted as 'norms' for state behavior (Mundy 1998). Not surprisingly, efforts to remake world order following World War II saw the inclusion of education as a universal right in the 1948 Universal Declaration of Human Rights (Article 26), and the establishment of UNESCO with its broad mandate to support (among other things) the universal right to education. UNESCO became neither center nor coordinator of the new regime. Instead, a rather diffuse regime for educational cooperation grew alongside the emergence of international development as a field of activity for United Nations organizations and for newly formed bilateral aid organizations. These organizations quickly took up the notion that education could be used as a tool in national development, and educational aid began to account for something between 5 and 10% of all aid flows.

Three key features of the education-for-development regime in the period from 1960 to 1995 deserve specific attention. First, although the notion of a universal right to education and of mass public education figured strongly in the international discourse (for example, in the UN Charter, UNESCO's mandate, and host of international declarations at regional meetings of developing country governments in the 1950s and 1960s) this was not what was supported by major flows of funding or technical expertise. Most aid flows to education were focused at levels beyond primary schooling. The reasons for this were threefold: (1) Donors assumed that national governments would/should fund and provide universal primary schooling. (2) Recurrent costs like teachers and textbooks, which are the largest piece of any public education budget, were seen as ineligible for aid funding – to fund recurrent costs would be 'unsustainable'. (3) The bilateral donors who dominated the field tended to want to tie aid to their own economic and political interests and thus were biased towards programs of post-primary training, foreign scholarships and institution-building (Table 1).

The second feature of the education-for-development regime was its profound decentralization and disorganization. At the level of norms and ideas,

Table 1. The Expansion of Educational Multilateralism, 1965–1995 (-n millions of constant 1994 US-$)

	1961	1965	1970	1975	1980	1985	1990	1995
1. Bilateral educational aid (OECD countries)	na	3412.5	3628.8	4038.1	5962.4	4596.9	4073.4	3985.0
2. World Bank lendingto education	0.0	230.3	409.5	636.9	772.9	1785.3	1663.6	1923.7
3. UNESCO								
(a) Total regular budget	228.3	298.6	401.2	483.8	532.1	721.4	423.8	417.9
(b) Education programs	52.1	69.5	84.5	105.0	98.5	169.3	81.7	89.3
(c) Extra budgetary support for education programs *(primarily UNDP)*	na	140.8	117.2	214.0	174.92	n/a	83.3	94.2
4. UNICEF	0.0	na	51.8	71.1	60.4	62.3	63.8	78.0
OECD/DAC GDP Deflator	14.24	16.41	19.29	35.14	56.94	51.97	89.36	109.5

Sources: OECD/DAC1995; Phillips 1987; UNESCO 1993; UNESCO Approved Program and Budget, various years; UNICEF, Annual Report, various years; World Bank, Annual Report, various years.

Notes: OECD/DAC Weighted GDP Deflator was used to calculate constant 1994 dollar amounts.

Row 1. Commitments, as reported in UNESCO 1993 and OECD/DAC 1996;

Row 2. World Bank Annual Report, "Trends in Lending" various years;

Row 3a. UNESCO Approved Program and Budget, various years. Figures refer to biennial budgets.

Row 3b. UNESCO Approved Program and Budget. Figures refer to biennial budgets.

Row 3c. Estimated Extrabudgetary Contributions as they appear in the Approved Program and Budgets. Figures refer to biennial budgets.

Row 4. Phillips 1987 and UNICEF Annual Report 1996.

one might argue that the institutionalization of state-led education systems in the Western world played a "chartering" or steerage role in the construction of an education-for-development regime (Meyers 1977; Anderson 1983). But as that regime developed, no formal system of governance or coordination among its many actors ever emerged. UNESCO, the putative leader in the field, kicked things off with ambitious regional conferences and targets for educational development. But it was weakened by limited resources and intense politicization in the 1970s and 1980s. Thus, UNESCO never developed the political capacity to coordinate the growing number of new agencies interested in educational development (Jones 1988; Mundy 1999). By the 1960s, UNICEF had begun to develop its own distinctive approach to educational development, acting on behalf of the world's children but not in coordination with UNESCO.

The World Bank entered the arena in the 1960s, and overtook UNESCO in terms of expertise and flows of funding by 1980. But the Bank paid little attention to coordinating the educational activities of other donors, instead concentrating on the development of an economic rationale for its educational activities to support its own distinct approach to educational development (Jones 1992; Mundy 2002). Alongside this fragmented multilateral effort, virtually every industrialized country also included education-sector programs in its bilateral aid program, at wildly varying levels of between 3 and 30% of total bilateral official aid. No single bilateral donor outweighed the others financially or could claim to provide intellectual or political guidance to the others – not even the United States, despite its status as hegemon in the global system. The net result was an education-for-development regime characterized by many small to medium-sized, short-term, bilateral transactions, often working at cross-purposes. For four decades – from the 1960s through the 1990s – ambitious attempts at global level coordination of education for development activities failed, and usually failed quite quickly. (Examples of failure include: UNESCO regional conferences of the 1960s; OECD DAC efforts to coordinate education-sector activities among OECD members in the 1970s; the World Bank's initiative in Sub-Saharan Africa in the 1980s; and the Jomtien World Conference on EFA in 1990).

The diffuse nature of the educational-aid regime also played out in its growth as an epistemic and professional community. From high-level manpower planning to vocational education, non-formal education, adult literacy, higher education and back again, a vague and expansive menu of what was 'needed' was reported or endorsed in a succession of international conferences and publications. A growing professional expert community on educational development, largely housed within international organizations and research institutions, could do little to harness donors behind a common agenda because their own assessment of priorities changed so rapidly or diverged quite widely (Chabbott 2003). Apart from major divisions between those who viewed education as a productive investment and those who saw it as a human right were many smaller divisions between those who saw in higher education, primary education, vocational and non-formal education etc. the next 'magic bullet' for development (Mundy 1998: 464). A fractious epistemic community allowed for a very loose coupling between rhetorical commitments and practical activities – creating in effect a smorgasbord of priorities and approaches from which donor countries might choose according to their own geopolitical and economic interests. Countries like France, England, and later Australia focused attention on scholarships and provision of teachers; others adopted vocational, adult and literacy education as the focus of their support (Nordics), all outside of any systematic or coordinated effort to support national planning for educational change (King 1991).

Finally, this regime had a fairly limited range of actors and a fixed array of aid modalities. It was dominated by 'official actors' – a handful of multilateral organizations (UNESCO, UNICEF, and the World Bank) and bilateral aid organizations. Southern governments were the targets (or recipients) of the regime, but often not active participants within it (Samoff 1999, 2001). Few non-governmental actors were involved or recognized within the official regime. They remained outside its conferences and conventions, despite the existence of international teachers unions and international humanitarian and religious organizations with an interest in education that predated official educational aid activities (Mundy and Murphy 2001). By and large, educational development was seen as the job of national governments, supported by bilateral donors and international organizations, with their funds and expertise. Aid modalities followed from this basic framework, and focused on bilateral grants or loans tied to the provision of 'technical cooperation' (read: Western training and provision of Western experts).

What emerged after World War II was a highly decentralized regime that reflected some of the fundamental structural features of the world polity. While the global importance of education was widely accepted, a set of common priorities for educational development never gained traction or played much of a steerage role among the growing group of international donor organizations active in educational development. Donor countries, worried about decolonization and the Cold War, engaged in a paradoxical pattern of involvement in the regime: on one hand offering rhetorical support for the idea of universal, equitable, mass public education, while on the other channeling their education development aid funding to post-primary education and programs of high-level expertise and training. International organizations developed competing programs, priorities and approaches to educational development with only the most minimal coordination.

Despite global commitment to the universal right to education, the highly state-centric structure of world politics limited appetite for collective action or coordination. Flows of expertise and funding were highly fragmented and often based on geo-political or economic interests of the bilateral donors and the idiosyncratic approaches of specific multilateral organizations, rather than on any collective prioritization of global educational needs, or coordinated effort within individual developing countries.

What has Changed: The New EFA Multilateralism

While it is important not to overstate the case, the education-for-development regime has experienced some sweeping changes over the last decade. These changes are particularly dramatic when placed alongside what has been was widely assessed to be the failure of the international community to achieve the goals established for education at the World Conference on EFA in Jomtien, Thailand in 1990 (Torres 2000; Chabbott 2003).

These changes may be grouped into the following categories: embedding education in a new consensus on global development; the construction of clear educational targets and monitoring efforts; new forms of donor coordination at the country level; the emergence of new actors and partnerships within the international education for development regime; and evolution of new aid flows and aid modalities.

Embedding Education in a New Consensus on Global Development

Since 1995, some of the most dramatic shifts in the education-for-development regime have come on the heels of renewed efforts to build consensus about priorities for international development. Partly spurred forward by international organizations and donor agencies, whose funding fell precipitously at the end of the Cold War, and partly by the development of new non-governmental networks highly critical of globalization, the 1990s saw education receive accelerating attention in a series of international conferences and proclamations (see Table 2).

Several authors have characterized this new 'consensus' as part of a broader rapprochement between the neo-liberal and pro-economic globalization approaches to development endorsed by the IMF and the World Bank in the 1980s–1990s, and the equity-and-globalization skeptical approaches adopted by the United Nations: a kind of global "third way" (Therien 2002, 2005; Ruggie 2003). It is very clear that both the United Nations and the Bretton Woods organizations have increasingly seen advantages in working on a common set of priorities. The Bretton Woods institutions now address poverty and equity issues regularly, while the UN organizations are less skeptical of the role of the market and private sector in development. Ruggie (2003: 305) describes this as the formation of a conceptual consensus that

> encompasses the centrality of governance, the rule of law, education, and health to economic success; the positive role of investment, including skills and technologies embodied in foreign direct investment; the need for further debt relief and other forms of development assistance for poor countries; the urgency of lowering trade barriers imposed on developing country exports by agricultural subsidies and other non-tariff barriers in the rich countries; the protectionist potential posed by pursuing social and environmental objectives through linkages to trade agreements; and the need for governments and international institutions alike to forge partnerships with the private sector and a wide range of civil-society actors.

Table 2. Evolution of basic education as a global development priority

	Year	Forum	Commitment or action
United Nations Conferences	1989	Children's Summit	Covenant on the Rights of the Child (right to free primary education) 190 states are signatory
	1990	World Conference On Education for All Jomtien, Thailand	World Declaration on EFA UPE by 2000
	1993	World Conference on Human Rights	Vienna Declaration and Program of Action States obliged to promote gender equality, esp. in education
	1995	World Summit for Social Development Copenhagen	"Universal and equitable access to education" is one of ten commitments
	2000	World Education Forum (Jomtien follow-up) Dakar Senegal	Dakar Framework for Action 1. Expand early childhood education 2. Free UPE by 2015 3. Access to life skills 4. 50% improvement in illiteracy 5. Eliminate gender disparity 2005 6. Improve quality of education World Bank presents idea of a Fast-track Plan: "no countries seriously committed to EFA will be thwarted by their lack of resources"
	2000	Millennium Summit and Millennium Declaration	Millennium Development Goals Goal 2: achieve UPE Goal 3: promote gender equality and empower women (Target 4: eliminate gender disparity in primary and secondary school)
	2002	United Nations Conference on Financing for Development, Monterrey Mexico	Commits governments, international financial institution and United Nations organizations to work through new forms of development partnerships and coordinate external aid in France and United States promise first increase ODA in a decade*

Table 2. Continued.

	Year	Forum	Commitment or action
G7/8 OECD	1996	OECD Development Assistance Committee "Shaping the 21st Century"	Commits OECD governments to coordination of aid at country level and to a common set of development priorities including universal access to primary education
	2000	G8 Ministerial Meetings	Commitment to fund viable national education plans Commitment to debt relief for education
	2001	G8 Ministerial Meetings	Re-affirmation of commitment to education Establishment of an education taskforce for 2002 G8 meeting
	2002	G8 Ministerial Meetings	Endorsement of EFA Fast-track Plan as funding mechanism for EFA Commitment to increase bilateral assistance for UPE
	2003	OECD DAC meeting	Rome Declaration on Harmonization (OECD/DAC 2003)
	2005	Commission for Africa Report	Endorses the idea that Northern governments should provide funding necessary for governments to abolish user fees
IGOs	1999	IMF/World Bank Poverty Reduction Strategy Initiative introduced	Establishes basic norms for educational expenditures in budgetary allocations linked to medium-term national development plans and expenditure frameworks; also gives criteria for debt relief
	2000	UNESCO appointed coordinator of interagency follow up on EFA and DAKAR	High level Task Force and EFA Working Group established EFA Global Monitoring Task Force to work with revitalized UNESCO Institute for Statistics In 2002, UNICEF, UNESCO endorse the EFA Fast Track Plan & call on G8 to do so
	2000	IMF, OECD, UN and World Bank	"A Better World For All" statement sets out agreed and common priorities and targets for development
	2001	Millennium Development Project Launched	Working groups to suggest ways of meeting MDGs and monitor one of 7 committees is for education
	2002	World Bank Board introduces new policy actively opposing user fees in education	
	2002	World Bank IDA introduces grant facility	For first time some education sector funding provided on grant rather than loan basis

Table 2. Continued.

Year	Forum	Commitment or action
2002	World Bank Managed Fast Track Initiative	Countries with credible (IMF/WB approved) poverty reduction strategy paper and an education sector plan can join, but fund remains limited to $ US 200m over 3 years
2004	Fast Track Initiative Re-endorsed	Funding for the Catalytic Fund rises to $243.4 million

*France announced increase of ODA to 5% in 5 years and 7% in 10 years; the United States promised to increase core funding to developing countries by 50% over 3 years.

Education early emerged as a central part of this new international consensus or compact about development. This is reflected not only in the priority given to education within the Millennium Development Goals, but also the near-revolutionary attention that the World Bank and the IMF now pay to the achievement of universal access to basic education in their country programs (Millennium Development Project 2005a, b).

The elevation of education within the new official development agenda is perhaps not so surprising, since education figures prominently in both equity and productivity conceptualizations of development. As such it straddles the divide between neoliberal and social welfare orientations. The following quotation from the World Bank (2002a, b: v), now regarded as one of the leading advocates for greater public spending on basic education, illustrates this straddling role played by education in the new official discourse of development:

> The expansion of educational opportunity, which can simultaneously promote income equality and growth, is a win-win strategy that in most societies is far easier to implement than the redistribution of other assets, such as land or capital. In short, education is one of the most powerful instruments known for reducing poverty and inequality and for laying the basis for sustained economic growth, sound governance and effective institutions.

Pronouncements and commitments by governments and multilateral institutions have further been matched by major endorsements from private sector and civil-society organizations – including members of the World Economic Forum, the new Global Campaign for Education and several US-based nongovernmental consortia (Mundy and Murphy 2001; World Economic Forum 2005). All of this signals the establishment of a global-level consensus about the role of basic education in development that is unprecedented in terms of scope, density, consistence and persistence. The solidity of the consensus is reflected in the seeming ease with which the Millennium Development Project Task Force on Education is now arguing for a new "Education Compact" to parallel the new development compact devised at Monterrey (Millennium Development Project 2005a, b):

> Bold political leadership is needed in a compact between developing countries and donors ... Under the compact each side is responsible for doing its part. Donors make a serious commitment to and respond to countries that are doing things right, assured that the external resources are being well used. Developing countries take on the tough political reforms in their systems with confidence that they will have sufficient and predictable financial support to deliver on promises made to their own citizens.

There is, nonetheless, still much to debate within this compact. For example, among the "tough political reforms" being referred to are: reducing unit costs of primary education, making good use of the private sector, introducing standardized testing regimes and decentralizing control, each reminiscent of the 1990s liberalization movement in education (Millennium Development Project 2005a, b). Furthermore, this compact suggests relatively little about how to work in contexts not characterized by 'good governance' – weak, corrupt, collapsed or post-conflict states are left off the map.

What is notable, however, is the degree to which the compact requires reforming "the donor business". For example, the Millennium Development Project urges donors to "commit new funds [7–17 billion US-$ per year] in a new way through a strong coordinated global effort that rewards and reinforces countries' measurable progress".

International Consensus about Selected Education Priorities

The new development consensus has established a clear hierarchy of global educational priorities, along with measurable time-bound targets for their achievement. The most widely and consistently endorsed goals are universal access (sometimes completion) to quality primary education, and the achievement of gender equity in education, beginning with the primary level (see Table 1). While a wider and more sophisticated array of goals was adopted at the World Education Forum (Dakar 2000) and at Jomtien (including the idea, for example, of publicly provided education and adult literacy and non-formal education), it is these two educational goals that have been endorsed as part of a common platform by heads of states and international organizations, these that are most often the focus on new pledges and commitments, and these that are the most closely and widely monitored.

The background to the establishment of these educational priorities can be traced to the OECD's Development Assistance Committee's endorsement of 'Shaping the 21st Century', in which OECD governments promised to increase bilateral aid, harmonize their activities, and focus on a handful of top development priorities – including universal education. This was followed by a joint declaration among the IMF, OECD, World Bank and UN in 2000 entitled 'A Better World for All' which promised closer coordination, more attention to country ownership of development and tighter focus on specific development priorities (including education).

Both agreements fed into the Millennium Development Summit and Millennium Development Declaration (2000), which aligned the United Nations (and its agencies), the Bretton Woods institutions, and OECD governments behind a unifying substantive framework. The Declaration sets out 8 Millennium Development Goals with time-bound, measurable targets. The MDGs include halving world poverty by 2015, reducing infant mortality by 2/3, halving the spread of HIV/AIDS, combating malaria, halving the number of people without safe drinking water and promoting gender equity and environmental sustainability. The achievement of universal primary education and gender equity in education are Goals Numbers 2 and 3 in the MDGs.

These documents and declarations move beyond the establishment of a common ideology and approach to global development within the international community. They suggest an unprecedented degree of interest in coordination among international aid organizations and governments of rich countries, as well as an unusual appetite for setting out a small focused list of priorities attached to clear targets. As we will see below, commitment to targeting and coordination is also being experimented with in new ways at the recipient country level.

Early evidence also suggests that the new consensus is being backed by both new efforts at monitoring progress (these include several efforts at closer monitoring of internationally set education targets. The UNESCO-led EFA Monitoring Group, for example, has tried to ensure that national EFA Plans are in place; and with the help of the UNESCO Institute of Statistics it collects data to monitor progress towards EFA goals, including donor funding. The United Nations, through its Millennium Development Programme, has established a Task Force under economist Nancy Birdsel to look at progress towards gender equity in education. The World Economic Forum's Global Governance initiative, which also plans to track the achievement of the multilateral development goals, has one of seven groups focused on education) and some new funding (see discussion below of the Monterrey Declaration on Financing for Development). Notably, education has been one of the first arenas to see a global initiative emerge that aims to operationalize the Monterrey commitments – in the form of a multilateral 'Fast Track Initiative' described below.

New Forms of Donor Coordination and Target Setting at the Country Level

One part of the new development consensus that has enormous implications for educational development is the new interest in achieving coordination of donor efforts within recipient countries. Coordination implies 'harmonization' of donor initiatives around a common framework of priorities and targets that can be used to hold recipient governments accountable. The first and possibly farthest reaching of these coordination efforts has been the introduction in 1999 of a World Bank and the IMF joint 'Poverty Reduction Strategy Initiative'. The initiative engages recipient governments in the development of a national development plan whose focus is not simply growth but poverty reduction. The 'Poverty Reduction Strategy Paper' in turn is intended to be pivotal in IMF and World Bank funding decisions (indicating eligibility for debt relief and other programs), and acts as a common platform for the contributions of bilateral donors.

The PRSP is novel in several ways (World Bank 2002b). It requires governments to formally integrate social development goals with plans for macroeconomic stability, liberalization and debt repayment into a medium-term expenditure framework that bridges what had previously often been quite separate planning exercises with WB, UN and IMF. It commits the IMF to a poverty and social development mandate and bridges the focus on growth, stability and equity that had previously divided donor organizations. It requires governments to conduct wider consultations about national plans than in the past, and to take more 'ownership' of development planning. But it also works in the opposite direction, by providing a common set of targets and plans that can be used by donors and citizens to hold governments accountable.

There is a large, fractious debate about the ultimate impact of PRSPs on national sovereignty and 'ownership', including an impressive empirical literature that suggests that PRSPs often impose specific (IMF-driven) targets that favor stability and liberalization over social development (McGee and Hughes, 2002; Gould and Ojanen 2003). For our purposes, what is worth noting is that the PRSP process has had the specific effect of bringing about the much tighter integration of educational-development planning into national development expenditure planning (Carnoy 1999). As part of this process the PRSPs create the need for much more sophisticated planning regimes within Ministries of Education, and also tend to establish certain 'indicative targets' for educational expenditures that both favor reallocation of resources to primary education, and to specific line items (i.e., from teachers' salaries to teaching materials) (Alexander 2002). On the other hand, the PRSP process has also helped to make this information available for public scrutiny in an unprecedented fashion (see Global Campaign for Education 2004). Alongside PRSPs have grown some interesting initiatives by non-governmental actors to track expenditures against PRSP commitments (Dyer et al. 2004).

In addition to the far-reaching PRSP process, a large number of additional initiatives among donors to achieve national level coordination of development efforts have cropped up in recent years. This includes the 'harmonization' initiative spearheaded by the Development Assistance Committee of the OECD (through which governments have formally committed to pool resources and coordinate aid), and formalized in the 2004 Rome Declaration on Harmonization (with the UN, Bretton Woods and OECD governments as signatories). It also includes widespread experimentation among bilateral aid donors with 'Sector Wide Approaches' (SWAps) in which individual bilateral programs of assistance are increasingly planned in the context of a coordinated plan for specific subsectors. In many SWAps, bilateral funds are pooled together to provide direct budgetary support. What is sometimes not recognized is how frequently education has emerged as the key sector in which donors experiment with these historically novel efforts at donor coordination and pooling of resources (see Riddell 2000; Samoff 2001, 2004).

Finally, two education-specific efforts at country-level coordination and target setting are worth mentioning. In the wake of the Dakar World Forum on Education, UNESCO has interpreted its mandate to include assisting nations and regions to develop and monitor the implementation of national

'EFA plans'. The World Bank, for its part, has spearheaded the Fast Track Initiative. Initially conceived of as a new, OECD-government sponsored, World Bank-hosted financing facility that would ensure that no developing countries with clear plans for achieving UPE would fail to make progress due to lack of resources, the Fast Track has not been funded at anticipated levels by governments of rich countries. It has now been re-conceptualized as a facility that gives governments additional resources to help them plan for, access and manage large programmes of pooled sector-wide funding from bilateral and multilateral donors.

To this end the Fast Track Initiative has introduced another internationally driven planning exercise into the education sector. Countries who apply must have a PRSP and a 'credible' national education plan for delivering publicly financed and free primary education that aligns with a matrix of specified norms for educational quality and access. Among the benchmarks for acceptance into the Fast Track are an appropriate ratio of primary to post-primary education sector expenditures, plans to achieve set teacher/student ratios, and specific levels of teacher remuneration (World Bank Development Committee March 2004). (As of January 2005, 16 of the original 18 applicant countries had been endorsed for Fast Track support, although the FTI still is not endowed to meet their resource needs.) Countries without a credible education sector plan, or without a track record of educational planning that could attract major donors, can apply to the Analytical Fast Track process (which provides technical assistance in getting a national plan in place) (since its creation in November 2003 in Oslo, the number of donors that have made pledges to the Catalytic Fund increased from four to five. Current contributors to the CF are Belgium, Italy, Norway, the Netherlands and the United Kingdom. Contributions and pledges for the calendar years 2004–2007 amount to a total of approximately US-$ 255 million (FTI Newsletter September 2004)). All Fast Track countries are supported in developing an empirical base for tracking and monitoring progress towards key Fast Track Initiative objectives.

A certain degree of fragmentation and inter-agency competition is apparent across these various initiatives – reminiscent of the diffuse system of the pre-2000 education-for development regime. Even coordination among IFI-led initiatives remains disjointed – thus, according to a recent World Bank report, "as yet there is no regular process to ensure that the connection is made between a country's PRSP, its MTEF [medium-term expenditure framework], its FTI program and its annual budget" (World Bank 2004b: 17). The Fast Track Initiative itself is not sufficiently funded to allow it to finance all the countries meeting its criteria, and has been subject to wide-ranging criticism regarding some of its benchmarks. Again, there is ample room for debate about the Fast Track. One part of the international community seems to view the Fast Track as a loose coordinating body to ensure donor coordination. Staff within the World Bank seem more interested in the way it can "become a force for building elements of output orientation, performance measurement, autonomy and accountability into schooling systems" (Pritchett 2004).

Despite such debate, the principles that underpin PRSPs and the Fast Track Initiative and the additional OECD/DAC mechanisms now in place to coordinate international educational for development efforts at the country level are remarkable. They imply a rather more elaborate, consistent and publicly transparent indicative framework for coordinating education sector aid than has been in place before. Such a framework, simple and transparent, yields much more easily to broad public debate. As an example, consider the tendency of international financial institutions to assert their view that the private provision of basic education is a crucial element in educational reforms. In the recently revised Fast Track Initiative benchmarks, strong debate led to the setting of a benchmark (10%) of primary pupils at privately financed schools (EFA/FTI Secretariat). These new coordinating mechanisms also imply an increasing willingness on the part of rich countries to forgo the traditional, sovereignty-based bilateral model of foreign aid in favor of collective action. (The United States and Japan, however, remain outliers. The former has become decidedly less multilateral in its aid provision, while the latter continues to focus on building schools, not sectors.) Experimentation with pooled funding, direct budgetary support, and funding of recurrent costs of primary level education each suggest that UPE is steadily being recognized by rich governments as a global public good in need of collective rather than unilateral action.

New Actors, New Partnerships, New Accountability Politics

Another aspect of the new educational multilateralism that is unprecedented is the inclusion of new kinds of actors in both international and national education-for-development policy arenas. It is not just that new partnerships with civil society and private sector organizations have come to be seen as essential by official political actors on the international stage (Ruggie 2003). There has also been a remarkable growth of effective transnational organizations representing coalitions of civil society and private sector actors. As Mundy and Murphy (2001) have shown, transnational advocacy networks on such issues as debt relief, ODA reform, and globalization have frequently taken up the issue of the universal right to education as one part of their broader advocacy efforts. In addition, a strong transnational advocacy network on EFA has also emerged. Initiated by OXFAM International, Action Aid and the international association of teachers' unions, Education International, the Global Campaign for Education now counts a large number of national civil-society EFA coalitions around the world, as well as some of the largest international non-governmental organizations involved in education (OXFAM, CARE, ActionAid, Global March). Originally viewed by the international community as an under-utilized resource in the provision of educational services, today INGOs have taken on new and unanticipated leadership in international EFA efforts. INGOs have asserted themselves as advocates and policy activists.

The GCE and other civil-society organizations have increasingly carved out a place for themselves as the makers and monitors of global EFA goals (Murphy and Mundy 2002). GCE in particular has been instrumental in pushing bilateral donors, international organizations and members of the Group of 8 industrialized countries to make concrete commitments of resources for EFA. They have also emerged as policy watchdogs at the international and national levels, raising issues of adequate financing and equitable distribution of opportunities in national educational planning exercises and in international forum. In the last 2 years, for example, GCE or its members have produced research and policy papers on the educational dimensions of PRSPs in individual; provided substantive criticism of the indicative framework for national educational planning set out in the Fast Track Initiative (Rose 2003); produced a 'report card' on developing-country and rich-country contributions to meeting EFA and MDG goals; and launched a campaign at the annual World Bank/IMF meetings to highlight the negative impact of IMF conditionalities on the achievement of EFA in Zambia (GCE 2004). GCE or its members are now represented on virtually every High Level Working Group or international forum on EFA. Their inclusion and action has introduced a new dynamism to international political alignments – they clearly hope to leverage greater and more coordinated collective action while at the same time introducing more accountability for recipient governments and donor governments to EFA commitments.

In addition to these non-governmental organizations and civil-society coalitions, several private-sector organizations have recently become active supporters of a global education for all initiative. These include the World Economic Forum, a consortium of business organizations which has spearheaded a Global Governance Initiative to monitor achievements of the MDGs (including education) and is actively pursuing discussions about private/public EFA partnerships; the Commonwealth Education Fund (which brings private sector and public sector funding in the UK), the International Business Leaders Forum, and a series of EFA research and advocacy initiatives funded by the Hewlett Foundation.

New Resources

The emergence of a common set of development priorities has set the stage for the first increases in official development aid from OECD countries in over a decade. Although levels still have not reached pre-Cold War highs, they have continued to make a modest advance over a 3-year period, and promise to increase further. The European Union and the United States have led the way in this regard, pledging their first substantive increase in ODA in more than a decade at the March 2002 Financing for Development conference in Monterrey.

The Development Assistance Committee of the OECD suggests that aid flows are set to rise to $75 billion by 2006, from $52 billion in 2001, according to pledges made in Monterrey. The following five countries: Belgium, Finland, France, Ireland and the United Kingdom have laid down a clear timetable for achieving the 0.7% of GDP target for official development aid. If all DAC countries were to meet their express commitments, the ODA to GNI ratio would increase to 0.30% by 2006, and 0.32% by 2010 (from 0.22 in 2001), with just under threequarters of the increase coming from the European Union (OECD/DAC 2004). Some G8 governments have recently promised an even greater acceleration of ODA commitments. There are also interesting proposals for increasing immediately available funding – as, for example, the United Kingdom's proposal for an International Financing Facility, and France's proposal for a new international tax (the IFF would take donor commitments and a down payment and use these to back international bonds that could generate an immediate expansion of funds for development).

A large number of OECD governments (including the six largest ODA donors) have now also made clear pledges committing themselves to increased funding for UPE, as can be seen in Table 3. However, the scope of these commitments is only beginning to be reflected in the actual disbursements of ODA, as shown in the OECD/DAC figures presented in Table 4. What can be seen here is that ODA for education is still lagging.

Several things are worth noting about changes in the overall flow of bilateral funding to basic education. First, the majority of aid to education still flows through bilateral, not multilateral channels. Second, while overall flows of aid to education are down, flows to basic education have grown very rapidly. Basic education now accounts for at least one-quarter of all aid to education, up by more than 60% in the period between 1998/9 and 2000/1, or from US-$ 486 to US-$ 800 million. Six countries account for more than three-quarters of all flows to basic education (France, Germany, Japan, the Netherlands, the United Kingdom and the United States), but more than one-half of all DAC countries have increased the proportion of ODA going to basic education. Finally, while these numbers suggest a positive trend, several analysts have suggested the US-$ 1.5 billion currently spent represents only a fraction of what would be needed to finance the achievement of UPE by the 2015 target, which a recent World Bank analysis estimates as requiring US-$ 3.7 billion per year through 2015 (Bruns et al. 2003).

It is now widely recognized that much of the additional funding for the achievement of basic education will require donor governments to assume some of the recurrent costs of the primary education systems of least-developed nations for an extended period of time. Again, in a sharp departure from past trends, donors have become increasingly willing to channel

Table 3. New EFA Actor and Initiatives Since 2000 and OECD/DAC Member support for basic education 2000–2004

New actors and initiatives	
Global Campaign for Education formed 1999	Membership organization of national and regional of NGOs and civil-society organization, INGOs with goal of leveraging achievement of funding for education for all. Includes Northern and Southern national and regional coalitions.
Commonwealth Education Fund	United Kingdom government and businesses fund NGO coalitions in education
World Economic Forum (Education initiatives launched 2002)	Global Governance Initiative: Tracks and monitors commitments to the MDGs. One of seven working on education. Workshop on private/public partnership in EFA (Nov. 2004)
United States Basic Education Coalition	NGO coalition to pressure more and better ODA for basic education, funded by the Hewlett Foundation
Universal Basic Education Project (UBASE), American Academy of Arts and Sciences	Multi-year research effort bringing together diverse social scientists to review best practices, effects of EFA, funding of EFA etc., funded by the Hewlett Foundation
United States Centre for Universal Education, Council of Foreign Relations	Lobby and research body advocates for more and better ODA for EFA, funded by the Hewlett Foundation
International Business Leaders Forum	Works with the Prince of Wales, UNDP to establish framework for global corporate social responsibility 2005: "Business and the Millennium Development Goals"
Donor countries	
Canada	2001: Canada says will double its resources for basic education to $100 million per year; Canada endorses Fast Track Initiative
Nordics	Norway pledges to increase ODA for basic education by 15%
Japan	Japan announces $2 billion for education over next 5 years
France	Commitment to the Fast Track Initiative
Netherlands	The Netherlands committed to 135 million euros for education initiatives 2003 – 2.5 billion ODA promised for education, 76% on basic education 2003 – Funds for Fast Track Initiative committed and funds for Global Campaign for Education committed

Table 3. Continued.

United Kingdom	UK announces increase in Aid for education
	UK establishes Commonwealth Education fund to support NGO advocacy in education
United States	1989 Basic Education Coalition of US NGOs established to lobby for more and better education aid
	2000 – US President signs legislation opposing 'user fees' in ODA
	2001 – Gene Sperling, former member of President Clinton's council of economic advisors, begins basic education project and US GCE coalition
	2001 – US announces an African Education Initiative ($100 million)
	2002 – US pledges $100 million more in education aid to Africa ($20 million for 5 years)
	2001 Universal Basic Education Project (American Academy of Arts and Sciences, funded by the Hewlett Foundation)
	2004 Tabling of the Clinton/Lowey EFA Act to provide $500 million by 2005 and 2.5 billion by 2009 for establishment of universal basic education systems; establishes high-level EFA interagency task force

Table 4. Official development assistance (ODA) for Education 1990–2002

	1990	1991	1992	1993	1994	1995	1996	1997	1998	1999	2000	2001	2002
Overall education (% bilateral ODA)	9.8	na	8.4	9.5	10.7	11.2	10.8	na	10.6	10.7	7.8	8.6	8.7
Basic Education(% bilateral ODA)	na	na	na	0.1	0.6	1.2	1.3	na	1	1.2	1.5	2.1	2.2
Total DAC ODA (bilateral and multilateral constant US-$ billion)	55.1	60.1	57.6	54.1	55.8	49.8	48.8	44.8	48.6	49.8	49.6	52.4	*(59.1)*

Source: OECD/DAC Reports, 1991–2003; EFA Global Monitoring Report 2003.
Note: 2002 figure for DAC ODA is in current dollars.

aid as direct budgetary support over somewhat longer time horizons. The European Union and the British now prefer this modality, and other donors (including France, and the United States through its Millennium Challenge Account) have begun experimenting with it. It is as yet unclear what criteria donors will use to decide the duration and extent of this new willingness to backstop national budgets.

Conclusion: EFA as a Measure of Change

In this contribution, we have sought to establish the basic parameters of an important series of shifts in the way that one aspect of multilateral activity in education is conceptualized, organized and enacted – that focused on assisting the poorest countries with their educational development. The present account points out several unprecedented shifts in this set of activities. Education is now embedded in a widening consensus on the core features of 'good' global development, a consensus that appears to bridge what had been a fundamental divide between those agents that have been more concerned with social equality and skeptical about the emergence of a global market, and those less concerned with equity, who view global economic growth through greater global integration as inevitably positive.

The international community has gone farther than in the past in establishing a clear, common set of priorities in education, focusing on time-bound targets for the achievement of universal basic education. New forms of donor coordination at the country level and global levels, and new aid modalities (most notably forms of pooled funding of recurrent budgetary costs of schooling) are now well established and growing. Transnational civil-society actors – from both the private sector and the non-governmental sectors – are on board. ODA funding itself seems set to increase.

What we can say with confidence about these changes is that many of them are surprising. They involved shifts that would not have been predicted a decade ago (e.g., increase in aid and aid to basic education; introduction of new actors). Furthermore, the degree to which the field of education has become an experimental ground for the new development compact is often underappreciated.

A move towards donor coordination, pooled funding and direct support of recurrent costs of primary education implies an important shift in the commitments of G8 governments to redistributive forms of multilateralism that are far different from the old bilateral regime of development. Yet these changes are recent, may actually be rather fragile, and are certainly open to considerable contestation. To paraphrase from Therien's critical reflections on the wider emergence of a global development compromise, the new focus on basic education as a strategy for poverty reduction may be seen as a victory for those who continue to frame the problem of development as one of individuals who are not well adapted to the demands of the market, and states that need to bear responsibility for development failures. It contrasts markedly from an understanding of development focused on structural inequalities that require both national and global measures of redistribution (Therien 2004/5; Maxwell 2005: 4). It is also at odds with the emergence, post 9/11, of renewed emphasis on using aid as a security perimeter by the United States. Finally, these changes in the aid-to-education regime are relative, not absolute shifts. Many of the older pathologies of educational ODA persist in the new regime. For example, the gap between rhetoric and resources, a hesitancy to empower multilateral channels of funding, and tensions between competing planning efforts (PRSPs, EFA, Fast Track Initiatives) and competing lead agencies (UNESCO, UNICEF, the World Bank) all remain.

Our initial sense is that what we are seeing is the opening up of an important and active phase in the re-structuring of governance at a global level. It is a phase that will almost certainly involve the redefinition of the appropriate scale, modes, and extent of global action in the field of education. With all its limitations and diverse interpretations, universal public access to free basic education has now achieved status and legitimacy as a global public good on a scale not realized during the 20th century.

References

Alexander, Nancy. 2002. *Paying for Education: How the World Bank and IMF Influence Education in Developing Countries*. Research Report, 1998, updated 2002. Washington, DC: Citizens' Network on Essential Services. Available at: http://www.campaignforeducation.org/resources/May2002/CNES%20Paying%20For%20Education.htm, accessed 4 October 2004.

Anderson, Benedict. 1983. *Imagined Communities*. London, New York: Verso.

Bruns, Barbara, Alain Mingat, and Ramahtra Rakotomalala 2003. *A Chance For Every Child: Achieving Universal Primary Education by 2015*. Washington, DC: World Bank.

Carnoy, Martin. 1999. *Globalization and Educational Reform: What Planners Need to Know*. Paris: IIEP.

Chabbott, Colette. 2003. *Constructing Education for Development: International Organizations and Education for All*. New York: Routledge/Falmer.

Commission for Africa. 2005. *Our Common Interest: Report of the Commission for Africa*. Available at: http://www.commissionforafrica.org/english/report/introduction.html, accessed 14 March 2005.

Dyer, Kate, and Chris Pain. 2004. Civil Society Budget Monitoring for National Accountability. Workshop Report, 17–19 February 2004. Lilongwe, Malawi.

EFA/FTI Secretariat. 2005. *Guidelines for Assessment and Endorsement of the Primary Education Component of an Education Sector Plan*. Available at: http://www1.worldbank.org/education/efaafti/documents/assessementguidelines.pdf, accessed 30 January 2005.

G8. 2001. G8 Communique. G8 Summit, Genova, Italy.

Global Campaign for Education. 2004. Undervaluing Teachers: IMF Policies Squeeze Zambia's Education System. Available at: http://www.campaignforeducation.org/resources/resources_listall.php, accessed 10 January 2005.

Gould, Jeremy, and Julia Ojanen. 2003. Merging in the Circle: The Politics of Tanzania's Poverty Reduction Strategy. Policy Paper 2. Institute of Development Studies, University of Helsinki.

IMF, OECD, World Bank, UN. 2000. *A Better World for All*. Washington, DC: Communications Development.

Jones, Phillip. 1988. *International Policies for Third World Education: UNESCO, Literacy and Development*. London, New York: Routledge.

———. 1992. *World Bank Financing of Education: Lending, Learning and Development*. London, New York: Falmer Press.

King, Kenneth. 1991. *Aid and Education in the Developing World: The Role of Donor Agencies in Educational Analysis*. Harlow, Essex: Longman.

Maxwell, Simon. January 2005. The Washington Consensus is Dead: Long Live the Meta-narrative. Working Paper 243. London: Overseas Development Institute.

McGee, Rosemary. and Alexandra Hughes. 2002. *Assessing Participation in Poverty Reduction Strategy Papers: A Desk-Based Synthesis of Experience in Sub-Saharan Africa*. Research Report 52. Sussex: Institute of Development Studies.

Meyer, John. W. 1977. The Effects of Education as an Institution. *American Journal of Sociology* 63: 55–77.

Millennium Development Project. 2005a. *Investing in Development: A Practical Plan to Achieve the Millennium Development Goals*. London: Earthscan and the UN Millennium Project. Available at: http://www.unmillenniumproject.org/, accessed 10 January 2005.

———. 2005b. *Toward Universal Primary Education: Investments, Incentives and Institutions*. Report from the Task Force on Education and Gender Equality. London: Earthscan and the UN Millennium Project. Available at: http://www.unmillennium-project.org/, accessed 10 January 2005.

Mundy, Karen. 1998. Educational Multilateralism and World Disorder. *Comparative Education Review* 42(4): 448–478.

———. 1999. UNESCO and the Limits of the possible. *International Journal of Educational Development* 19(1): 27–52.

———. 2002. Education in a Reformed World Bank. *International Journal of Educational Development* 22(5): 483–508.

———. and Lynn Murphy. 2001. Transnational Advocacy, Global Civil Society: Emerging Evidence from the Field of Education. *Comparative Education Review* 45(1): 85–126.

Murphy, L., and Mundy Karen. 2002. *New Roles of INGOs in the Education for all Movement*. Paris: UNESCO.

OECD/DAC. 1995. *Annual Report of the Development Assistance Committee*. Paris: OECD.

OECD/DAC. 1996. *Shaping the 21st Century: The Contribution of Development Cooperation*. Paris: OECD.

OECD/DAC. 2004. *Annual Development Co-operation Report*. Available at: http://www.oecd.org/document/19/0,2340,en_2649_37413_25612371_1_1_1_37413,00.html, accessed 10 January 2005.

Phillips, H. M. 1987. *UNICEF and Education: A Historical Perspective*. New York: UNICEF.

Pritchett, Lant. 2004. *Towards a New Consesus for Addressing the Global Challenge of the Lack of Education*. Available at http://www.copenhagenconsensus.com/Default.aspx?ID = 224, accessed 10 January 2005.

Riddell, Abby. 2000. Implications for Agencies of Pursuing Sector Wide Approaches in Education. Unpublished paper.

Rose, Pauline. 2003. *The Education Fast Track Initiative*. Report prepared for ActionAid on Behalf of the Global Campaign for Education. London: ActionAid.

Ruggie, John. G. 2003. The United Nations and Globalization: Patterns and Limits of Institutional Adaptation. *Global Governance* 9: 301–321.

Samoff, Joel. 1999. No Teacher Guide, No Textbooks, No Chairs: Contending with the Crisis in African Education. In: *Comparative Education: The Dialectic of the Global and the Local*, ed. by Robert Arnove et al., 393–431. Boulder: Rowman and Littlefield.

———. 2001. The Evolution of Education Aid to Africa: Changing Terminology, Persisting Practice. Paper presented at the Annual Meeting of Comparative and International Education Society, Washington, DC, March.

———. 2004. From Funding Projects to Supporting Sector?. *International Journal of Educational Development* 24(4): 397–427.

Sperling, Gene. 2001. The Developing World's Quiet Crisis. *The Financial Times*. Washington, D.C.

———. 2001. Toward Universal Education: Making a Promise and Keeping it. *Foreign Afairs* 80(5): 7–13.

Therien, Jean-Phillipe. 2002. Multilateral Institutions and the Poverty Debate. *International Journal* 57(2): 233–252.

———. 2004/5. The Politics of International Development: Towards a New Grand Compromise? *Economic Policy and Law: Journal of Trade and Environmental Studies* Special Issue. Available at: http://www.ecolomics-Internationa.org, accessed 15 March 2005.

Torres, Rosa Maria. 2000. *One Decade of Education for All: The Challenge Ahead*. Buenos Aires: International Institute of Educational Planning.

UNESCO. 1993. *World Education Report*. Paris: UNESCO.

———. 2004. *EFA Global Monitoring Report 2003/4: Gender and Education for All: the Leap to Equality*, UNESCO, Paris.

———. 2005. *EFA Global Monitoring Report 2005. The Quality Imperative*. Paris: UNESCO.

United Nations. 2004. *Interim Report on Achieving the Millennium Development Goal of Universal Primary Education*. Report of the Millennium Development Project. Paris. UNESCO. Available at: http://www.unmillenniumproject.org, accessed 10 September 2004.

World Bank. 2002a. *Achieving Education for All By 2015: Simulation Results for 47 Low Income Countries*. Washington, DC: World Bank.

———. 2002b. Review of the Poverty Reduction Strategy Paper Approach: Main Findings. Washington, DC: World Bank.

———. 2004. *Fast Track Initiative News* August, September, October 2004. Washington, DC: World Bank.

World Bank Development Committee. March 26, 2004c. *Education for All Fast Track Initiative. Progress Report*. Washington, DC: World Bank.

World Economic Forum. 2005. *Global Governance Initiative Annual Report 2005*: 51–63. Available at: http://www.weforum.org/site/homepublic.nsf/Content/Global + Governance + Initiative, accessed 15 March 2005.

World Education Forum. 2000. *The Dakar Framework for Action, Education for All: Meeting our Collective Commitments*. Dakar: Senegal.

The Author

Karen Mundy is Associate Professor and Canada Research Chair in Global Governance and Educational Change at the Ontario Institute for Studies in Education of the University of Toronto, where she also directs the Comparative, International and Development Education Programme. Her research focuses on educational change in sub-Saharan Africa, the evolution of international governmental and non-governmental organizations in education, and the politics of foreign aid to education.

Contact address: Canada Research Chair in Global Governance and Comparative Education, OISE-University of Toronto, 252 Bloor Street West, Toronto, Ontario, Canada. M5S 1V6, E-mail: kmundy@oise.utoronto.ca.

"IF ONLY MY EYES WERE DIFFERENT": THE LOSS OF IDENTITY AND THE UNDER-UTILIZATION OF BLACK CHILDREN'S EDUCATIONAL POTENTIAL – RETHINKING SOCIAL JUSTICE AND ASSIMILATION

KASSIE FREEMAN

Abstract – This study explores how social identity is formed in the United States of America. In particular, it examines the social, economic and educational problems experienced by underachieving Black American children and issues of social inequality along with their implications for social justice. Against the background of matters of group identity and its maintenance or loss, the author reflects on the under-utilization of Black American children's educational and human potential. She also suggests a rationale for re-conceiving the goal of social justice and how it is to be achieved, as well as the paradigm of cultural assimilation.

Zusammenfassung – "WENN DOCH MEINE AUGEN ANDERE WÄREN": DER VERLUST VON IDENTITÄT UND DIE MANGELNDE NUTZBARMACHUNG DES BILDUNGSPOTENTIALS SCHWARZER KINDER – EINE REVISION DER SOZIALEN GERECHTIGKEIT UND ASSIMILATION – Diese Untersuchung erforscht, wie sich soziale Identität in den Vereinigten Staaten von Amerika bildet. Im Besonderen werden die sozialen, ökonomischen und pädagogischen Probleme untersucht, die von leistungsschwachen schwarzen amerikanischen Kindern erfahren werden, sowie die Probleme sozialer Ungleichheit in Verbindung mit ihren Implikationen für die soziale Gerechtigkeit. Vor dem Hintergrund der Dynamik von Guppenidentität sowie deren Erhaltung oder Verlust reflektiert die Autorin über die mangelnde Nutzbarmachung des Bildungs- und des menschlichen Potentials schwarzer amerikanischer Kinder. Sie entwickelt auch Vorschläge, wie die soziale Gerechtigkeit wieder als eine Zielvorstellung zu errichten und wie diese zu verwirklichen ist, ebenso wie das Paradigma der kulturellen Assimilation.

Résumé – « SI SEULEMENT MES YEUX ÉTAIENT DIFFÉRENTS »: LA PERTE D'IDENTITÉ ET LA SOUS-UTILISATION DU POTENTIEL ÉDUCATIF DES ENFANTS NOIRS : REPENSER LA JUSTICE SOCIALE ET L'ASSIMILATION – Cette étude explore comment l'identité sociale est constituée aux États-Unis d'Amérique. En particulier, elle examine les problèmes sociaux, économiques et éducatifs vécus par les enfants noirs-américains aux acquis insuffisants, et les questions de l'inégalité sociale en même temps que leurs implications pour la justice sociale. Sur l'arrière-plan des questions de l'identité de groupe et de son maintien ou de sa perte, l'auteur réfléchit sur la sous-utilisation du potentiel humain et éducatif des enfants noirs-américains. Elle suggère également une analyse raisonnée pour reconcevoir la finalité de la justice sociale et sa réalisation, aussi bien que le paradigme de l'assimilation culturelle.

Resumen – "SI TAN SÓLO MIS OJOS FUESEN DIFERENTES": LA PÉRDIDA DE IDENTIDAD Y EL DESAPROVECHAMIENTO DEL POTENCIAL DE

J. Zajda (ed.), Education and Social Justice, 39-55.

EDUCACIÓN DE NIÑOS DE RAZA NEGRA – RECONSIDERACIÓN DE LA JUSTICIA SOCIAL Y DE LA INTEGRACIÓN – Este trabajo investiga cómo se forma la identidad social en los Estados Unidos de América. En particular, examina los problemas sociales, económicos y educativos que tienen los niños norteamericanos de raza negra que no alcanzan los objetivos de aprendizaje, y temas de desigualdad social y sus implicaciones en cuanto a la justicia social. Ante el trasfondo de la identidad de grupos y conservación o pérdida de la misma, la autora reflexiona sobre el desaprovechamiento del potencial educativo y humano de los niños norteamericanos de raza negra proponiendo, además, un fundamento para reconcebir el objetivo de justicia social y cómo lograrlo, al igual que un nuevo modelo de integración cultural.

Резюме – «ЕСЛИ БЫ У МЕНЯ БЫЛИ ДРУГИЕ ГЛАЗА»: УТРАТА ИДЕНТИЧНОСТИ И НЕПОЛНОЕ ИСПОЛЬЗОВАНИЕ ОБРАЗОВАТЕЛЬНОГО ПОТЕНЦИАЛА ЧЕРНОКОЖИХ ДЕТЕЙ – ПЕРЕСМОТР СОЦИАЛЬНОЙ СПРАВЕДЛИВОСТИ И АССИМИЛЯЦИИ – В данном исследовании изучается проблема формирования социальной идентичности в Соединенных Штатах Америки. В частности, здесь рассматриваются социальные, экономическе и образовательные проблемы, возникшиеся перед американскими чернокожими детьми, а также проблема социального неравенства и ее влияние на социальную справедливость. На фоне вопросов о групповой идентичности и ее сохранении или утраты, автор статьи рассуждает о неполном использовании образовательного и человеческого потенциала американских чернокожих детей. Автор также предлагает логическое обоснование для пересмотра целей социальной справедливости и способов ее достижения, а также парадигму культурной ассимиляции.

The present study takes the first part of its title from Toni Morrison's novel *The Bluest Eye* (1970). In this novel, Toni Morrison describes a character nicknamed Soaphead Church, who was born of mixed blood and settled in Lorain, Ohio, in 1936. Not being able to understand him, the women of the town decided that he must be supernatural rather than unnatural. Pecola Breedlove, the 12-year-old heroine of the novel, heard of this man's powers and came to him with one request (p. 138):

> "I can't go to school no more. And I thought maybe you could help me."
> "Help you how? Tell me. Don't be frightened."
> "My eyes."
> "What about your eyes?"
> "I want them blue."

Soaphead thought that "Of all the wishes people had brought him – money, love, revenge – this seemed to him the most poignant and the one most deserving of fulfillment. A little Black girl who wanted to rise up out of the pit of her blackness and see the world with blue eyes." Pecola symbolizes all the Black children who have come to believe that if only they could be different they would be valued, and Soaphead symbolizes all those who believe in the undervaluing of difference. In their exchange, two very important dynamics occurred. Soaphead felt, as Morrison describes, that all that was worth learning was to separate body, mind, and spirit from all that suggested Africa: to cultivate the habits, tastes, and preferences of non-Blacks. The second noteworthy dynamic was that Pecola began with "I can't go to school no more." These dynamics are important because they describe the loss of Black children's identity and the resulting under-utilization of their potential. Building on this story, briefly, the present study discusses three crucial points:

1. how a group's loss of identity occurs and how that leads to the under-utilization of its educational/human potential;
2. the resulting non-monetary costs of the under-utilization of human potential to societies;
3. the rationale for rethinking social justice and the assimilation paradigm.

I am using a racial definition for Black,that is, the physical characteristics that identify Blacks, such as colour, hair, and/or other distinguishing features that define race. Although most recently ethnicity has been used to define a group's identity and experiences in educational research, I use race because in comparative and international research race more accurately describes the similarity of Black experiences.

"If Only My Eyes Were Different"

What could be the common characteristics globally that would make Black children want to see the world through blue eyes? In order for Black children to assimilate into the dominant culture in different countries, historically, their cultural values have been minimized or, in some cases, attempts have been made to separate them altogether from their cultural group. This process of cultural assimilation or alienation has had a devastating effect on Black children's educational opportunities around the globe, particularly as it relates to the loss of their identity and to the under-utilization of their human potential and to the resulting costs to societies. A group's loss of identity occurs through a process of cultural alienation and annihilation and through a culture of exclusion.

Cultural Alienation and Annihilation: Implications for Social Justice

According to Anderson (1994: 82), one way that the use of power over a less powerful group takes form is "the group with the greater power annihilates the powerless group or drives them out of the territory". Thus, cultural alienation and annihilation can be defined as that process that controlling populations use to minimize or eradicate the culture of minority populations. Generally, this process is synonymous with assimilation, acculturation, or deracination, the term Mankiller (1993) used to describe the mission of boarding schools to annihilate the American Indian culture, or the uprooting or destruction of a race and its culture. In order for Blacks to assimilate into the dominant culture in different countries, they were often separated or alienated from their own cultural group or an attempt was made to eliminate (annihilate) their culture altogether. Clear examples of cultural alienation and annihilation can be found across Black populations. In Australia, for example, "between 1910 and 1970 it [the Australian government] forcibly stole up to 100,000 aboriginal children from their families to live with whites in an attempt at forced integration – 'to breed the black out,' as politicians of the day expressed it" (Evenson 1998: A10). As it related to the experience of Black Britons, Fryer (1992: 70) indicated that most Black Londoners "had been torn from their parents and ethnic groups while still children. They were atomized in separate households, cut off from the cultural nourishment and reinforcement made possible by even the most inhumane plantation system". As Claude Steele (1999: 58), a Black Briton, stated in the popular press: "I have done a lot of thinking about issues of assimilation and national identity. And I'm beginning to suspect that immigrants can only blend totally into their host environment if they are the same colour as the host or dominant population."

Similarly, African American families were divided. Franklin and Moss (1988: 106–107) described the process of dividing Black slave families in the United States: "Since the domestic slave trade and slave breeding were essentially economic and not humanitarian activities, it is not surprising to find that in the sale of slaves there was the persistent practice of dividing families. Husbands were separated from their wives, and mothers were separated from their children." Although the dividing of families might have been justified for economic reasons, it also served the function of cultural annihilation and/or alienation. That is, when families were divided, they had to reconstruct their social institutions into new forms.

Education has been used as one of the primary channels through which cultural alienation and annihilation have occurred. This has serious implications for social justice. In addition to using education as a divisive tool based on color among Blacks, cultural alienation and annihilation have occurred through the transmission of education. That is, the way in which education has been transmitted (teaching style) and the content of educational materials (curriculum) have discounted the social and cultural capital of Black populations (consciously or subconsciously) and have therefore minimized the culture of Black populations. Who has taught, what has been taught, and how it has been taught over time have severely eroded the cultural identity and educational opportunities of Blacks. Although this has been the case historically, Black educators and researchers, particularly in the United States, are currently extensively examining and discussing ways to undo the intellectual damage to Black children by demonstrating the importance of valuing the culture of Blacks rather than eradicating their culture. For example, several researchers and educators have written about the influence of the curriculum (what is being taught) on the education of Black children (e.g., Banks 1988; Hollins 1996; King 1995). At the same time Black educators in the United States have focused their research on the inclusion of a Black perspective and valuing Black culture in the educational system, Black researchers in other countries have also begun to address these same issues. Searle (1994: 25) stated about the British system: "The ignorance of teachers and the school system generally about the communities which they serve is still a vital factor which promotes conflict and misunderstanding between teachers and students."

Bridges (1994: 4), another British educator, supported Searle's assertion. He indicated that more Black teachers were employed as a way "of counterbalancing the under representation of black teachers in the borough and, through this, to attack the real problems of underachievement among black children." Cultural alienation and annihilation have had a devastating effect on Black students' participation in education. Over time, the process of trying "to breed the black out" (assimilation), whether through the devaluation of the cultural capital of Blacks or the what and who of the transmission of knowledge, has severely impacted on the Black students' sense of self and achievement. There should be little doubt that cultural alienation/annihilation has led to a 'culture of exclusion' for Black populations globally, which is at odds with the principles of democracy and social justice in particular.

Culture of Exclusion

Drawing on the research of Searle and Bridges (1994: 11), a culture of exclusion, then, can be defined as that process whereby Black children are excluded from schooling, whether through suspension or expulsion or place ment in the lower tracks (or streaming by ability) of schooling – which would be referred to as 'internal expulsion'. Educational expulsion (suspension) is a phenomenon that is similarly faced by Black populations globally. For example, Fernando Ka (1998: 2), in a report on the conditions of Blacks in Portugal, indicated the following:

> "The black community in general – and the children and young people in particular – are victims of educational expulsion. The number of those that manage to complete compulsory education (up to the 9th grade) is frightfully low, and even worse if we consider the number of those who manage to complete secondary education (12th grade)"

In the United States, as in Britain and Portugal, a greater number of Black children are subjected to suspension or expulsion. For example, a comprehensive study conducted by the Children's Defense Fund (1975: 12) in the 1970s reported the following:

> "No one is immune from suspension, but black children were suspended at twice the rate of any other ethnic group. Nationally, if they had been suspended at the same rate as whites, nearly 50 percent or 188,479 of the black children suspended

> would have remained in school. Although black children accounted for 27.1% of the enrollment in the districts reporting to OCR, they constituted 42.3% of the racially identified suspensions."

However, the greatest number of African American students are subjected to 'internal expulsion'. A recent report (Klenbort 1999) presented, as an example, a statement from a high-school sophomore who spent his schooling in the lower-level track: "You live in the basement, you die in the basement. You know what I mean?" Researchers such as Oakes (1985), Wheelock (1992), Braddock and Slavin (1995) support this student's description of tracking or what can be referred as 'internal expulsion'. Whether internally excluded or suspended or expelled, Black students globally share similar experiences. At least as described in Britain, Portugal, and the United States, Black students comprise the majority of students facing a 'culture of exclusion'. This has led to the under-utilization of Blacks in education which, in turn, has implications for societal and individual costs.

Non-Monetary Costs of Under-Utilization of Human Potential

Through the historical experiences of Black populations, the pattern of cultural alienation and annihilation and the culture of exclusion surrounding their schooling, a clear pattern emerges as to how their human potential has been under-utilized. The under-utilization of Blacks' human potential has not been without costs to individuals or societies. What is the under-utilization of potential and how has it been manifested as it relates to Black populations? The under-utilization of human potential is defined as a too-narrow definition of talents (what constitutes merit), matching of abilities with tasks (under-employment), or the lack of use of talents (unemployment) which prevents individuals or groups from maximizing their capabilities and/or productivity (Freeman et al. 1999). The under-utilization of human potential takes on many dimensions across cultures. For example, it can occur in the case of discrimination, differential educational opportunities among individuals and/or groups, the inappropriate training for the market, or a division in the distribution of technological knowledge – the digital divide. Schultz (1961: 320) commented on one aspect of this issue of the under-utilization of human potential in the early 1960s when he stated: "Human capital deteriorates when it is idle because unemployment impairs the skills that workers have acquired." Additionally he remarked that there are many hindrances to the free choice of professions due to discrimination, whether ethnic, class, gender, or religious. Understanding the under-utilization of human potential has merit because it can help us better grasp educational inequality, the under-employment and unemployment of different groups, the differences in roles in societies, and the economic division between the "haves" and "have-nots".

Farrell (1992) outlined a model in which he described four points where inequality as it relates to educational opportunities is likely to occur:

- Access: the differences in children from different groups getting into the school system
- Survival: once in school the differences in children from various groups staying in the school system to some defined level, usually the end of a cycle (primary, secondary, higher)
- Output: the differences in children from different groups learning the same things to the same level
- Outcome: the differences in children from different groups living relatively similar lives subsequent to and as a result of schooling (having equal income, having jobs of the same status, having equal access to positions of political power, etc.).

Drawing on Farrell's (1992) research, other researchers (Freeman et al. 1999) found that there are four points at which under-utilization of human potential typically occurs:

1. the transition of students into schooling;
2. the experiences of students within the educational setting;
3. the transition of students to the labor market; and
4. the experiences in the workplace.

In a recently completed cross-cultural study, we found that minority groups tended to be under-utilized across societies at each point (Freeman et al. 1999). At each of these points, under-utilization of potential occurs for Black populations because of a too-narrow definition of merit and because of who is defining merit for different groups. That is, at the point of entrance to schooling, as pointed out in this research, the culture of Black populations undergoes a process of being discounted, whether through alienation or annihilation. This in turn leads to a culture of exclusion, where students are turned off from schooling, which limits labour market opportunities. As demonstrated in this research, this cycle of under-utilization has historically been and continues to be the case with Black populations globally. This cycle of under-utilization of human potential understandably has costs for individuals and societies.

Economics of education theorists typically divide costs and benefits of education into monetary and non-monetary (Johns, Morphet and Alexander 1983; Merisotis 1998; Schultz 1961; Thurow 1972). They generally assess monetary and non-monetary costs by societal and private-individual factors (Johns et al. 1983). The monetary costs (i.e., unemployment and under-employment which leads to lower productivity and reduced tax revenue) associated with the under-utilization of the potential of Blacks have been generally well documented (Carnoy 1994; Schultz 1961; Thurow 1972). Furthermore, Levitan, Magnum and Marshall (1972: 427) reported that "under-utilization and underdevelopment not only deprive Blacks of opportunities to improve their material welfare but also cost the nation the economic contribution they could make if they had better employment and income opportunities". However, the current costs associated with unemployment and/or underemployment of Blacks continue to be extremely costly to societies. In Australia, for example, the *Daily Telegraph* (1999: 10) reported that the unemployment rate among Aborigines (23%) was three times the general rate and was growing twice as fast. Although the Australian government subsidizes approximately 70% of Aboriginals who work, the article concluded that instead of subsidies, "better education and training are needed".

In Portugal, Ka (1998: 7) stated concerning Blacks' participation in the labour market: "It is not easy for a Black person to find a decent job in this country, even if s/he has good academic and/or professional qualifications. The colour of the skin is always a barrier, often difficult to transpose." Similarly, the latest report from the United States Department of Labor (1999: 11–12) indicated that although the unemployment rates for African Americans and Hispanics have declined in the past 2 years, the "unemployment rate of African American men is still twice that of white men. For African American teens, unemployment has fallen dramatically over the past 6 years but remains around 25% or higher".

Although the costs associated with the under-utilization of the potential of Blacks have been documented, considerably less has been written about the non-monetary costs associated with education, particularly as it relates to the under-utilization of Black populations. This is particularly troubling given that non-monetary costs to societies and individuals are much more difficult to penetrate and eradicate. What are the non-monetary costs associated with the under-utilization of Blacks' human potential? Non-monetary costs are usually those costs that are more indirect and are usually seen over time. Merisotis (1998) defines non-monetary costs as costs that accrue to individuals, to groups of people, or to society broadly that are not directly related to economic, fiscal, or labor market effects.

Societal Non-Monetary Costs

Societal non-monetary costs would include such things as lack of the benefits of an intergenerational effect, increased crime, and decreased adaptability to lifelong learning and use of technology – that is, a mismatch between skill levels (Johns et al. 1983; Merisotis 1998). Due to the very nature of non-monetary costs, it is difficult to affix a price tag. Nonetheless, as Bowen (1977: 458) has indicated, the importance of better understanding the non-monetary benefits to societies and individuals is crucial:

> The monetary returns alone, the forms of enhanced earnings of workers and improved technology, are probably sufficient to offset all the costs. But over and above the monetary returns are the personal development and life enrichment of millions of people, the preservation of the cultural heritage, the advancement of knowledge and the arts, a major contribution to the national prestige and power, and the direct satisfactions derived from college attendance and from living in a society where knowledge and the arts flourish. These non-monetary benefits surely are far greater than the monetary benefits – so much greater, in fact, that individual

and social decisions about the future of higher education should be made primarily on the basis of non-monetary considerations and only secondarily on the basis of monetary factors.

Intergenerational Effect

The intergenerational effect, according to Johns et al. (1983), can be understood as a process whereby the quality of life of children whose parents have attended college and value education is transmitted between generations. That is, the higher the level of education, the higher the value of education that parents instill in their children. For example, college-choice theorists (e.g., Hossler and Gallagher 1987; Hearn 1991) have documented that the children of college-educated parents are more likely to choose higher-education participation than those of parents who have not participated in higher education. Therefore, the fact that Black families have been under-educated is costly to societies because it causes generations of children to be under-utilized primarily at the first and second points of under-utilization (i.e., the transition of students into schooling and their experiences once in school). As Figure 1 below demonstrates, the transition into school and the experience in schooling have a reciprocal impact on the intergenerational effect. That is, because generations of Black populations have not been the beneficiaries of education, in many cases, they are unable to transmit education to their children, which impacts students' transition into school and their experiences once in school (e.g., different cultural capital and lack of information), which in turn affects the educational outcomes of future generations. This would be considered a non-monetary cost because what is hurt most is the ability of generations who are uneducated to instill the aspiration and motivation to continue schooling.

Increased Crime

Increases in crime rates in communities with less-educated populations are also associated with under-utilization of human potential and therefore increased costs to society. For example, Merisotis (1998: 3) suggested that "there are far fewer prisoners with at least some college education compared with those with high school or less". It should be no surprise that with a 'culture of expulsion', more Blacks become disinterested in schooling. As Figure 1 demonstrates, the schooling experience is directly linked to increases in crime, which impacts on students' inability to transition to the labor market. For example, when *The Economist* (1999: 2) discussed British Prime Minister Tony Blair's war on poverty, the article indicated that the government's micro-initiative would be aimed at trouble spots such as "crime and educational failure". It is widely accepted across societies that increased crime among different segments of populations is associated with decreased educational opportunities. In speaking about social costs related to poverty and education, Carnoy (1994: 240–241) summed up the linkage between costs, education, and crime in this way:

> The middle class is a 'hostage to worry' about crime, and spends more and more each year on guns, self-defense courses, and other paraphernalia related to warding off assailants ... All this means that whatever the costs of increasing crime, they are being privatized, and they are rising ... The rising social costs of poverty should be convincing argument for the need to reduce racial inequality.

Adaptability to Lifelong Learning and Technology

Individuals who are adaptable to changing skills and understanding of techniques of lifelong learning while being acutely aware of technology are what all societies will increasingly require. Because the potential of Black populations has been under-utilized at all four points, societies face enormous costs associated with increasing Black students' motivation and aspiration to participate in higher levels of schooling at the same time that higher skills are already necessary. These societal costs have also had consequences for Black individuals across societies. The report from the United States Labor Department (1999: 4–5) sums up the importance of adaptability to lifelong learning and technology:

> In the information-based, skills-intensive economy of the twenty-first century, one thing is clear: knowing means growing ... While many workers will continue to be in occupations that do not require a bachelor's degree, the best jobs will be those requiring education and training ... Lifelong learning for workers will become more important as a result"

This report indicated that because African Americans lag behind Whites in college attendance, this group lacks access to many of the necessary skills that higher education provides. Similarly in Portugal, Ka (1998: 5) stated, "Few are the Black persons that can benefit from adequate professional training, although Portugal has been one of the European Union countries that received the largest amounts in subsidies for that end." Therefore, it is easy to see how, relative to adaptability to lifelong learning and technology, the potential of Blacks has been and continues to be underutilized at the points of transition into the labour market and in the labor market itself (see Figure 1).

Individual Non-Monetary Costs

Relating to the benefits of education to the individual, Bowen (1977: 38) argued: "Education should be directed toward the growth of the whole person through cultivation not only of the intellect and practical competence but also of the affective dispositions, including the moral, religious, emotional, and esthetic aspects of the personality." Unfortunately, as pointed out historically, education has not necessarily served Black individuals in this

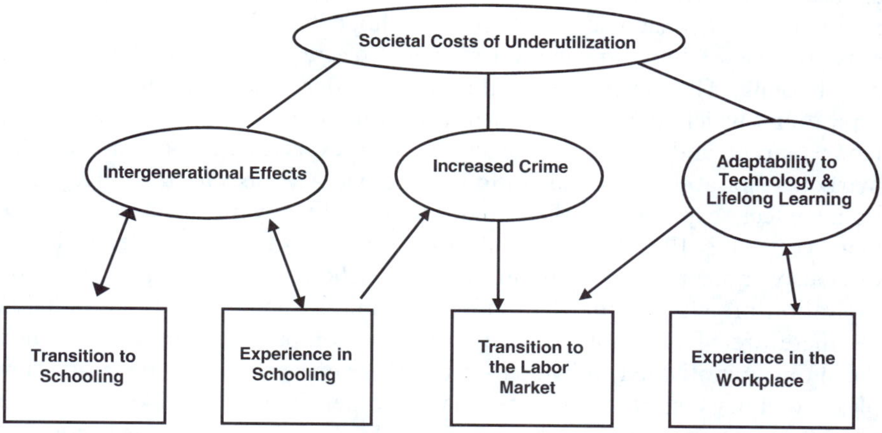

Figure 1. Linkages between societal costs of under-utilization and the four points of under-utilization

way. In fact, individual costs to Blacks would include psychological barriers – affective dispositions, as Bowen stated, such as decrease in motivation and aspiration to participate in education (Freeman 1997) and what Steele (1999) refers to as "stereotype threat". Having their talents under-utilized over the centuries has impacted the psychological well-being (self-esteem and confidence) because the costs of underutilizing their potential has gone to the heart and soul of Blacks; overcoming this phenomenon will not be easy.

Aspiration and motivation

In a qualitative study Freeman (1997: 537) conducted among Black high-school students to assess college choice (i.e., why some African Americans

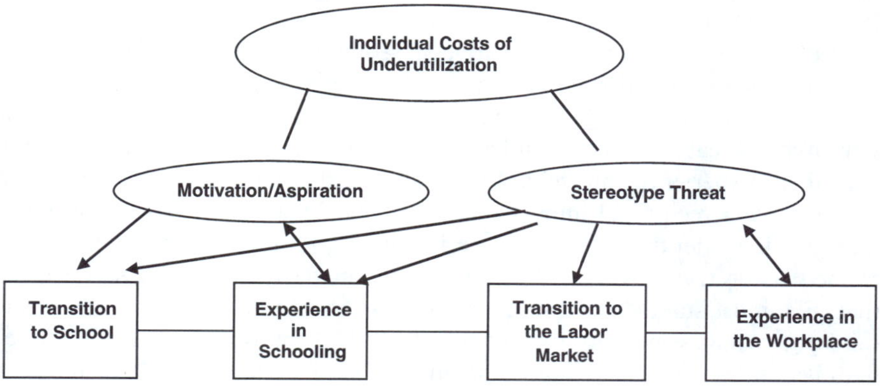

Figure 2. Linkages between individual costs of under-utilization and the four points of under-utilization

choose to participate in higher education and some do not), a student responded, rather laconically: "They lose hope." As Figure 2 suggests, that sense of loss of hope impacts on students' desire to move to the next level of schooling. The experiences within school affect students' motivation and aspiration, which impacts on their acquiring the skills to proceed to the labor market and also can impact on their experiences once in the labor market. Aspiration and motivation are obviously tied to the intergenerational effect, explained earlier, and are associated with academic achievement (Freeman 1995): Children who do not perform well academically are obviously more prone to disconnect from schooling. Also, motivation and aspiration are closely linked to cultural affinity. That is, the more individuals there are of the same cultures who are not participating in education, the more unmotivated individuals from the same group will be. For example, individuals start to assume that if other individuals like themselves who have participated in the labor market have not obtained positions commensurate with their level of schooling, there is no reason to bother with education.

The costs to societies of individuals who lose their motivation and aspiration to participate in schooling at any level, while difficult to assess, are high. The questions become: How do societies go about first impacting motivation and aspiration, and next, how do societies place a price tag on impacting the change of a process that has been historically implemented? In other words, how do we implement the notion of social justice which is authentic and genuine in empowering classroom pedagogy?

Stereotype Threat

In the same way that Black individuals' motivation and aspiration have been impacted by the under-utilization of Blacks over time, Steele (1999) more recently has documented a process that he refers to as "stereotype threat" that can also influence the costs of the under-utilization of the potential of Blacks. Steele (p. 45) describes "stereotype threat" as "the threat of being viewed through the lens of a negative stereotype, or the fear of doing something that would inadvertently confirm that stereotype – something external, the situational threat of being negatively stereotyped". Figure 2 depicts that stereotype threat influences students at the point of transition to schooling and their experiences in school and shows that students' experiences in school have a reciprocal impact on stereotype threat. Steele (p. 50) reported that Black students taking an experimental test "under 'stereotype threat' seemed to be trying too hard ... The threat made them inefficient on a test that, like most standardized tests, is set up so that thinking long often means thinking wrong, especially on difficult items like the ones we used". Steele's findings cut across social class, and in fact, he indicated (p. 50) that "what exposes students to the pressure of 'stereotype threat' is not weaker academic identity and skills but stronger academic identity and skills. In addition to the academic costs to Blacks that accompany stereotype threat, Steele (pp. 50–51) stated:

> Sadly, the effort that accompanies 'stereotype threat' exacts an additional price. We found the blood pressure of black students performing a difficult cognitive task under 'stereotype threat' was elevated compared with black students who were not under 'stereotype threat' or white students in either situation.

Unlike societal non-monetary costs, individual costs are often ignored or underestimated. Certainly, there are enormous costs associated with the damage exacted on the individual psyche of Blacks by having their potential under-utilized. Unless and/or until individual costs are addressed, programs or models will have a difficult time being effectuated. As Henry Levin (2004) stated: "Individuals act on what they perceive, not necessarily on what others say is." Through societies' under-utilization of the human potential of Blacks, the non-monetary costs have been high and the effects are still growing. How do all of these pieces tie together to demonstrate a composite of the costs associated with the under-utilization of Black populations? How do these pieces fit together to make the case for an expanded research agenda?

Black Children's Educational Potential: Rethinking the Assimilation Paradigm

As research demonstrates, Black children globally are under-achieving academically. Their educational potential is severely limited due to the minimizing of their identity through the process of cultural assimilation and alienation. This loss of identity has led to the under-utilization of Black children's potential, thereby often leading to their being disinterested in school, under-achieving academically, or dropping out of school. In order to fully value and capture the potential of Black children, a different paradigm is necessary.

First, it is important that schools and societies value the culture of all children. As pointed out, school curriculums must be reflective of the histories and heritage of all groups in society. All children bring cultural and social capital to schools and other settings that must be recognized and valued, not minimized or 'bred out'. Second, the process of exclusion in school has to be factored into Black children's loss of identity and into the under-utilization of their educational potential. What are methods to prevent students from internal and external expulsion? Better still, what are alternative ways of stimulating and developing Black children's interest in school as opposed to expelling them? Each time students are expelled from school, their potential is being under-utilized. To better understand the barriers constructed across cultures to under-utilize the potential human potential of Blacks in countries where non-Blacks are the controlling populations, much more research needs to be conducted. In order to more fully understand this process, more research on each point where under-utilization occurs has to be explored. This research demonstrates how each aspect of the Black experience impacts on each experience and level of schooling. Understanding the costs, particularly the non-monetary costs as indicated by Bowen (1977), associated with the under-utilization of Black potential is imperative so that countries better understand how everyone is losing.

Finally, though, it is not enough for countries to assess the costs associated with the under-utilization of the potential of Black populations, for this research suggests that at each point Blacks have been under-utilized. At the beginning of the 21st century, countries will find it necessary to develop strategies to address the societal and individual costs associated with Black populations' under-utilization while simultaneously increasing the utilization of the potential of Blacks. Carnoy (1997: 241) describes the way the process of increasing the spending on the under-utilization of Blacks should work: "The vicious cycle of increasing social costs will gradually break. Down the road, as early-childhood investment reduces spending on adult social problems, more public funds will become available for general education and other activities that improve worker productivity and growth rates." However, countries have not yet been able to develop a formula for assessing the individual and societal costs and therefore to appropriately target their spending.

Conclusion

The goal of social justice should be the full utilization of the potential of all people. To attempt to force all cultural groups to assimilate into one model inevitably will lead to the under-utilization of a cultural group, in this case Black populations, which creates social and economic problems which are detrimental to the whole of society. In order that globalization might be successful for individual countries and countries collectively, the potential of all of their citizens must be utilized. In order to balance this imperative, different paradigms and players have to be a part of the research agenda, particularly as it relates to Black children and social justice. The reality is that Black children's eyes are not going to be different, as Pecola Breedlove so desperately wanted. But neither should societies be structured, as Soaphead Church believed and practiced, to enforce all individuals to assimilate into one model, while ignoring human rights and social justice in the global economy.

References

Anderson, Claud. 1994. *Black Labor White Wealth: The Search for Power and Economic Justice*. Edgewood, MD: Duncan and Duncan.

Anderson, James D. 1988. *The Education of Blacks in the South, 1860–1935*. Chapel Hill, NC: The University of North Carolina Press.

Banks, James A. 1988. *Multiethnic Education*. 2nd ed. Boston: Allyn and Bacon.

Braddock, Jomills, and Robert E. Slavin. 1995. Why Ability Grouping Must End: Achieving Excellence and Equity in American Education. In: *Beyond Tracking: Finding Success in Inclusive Schools*, ed. by Harbison Pool and Jane A. Page, 7–19. Bloomington, IN: Phi Delta Kappa Educational Foundation.

Bridges, Len. 1994. Exclusions: How Did We Get Here? In: *Outcast England: How Schools Exclude Black Children*, ed. by Jenny Bourne, Lee Bridges and Chris Searle, 1–16. London: Institute of Race Relations.

Bowen, Howard. 1977. *Investment in Learning*. San Francisco: Jossey-Bass.

Carnoy, Martin. 1992. Education and the State: From Adam Smith to Perestroika. In: *Emergent Issues in Education*, ed. by Robert Arnove, Philip Altbach and Gail Kelly, 143–159. Albany, NY: State University of New York Press.

———. 1994. *Faded Dreams: The Politics and Economics of Race in America*. Cambridge: Cambridge University Press.

Children's Defense Fund. 1975. *School Suspensions: Are They Helping Children?*. Washington, DC: Children's Defense Fund.

Cicourel, Aaron, and Hugh Mehan. 1985. Universal Development, Stratifying Practices, and Status Attainment. *Research in Social Stratification and Mobility* 4(5): 728–734.

Clarke, John. 1972. Introduction. In: *World's Great Men of Color*, ed. by Joel A. Rogers, ix–xvi. New York: Macmillan.

Coleman, James. 1988. Social Capital in the Creation of Human Capital. *American Journal of Sociology* 94: 95–120.

———. 1990. *Foundations of Social Theory*. Cambridge, MA: Belknap Press.

The Daily Telegraph. 1999. Working Towards a Solution. *The Daily Telegraph May* 26: 18.

DiMaggio, Paul, and John Mohr. 1985. Cultural Capital, Educational Attainment, and Marital Selection. *American Journal of Sociology* 90(6): 1231–1261.

Evenson, B. 1998, February 23. Land Crisis Brewing Down Under: A 1996 Court Ruling Means Aboriginals Could Claim 80 per cent of Australia's Land Mass. *The Ottawa Citizen*, p. A10.

Farrell, Joseph. 1992. Conceptualizing Education and the Drive for Social Equality. In: *Emergent Issues in Education*, ed. by Robert Arnove, Philip Altbach and Gail Kelly, 107–122. Albany, NY: State University of New York Press.

Foster, Michele. 1997. *Black Teachers on Teaching*. New York: The New Press.

Franklin, John, and Alfred Moss. 1988. *From Slavery to Freedom: A History of Negro Americans*, 6th ed. New York: McGraw-Hill.

Freeman, Kassie. 1999. My Soul is Missing: African American Students' Perceptions of the Curriculum and the Influence on College Choice. *Review of African American Education* 1(1): 31–43.

———. 1997. Increasing African Americans' Participation in Higher Education: African American High School Students' Perspective. *The Journal of Higher Education* 68(5): 523–550.

———, et al. 1999. *Economic Development and the Utilization of Human Potential: Bridging the Gap Between Higher Education, Economics, and Culture*. Nashville, TN: Vanderbilt University, Department of Leadership and Organizations.

Fryer, Peter. 1992. *Staying Power: The History of Black People in Britain*, 6th ed. London: Pluto Press.

Hearn, James. 1991. Academic and Nonacademic Influences on the College Destinations of 1980 High School Graduates. *Sociology of Education* 64: 158–171.

Hollins, Etta R. 1996. *Culture in School: Revealing the Deeper Meaning*. Mahwah, NJ: Lawrence Erlbaum Associates.

Hossler, Don, and Karen Gallagher. 1987. Studying Student College Choice: A Three-Phase Model and The Implications for Policymakers. *College and University* 62(3): 207–221.

Irvine, Jacqueline. 1990. *Black Students and School Failure: Policies, Practices, and Prescriptions*. Westport, CT: Praeger.

Johns, Roe, and Edgar Morphet. 1983. *The Economics and Financing Of Education*, 4th ed. Englewood Cliffs, NJ: Prentice-Hall.

Ka, Fernando. 1998. Black People's Situation in Portugal. Paper prepared for Fisk University Race Relations Institute Conference, Nashville, Tennessee, 5–8 July.

King, J. E. 1995. Culture-Centered Knowledge: Black Studies, Curriculum Transformation, and Social Action. In: *Handbook of Research on Multicultural Education*, ed. by James Banks and Cherry Banks. New York: Macmillan.

Kogbara, Donu. A Sense of Elsewhere. *Mail on Sunday* August: 58–59.

Ladson-Billings, Gloria. 1994. *The Dreamkeepers: Successful Teachers of African American Children*. San Francisco: Jossey-Bass.

Levin, Henry. 2004. Personal communication with the author.

Levitan, Sar, Garth Mangum, and Ray Marshall. 1972. *Human Resources and Labor Markets: Labor and Manpower in the American Economy*. New York: Harper and Row.

Lorde, Audrey. 1992. Foreword to the English Language Edition. In: *Showing Our Colours: Afro-German Women Speak Out*, ed. by May Opitzsto and Catherina Oguntoye, xi–xviii. London: Open Letters.

Mankiller, Wilma. 1993. *Mankiller: A Chief and Her People*. New York: St. Martin's Press.

Merisotis, Jamie P. 1998. Who Benefits from Education? An American Perspective. International Higher Education 1–2. Chestnut Hill, MA: Department of Higher Education, Boston College.

Morris, John, and Ellen Goldring. 1999. Are Magnet Schools More Equitable? An Analysis of the Disciplinary Rates of African American and White Students in Cincinnati Magnet and Nonmagnet Schools. *Equity and Excellence in Education* 32(3): 59–65.

Morrison, Toni. 1970. *The Bluest Eye*. New York: Rinehart and Winston.

Oakes, Jeannie. 1985. *Keeping Track*. New Haven, CT: Yale University Press.

Opitzsto, May, and Catherina Oguntoye (eds.). 1992. *Showing Our Colours: Afro-German Women Speak out*. London: Open Letters.

Pool, Harbison, and Jane Page. 1995. Tracking and its Effects on African–Americans in the Field of Education. In: *Beyond Tracking: Finding Success in Inclusive Schools*, ed. by Harbison Pool and Jane Page, 71–77. Bloomington, IN: Phi Delta Kappa Educational Foundation.

Pilkington, Doris. 1996. *Follow the Rabbit-Proof Fence*. Queensland, Australia: University of Queensland Press.

Saunders, A. C. de C. M. 1982. *A History of Black Slaves and Freedmen in Portugal 1441–1555*. Cambridge: Cambridge University Press.

Schultz, Theodore W. 1961. Investment in Human Capital. *American Economic Review* 51: 1–17.

Searle, Chris. 1994. The Culture of Exclusion. In: *Outcast England: How Schools Exclude Black Children*, ed. by Jenny Bourne, Lee Bridges and Chris Searle, 17–28. London: Institute of Race Relations.

Steele, Claude M. 1999. Thin Ice: "Stereotype Threat" and Black College Students. *The Atlantic Monthly* 284(2): 44–58.

Thurow, Lester. 1972. Education and Economic Equality. *Public Interest* 28: 66–81.

The Economist. 1999. Tony Blair's War on Poverty. *The Economist* 352(8138): 18–19.

United States Department of Labor. 1999. *Labor Day 1999 Executive Summary. Future Work: Trends and Challenges for Work in the 21st century*. Washington, DC: Department of Labor.

Walker, Vanessa. 1996. *Their Highest Potential: An African American School Community in the Segregated South*. Chapel Hill, NC: The University of North Carolina Press.

Wheelock, Anne. 1992. *Crossing the Tracks: How "Untracking" Can Save America's Schools*. New York: The New Press.

The Author

Kassie Freeman is Professor of Education and Dean for Academic Advancement at Bowdoin College. Her recent research has focused on teacher education and African American males, as well as the under-utilization of human potential and the transition of higher-education students to the labor market.

Contact address: Bowdoin College, 5700 College Station, Brunswick, ME, 04011-8448, USA. E-mail: kfreeman@bowdoin.edu.

FREEDOM'S CHILDREN: A GENDER PERSPECTIVE ON THE EDUCATION OF THE LEARNER-CITIZEN

MADELEINE ARNOT

Abstract – Drawing on Ulrich Beck's theory of "freedom's children", the present contribution examines contemporary concerns about educating young people *for* citizenship as well as educating them *about* citizenship. Under the first theme, the author focuses on the *citizen as learner*, highlighting some of the gender- and class-related inequalities that are typically associated with individualisation. Under the second theme, she looks at the *learner as citizen* in view of the fact that citizenship education courses often prepare learners for a gender-divided world – even though the processes of individualisation have themselves significantly reshaped contemporary gender relations. In light of current challenges facing citizenship education, the study concludes by reflecting on gender-related dimensions of individualisation and their implications for democracy and the learner-citizen.

Zusammenfassung – DIE KINDER DER FREIHEIT: EINE GESCHLECHTSBEZOGENE PERSPEKTIVE AUF DIE BILDUNG DES LERNENDEN BÜRGERS – Indem er sich auf Ulrich Becks Theorie der "Kinder der Freiheit" stützt, untersucht der vorliegende Beitrag zeitgenössische Bemühungen, junge Menschen sowohl *zur* Staatsbürgerschaft hin zu erziehen als auch sie *über* die Staatsbürgerschaft zu belehren. Unter der ersten Überschrift konzentriert sich die Autorin auf den Bürger als Lernenden, indem sie einige der geschlechts- und klassenspezifischen Ungleichheiten betont, die typischerweise mit der Individualisierung verbunden werden. Unter der zweiten Überschrift wirft sie einen Blick auf den Lernenden als Bürger, und zwar unter Berücksichtigung der Tatsache, dass Lernende in Kursen für staatsbürgerliche Erziehung häufig auf eine Welt vorbereitet werden, die nach Geschlechtern getrennt ist – auch wenn die Prozesse der Individualisierung ihrerseits die gegenwärtigen Beziehungen zwischen den Geschlechtern in bedeutender Weise umgeformt haben. Im Licht aktueller Herausforderungen, mit denen die staatsbürgerliche Erziehung konfrontiert ist, schließt die Untersuchung, indem sie über die geschlechtspezifischen Ausmaße der Individualisierung und ihre Implikationen für die Demokratie sowie den Bürger als Lernenden reflektiert.

Résumé – LES ENFANTS DE LA LIBERTÉ : UNE PERSPECTIVE SEXUELLE SUR L'ÉDUCATION DE L' APPRENANT-CITOYEN – Partant de la théorie d'Ulrich Beck sur les « enfants de la liberté », la présente contribution examine les préoccupations contemporaines à propos de l'éducation des jeunes gens *à* la citoyenneté et *autour* de la citoyenneté. Quant au premier thème, l'auteur se concentre sur *le citoyen en tant qu'apprenant*, mettant sur le devant de la scène certaines des inégalités relatives aux différences de sexe et de classes sociales qui sont associées de façon typique à l'individualisation. Avec le deuxième thème, elle se tourne vers *l'apprenant en tant que citoyen* eu égard au fait que les cours d'éducation à la citoyenneté préparent souvent les apprenants à un monde divisé en sexes différents – même si les processus d'individualisation ont eux-mêmes refaçonné significativement les relations contemporaines en

J. Zajda (ed.), Education and Social Justice, 57-77.

matière de différences sexuelles. Au vu des défis actuels face à l'éducation à la citoyenneté, l'étude conclut sur une réflexion sur les dimensions relatives à la différence de sexe de l'individualisation et leurs implications pour la démocratie et l'apprenant citoyen.

Resumen – HIJOS DE LA LIBERTAD: LA PERSPECTIVA DE GÉNERO EN LA EDUCACIÓN DE LOS CIUDADANOS – Haciendo referencia a la teoría de Ulrich Beck contenida en su libro *Hijos de la libertad*, esta contribución examina asuntos de relevancia actual relacionados con la educación de las personas jóvenes *para* la ciudadanía *y sobre* la ciudadanía. Bajo el primer aspecto, la autora se concentra en el *ciudadano como alumno*, realzando algunas de las desigualdades de género y de clases, típicamente relacionadas con la individualización. Bajo el segundo aspecto, la autora enfoca al *alumno como ciudadano*, en vista del hecho de que los cursos sobre ciudadanía muchas veces preparan a los educandos para un mundo dividido en géneros, pese a que los procesos de individualización les hayan deparado unas relaciones entre los géneros sustancialmente remodeladas. A la luz de los retos que actualmente debe afrontar la educación ciudadana, el estudio termina con una reflexión sobre las dimensiones de la individualización en cuanto a su relación con los géneros y a los efectos que pueden tener para la democracia y los ciudadanos en formación.

Резюме – ДЕТИ СВОБОДЫ: ГЕНДЕРНАЯ ПЕРСПЕКТИВА В ОБРАЗОВАНИИ ГРАЖДАНИНА-УЧАЩЕГОСЯ – Основываясь на теории Ульриха Бека о «детях свободы», в данной статье исследуются современные проблемы воспитания молодых людей в духе гражданственности, а также обучения основам гражданственности. В первой части статьи автор уделяет внимание *гражданину как учащемуся*, выделяя некоторые гендерные и классовые неравенства, которые обычно ассоциируются с индивидуализацией. Во второй части статьи автор рассматривает *учащегося как гражданина* в свете того факта, что курсы обучения гражданственности часто готовят учащихся к гендерно-разделенному миру – несмотря на то, что сам процесс индивидуализации значительно изменил современные гендерные отношения. В свете последних вызовов, стоящих перед обучением гражданственности, в данной статье делаются выводы о масштабах гендерных вопросов индивидуализации и их влиянии на демократию и на самого гражданина-учащегося.

The present study uses the concept of social change provided by the German social theorists Ulrich Beck and Elizabeth Gernsheim Beck (2002) as a yardstick with which to assess current educational practice particularly in relation to citizenship. Taking a rather optimistic tone, they argue that two "epochal forces of modernity", above all others

> individualisation and globalisation, are changing the foundations of living together in all spheres of social action. Both only superficially appear to be threats they force but they also permit society to prepare and reshape itself for a second modernity ... [C]ultural individualisation and globalisation create precisely that historical orientation and those preconditions for an adaptation of institutions to a coming second modernity (Beck and Beck-Gernsheim 2002: 169).

The aim here is to focus on the processes of individualisation since this concept is increasingly being used to explain young people's attitudes to their futures. Youth cultural researchers have found that young people today employ the language of individualisation, the concepts of freedom and choice, to justify their life styles and decisions. There is, therefore, great interest in the ways in which individualisation is being worked on by the younger generation. In contrast, there appears to be relatively little sociological analysis of how individualisation as an epochal process has shaped the educational world especially its curriculum and pedagogy. In the present work, I suggest the way such processes of individualisation can be brought into an analysis of education, and how such a study can assess the contribution of individualisation to the alleviation of social injustice and the promotion of democratic education. A key question I address is what sort of citizen will be needed in the future and how best should youth be prepared for such a major social change.

The concept of the learner-citizen is useful for this task since it signals the important role that the education system plays in educating young people *for* citizenship and educating them *about* citizenship. Drawing on John Beck's (1998) distinction between education *of* the citizen and education *for* citizenship, I separate out analytically the study of the *citizen as learner* and the study of the *learner as citizen*. In terms of the first concept, I focus on the emergence of individualised learners and their rights in the classroom. Under the second theme, I focus on the learner as a future citizen who is prepared through citizenship education courses within schools. In both cases I will use empirical research findings to bring a gender and class analysis into play.

One of the arguments I want to make is that these debates about new notions of pupil rights in classroom learning and the development of new citizenship education courses are linked together. Both reflect, although often neither explicitly nor directly, the growing individualisation of society. In the first case, we find the extension of individualisation in the classroom setting, and in the second case we find the reactions by governments to attempt to hold back change by reasserting traditional values, in effect redressing the negative effects of individualisation in society. These linked scenarios are troubling ones – they challenge us to consider whether or not democratic educators should support the notion of individualisation.

Individualisation as Constraint or as Freedom?

Leif Moos, a Danish educationalist writing in a new anthology on *Democratic Learning* (MacBeath and Moos 2004) draws to our attention Habermas' (2001) four defining characteristics of globalising societies – all of which do not bode well for democratic education or for those committed to using education to alleviate social inequalities and promoting social justice. The four characteristics are

- an anthropological view of human beings as rational instruments willing and able to make informed decisions and to offer their labour freely in the marketplace;
- an image of a post-egalitarian society that tolerates social marginalisation, expulsion and exclusion;
- an image of a democracy where citizens are reduced to consumers in a market society, and where the role of the state is redefined to that of a service agency for clients and consumers;
- a view that policy should be aimed at dismantling state regulation (Moos 2004: 2).

In such globalising societies, governance is about market efficiency, not about promoting the sort of civil society which is regulated by "communication and community, orality and ethics, and trust and reciprocity between subjects" (Moos 2004: 2). As Moos points out, in this new scenario, governance shifts from the state down to the classroom and to the individual. Governance is through the promotion of self-managing individuals:

> No longer are citizens presumed to be members of a political community, which it is the business of a particular form of governance to express. The old and presumed shared political process of the social contract disappears in favour of a disaggregated and individualised relationship to governance (Peters et al. 2000: 118, quoted in Moos 2004: 3).

For some, the concept of individualisation and the self-managing individual is associated with greater democratic freedom. Countering those who see the negative destructive effects of globalised economies and a risk society, Beck and Beck-Gernsheim (2002) and Beck (1992), for example, describe what they call "Freedom's Children" – children who have been brought up, unlike their parents, to become choosers, or consumers of what life has to offer. This new culture is described as *a self-culture* which combines the "indeterminancy of self and of the ensuing conflicts, crises and developmental opportunities and a binding or bonding of self-oriented individuals to, with and against one another" (Beck 2002: 42). Central to this self-culture are the processes of reflexive individualisation in which individuals come to see themselves as centres of their own life-world. People's lives become an art form – something to be created. In the first stage of modernity, the ethos was of 'being individual' and reflective – in contrast, the new generation of youth are now "becoming individual" through reflexivity. The new credo is not "I think, therefore I am" but rather "I am I" (Lasch 2002: ix).

Beck and Beck-Gernsheim argue that, as a result, in this new "second" stage of modernity, the "quality of the social and the political" will be changed so that individuals no longer locate themselves in traditional communities, with traditional identities of class, gender and ethnicity. They argue that ascribed statuses, such as class, gender ethnicity and regionality (which traditionally have been associated with social inequality) will pale into significance – *normative* biographies will be replaced by *choice* biographies and new alliances will be formed by individuals on the basis of shared common risks rather than any restrictive notion of social contract (Beck 1992).

The political implications are likely to be major. In this century, Freedom's Children will experience difficulty in being directed from above or being forced into particular identities or types of commitment, preferring their own self-organisation and political action which is focused on different activities rather than participation in a given democratic order. They have already moved outside the left–right spectrum, their identifications are already more fluid. Young people's politics now involve "complaining, campaigning and acting about all things possible and impossible", developing through the centrifugal dynamic of a "life of one's own". Such politics are not trapped within traditional conventions or boundaries. The form of civic participation for young people is not the ballot box, but rather the right to take charge of matters that are thought to be important. The self-culture represents *a third sphere* or sector – outside the money economy and political ballot box.

According to Beck and Beck-Gernsheim, evidence of the development of this self-culture is already visible in a variety of social changes: the new forms of social movement that act as forms of "resistance within civil society"; "the many kinds of moral and aesthetic experimentation" by people on how they live their lives, with their emotions, their personal relationships, "parenthood, sex and love"; the "great unfinished experiment" with healthy eating shifting people's relationship to nature and their bodies; "the new forms of active empathy" with animal rights, asylum seekers, AIDS victims, drug addicts; the new forms of vigilantes protecting "niches of prosperity"; the conflicts, great and small, between men and women in all spheres (Beck and Beck-Gernsheim 2002: 44).

What characterises this culture is an "internationalised practising consciousness of freedom" (Beck and Beck-Gernsheim 2002: 43). This increase in freedom, Beck and Beck-Gernsheim argue, is not a crisis – it is only a crisis if such freedom is understood as a threat to the traditional authority structures and forms of social privilege which sustained the first stage of modernity. Changing values (especially those of self-development) and acceptance of democracy arguably can go hand-in-hand. There is no necessary connection between this legally sanctioned individualism and either an inflation of material demands or a breaking-down of altruism and community. Indeed such individualisation might even lead to a rejection of the domination of a work-focused "growth oriented labour society" (Beck and Beck-Gernsheim 2002: 162) a questioning of the custodians of public interest and a great desire for more personal fulfilment, time and pleasure. Reflexive individualisation could also, if focused, ensure more co-operative or altruistic individualists who are able to think for themselves and live for others at the same time. Beck argues that if we are fortunate, in the new world, traditional certainty will perish and be replaced by "legally sanctioned individualism for everyone" (Beck and Beck-Gernsheim 2002: 157). The new forms of society will provide the conditions for an *internalised democracy which* is an extension of the Western heritage – another stage in the pursuit of individual development and social fulfilment. In this context, Western European democracy reaches its zenith.

Clearly, educating Freedom's Children with new sets of values and a sense of belonging represents quite a challenge. Crude moral codes or simple national identities already look very dated and inappropriate, but then so do the forms of educational knowledge in current curricula. Critical thinking would be needed to address major cross-generational chasms about what forms of knowledge are valued. In the new social order, educational institutions would need to provide basic social and political rights and offer opportunities to develop an informational base; acquire the skills of preparedness for conflict, capacity for compromise, civic courage, curiosity, tolerance of ambiguity and the making of alliances. These forms of education would also have to stress the malleability of knowledge, the uncertainty of explanations and the relativity of perspective. Knowledge would be non-linear, as would institutions. There would not necessarily be an interlocking system of institutions since strong connections would be established between individuals and the socio-technical world (Bauman 2002). In such a future it may make little sense to talk about knowledge as property or subject positions – rather reflexive modern individuals could be offered knowledge that was "possibilistic, probabilistic and uncertain" (Lasch 2002). In the future, learning is likely to be intense, at speed, with ranges of choice and opportunities for immediate decision-making. The individual would be nomadic, finding the rules and roles him or herself – there would be *a de-normalisation of roles*.

This transformation of the learner-citizen is to some extent now underway but not necessarily in the utopian fashion described by these theorists. As Bernstein (2000) argued, the United Kingdom has recently seen a major shift away from child-centred progressive pedagogies towards the paradoxical if not pathological/schizoid position associated with the visible performance-based pedagogies of the late 20th century. Today we have a unique coupling – a "pedagogical Janus" involving, on one hand, market-oriented modes and, on the other, political discourses which exploit the language developed by egalitarian critiques of such markets. Thus neoliberal agendas can be found clustered around the complex and often contradictory notions of possessive individualism coupled with moral agendas worrying about social exclusion and creating new citizenship identities to hold society together, whilst tearing apart the social fabric.

The freedom associated with individualisation is in good hands, according to Beck, if institutions react with "composure". However, it is hard to say that the UK government has acted with composure. Whilst promoting freedoms especially in the discourses around choice and consumer needs, it has nevertheless been fearful of the consequences of such freedom. Education is associated now with increased rather than less regulation. Such institutional and political responses create what Beck and Beck-Gernsheim (2002: 165) called the "ugly citizen" – where civic virtues turn ugly and aggressive (Beck and Beck-Gernsheim 2002: 165). Freedom is associated, for example, with the possessive and egoistic individualism of 1980s neoliberalism (Thatcher, Reagan, Bush). It is in this somewhat complex and problematic context that democratic educators have had to come to terms with the individualising processes. New discussions about citizenship education, about democratic learning and about pupil voice and consultation are trying to revitalise democratic discussions – debates about freedom, rights, solidarity and social justice – over and above such increases in state regulation and surveillance. One of the levels at which these tensions between individualisation and democracy have been played out is that of classroom learning, to which I shall now turn.

The Citizen as Learner

Individualisation has already affected schooling in a diverse range of ways – from the idea of a flexible school and the introduction of ICT learning which can be highly individualised to the flexibility of the curriculum and the discursive construction of the independent learner. All in their different ways imply the individualisation of learner. Children are encouraged to see themselves as choosers making their own decisions about school, about work and about their life plans. However, the process of reflexive individualisation when recontextualised within essentially modernist institutional settings and regimes look rather different from that described by Beck and Beck-Gernsheim. Rather than generate counter-narratives and alternative "mindsets" (Rowan et al. 2002) exploring the "kindness and beauty" of the citizen (Beck and Beck-Gernsheim 2002: 165), the processes of individualisation are associated with high-performance cultures and expectations and exclusionary processes.

Individualisation, from this point of view, becomes a mechanism of surveillance and regulation more than democratic freedom. Individual learner-citizens are now expected to assess and evaluate their own learning and have been given the responsibility of improving their own performance – they are expected to act as clients or patients in charge of their own treatment. At the same time, they are not expected to take control of the nature of their learning and its processes. Such individualisation, therefore, is not necessarily coupled with strong notions of civic agency in relation to learning and the learning experience. Indeed, the transition from pupil to citizen may involve a loss of agency. The abstract notion of the citizen inscribed in schooling, as the Finnish sociologists Tuula Gordon and Elina Lahelma, and Janet Holland, a British sociologist, argued (2000: 188–189), implies equality:

> Education prepares children to take up their place as future citizens. A process of normalisation takes place in schools, which is based on conceptions of proper

> adulthood and the rights and duties of citizens. In this process, children and young people are seen as abstract "pupils", abstracted from diverse social and cultural contexts, and trained equally to become the future citizens.

However, these authors found that there were few spaces in the schools in the United Kingdom, for example, where pupils can achieve what they call "agentic embodiment" – opportunities to enact their agency. In the English and Finnish secondary schools they researched, young people followed the route from pupil to citizen within the official school, the informal school and the physical school without being able to control the forms of educational knowledge taught to them, or the curriculum of the body which organised them through varied time–space paths. The authors point out that the spaces for agency, negotiation, avoidance, opposition and resistance were limited. When exercised such spaces were significant in the context of tensions between emancipation and regulation, control and agency (pp. 187–188). Within the strongly externally controlled pedagogies of marketised economies, the route to citizenship is socially differentiated. Boys, for example, were provided with more space to exercise agency, whilst far less physical and emotional space was offered to girls. "Patterns of student agency are thus prefigured by existing gender inequalities" (p. 200; see also Dillabough and Arnot 2002).

Such research reveals that social differences such as those of gender, ethnicity and class from the "external environment" (Jorgensen 2004) enter into the learning process and deeply distort the "inner environment" of learning outcomes often and perhaps increasingly in very subtle ways. Traditional social inequalities appear not only to have shaped such processes of individualisation but to be "masked" in the pedagogic relationships of individualised learning. At the heart of market-oriented performance pedagogies lie socially constructed and value-laden concepts of the learner and appropriate learning relationships. However, we are not necessarily able to see or recognise such social constructions. Learning styles, assessment modes, even the seemingly democratic process of student consultation on which contemporary notions about "the independent learner" are based encourage us to misrecognise learning as socially neutral cognitive processes. They redirect attention away from the fundamentally social nature of knowledge transmission and acquisition (Bernstein 2000).

Those interested in independent learning and the self-managing learner focus attention particularly on the importance of eliciting and working not just with pupils' agency but also with pupil voice as a means of improving individual learning (Arnot and Reay 2004). Thus, the voice of the child currently has symbolic significance for supporters of a range of democratic educational agendas. Increasingly the United Nations Convention on the Rights of the Child (1989) is brought to bear on educational debates (Rudduck and Flutter 2004: 125). Article 12 is of especial relevance today since it declares the right of children to participate in their own lives – in accordance with age and maturity; children should be heard and taken seriously in all matters affecting them, including judicial and administrative matters. This declaration implies that pupils should have not just a voice in relation to their own learning but also have the capacity and confidence to intervene in the principles which govern their learning experience.

However, in the context of socially inequitable societies, the notion of pupil voice can become converted into alternative purposes. For example, pupils can be consulted in order to judge the effectiveness of the school's engagement with performance cultures – their voices can become the means by which teachers and pupils themselves are individually surveilled and regulated (Fielding 2001). Rather than promoting higher levels of reflexive subjectivity, participation and self-direction, pupils can become incorporated in the project of social control. In this context it becomes extremely important to consider, as Bernstein (2000: xxi) argued, whose voice is heard and whose voice is listened to in what he called the "acoustic of the school".

Findings from a recent study on pupil consultation address some of these questions (Arnot and Reay 2004). This project involved group discussions with 14–15-year-old male and female, higher- and lower-achieving pupils from different ethnic and class backgrounds. We focused on all pupils in one tutor group in each of the two secondary and two primary schools. Sixty-two children were involved in a total of 24 discussion groups. Five lower achieving pupils were observed in maths and English classes and were interviewed individually. Later, we asked the form tutors and maths and English teachers to build strategies of pupil consultation into their lessons and we evaluated these initiatives (Arnot and Reay 2004; Reay and Arnot 2004). We asked pupils to comment on the degree to which they felt able to describe their own abilities and learning progress. Did they feel included and respected by teachers in classroom learning? Did they feel they could control the pace and content of their learning and the rules of the pedagogic encounter? Our discussions focused on whether the pupils were ever consulted about how they learnt, about whether they could communicate their needs (in terms particularly of the pace of learning) to teachers, about whether they were consulted about what they learnt and why. What we were reflecting on was whether they were really self-managing pupils, or independent learners.

Our research findings highlight the fact that independent learners are neither class- nor gender-neutral. The forms of pedagogic communication typical of today's classrooms are heavily class- and gender-nuanced. Many pupils in our study were aware that neither they nor teachers had control over the content of lessons, and this affected the motivation of working class pupils who wanted what they saw as "useful" knowledge. If any pupils were likely to gain some limited (discretionary) control over the choice of activity, the pace of classroom learning or even their seating, it was the higher-achieving upper-middle-class pupil (especially the girls). Irrespective of the perceived relevance or irrelevance of the curricula, the highest-achieving (often professional-middle-class) girls were found to be able to exploit the pedagogic agendas of the individualised learner and at the same time uncouple themselves from constraining and stereotypical models of femininity.

Higher-achieving professional-middle-class girls seemed to have an appropriate pedagogic language and emotional competence when relating to teachers. They were rather nonchalant about consultation, possibly because they felt that, unlike less successful pupils, they had a voice and felt more in tune with the school's purposes. They were able to manage informal dialogue between themselves and their teachers. As a result they were asked, listened to and heard. These pupils thought themselves to be in control of their learning even within the constraints of the compulsory curriculum. They worked with notions of individual choice in terms of when to co-operate, when to slow down, speed up (or zoom) through their work. They worked independently but they also made considerable demands on the teacher to deal with their needs for extension work.

The threat to these girls' control of their learning were teachers who failed to cope with their needs, especially in a mixed-ability, mixed-sex environment where they had to cope with the demands of boys, especially working-class lower-attaining boys. The threats to upper-middle-class girls' control over their learning were therefore male powers of manipulation using disaffection, endless demands for attention, disruption of the rules, requests to repeat work from earlier stages and teachers' acquiescence. Perceiving these issues, girls proposed segregation by ability. In contrast, black working-class girls suggested a change in their own attitudes to try and understand the boys, and the rest of the girls expressed frustration; lower-achieving white working-class girls were left to negotiate personal relationships with teachers and rely on interpersonal skills to acquire some modicum of control in the classroom setting. Both these latter groups had little real sense of control over their school learning.

The issue of whether to gain control over the pace and level of work for working-class boys appeared to be deeply affected by the image of the curriculum as irrelevant to their interests and needs. They attempted to be independent, but they were, in effect, deeply dependent learners – assuming, on one hand, that intelligence was the key to achievement (not hard work) and that it was the teachers' responsibility to help them and get it right. Learning was a risky business since they might not be able to perform well publicly and could be ridiculed by the teacher and other boys. There were only negative academic and social consequences if they said the work was too easy or too difficult, the pace too fast or too slow. One of the only possible ways for them to get control was to break behavioural rules.

Despite girls' view of boys' power within the classroom setting, these working-class boys experienced strong regulation by teachers who intervened on their seating, their learning patterns, and largely failed to meet their demands. These boys appeared to be the least able to communicate with teachers and received the least help. Thus, those who most needed to have control over their learning had the least control. As a result they used physical disruption of the classroom in an attempt to regain control over their learning. Thus, whilst teachers struggled to maintain control, these lower-achieving boys were trapped in a dynamic that was hard to break. Their lack of power was expressed in dysfunctional attention-seeking and classroom dominance. They were clearly not independent learners nor did they appear to have the means of becoming such learners.

The model of the independent learner we observed implied that all students can speak the language of learning – the sorts of pedagogic language being used by teachers in the classroom (whether traditional or progressive in style). However, being a learner involves considerable skill and familiarity with the expectations of such a communicative setting. It does not just entail having the appropriate vocabulary that a teacher can recognise, but also having an appropriate relationship with the teacher in order to be able to communicate effectively. Paradoxically the most dependent learners needed to have great maturity in handling their relationships with teachers, since their work and classroom behaviour was often not in line with teacher expectations. Of particular importance, therefore, was the problem for pupils of achieving some sort of communicative competence and effective pedagogic relationships in the classroom setting. Pupils when consulted recognised that a number of elements would be needed to ensure successful communication about learning (see also Arnot and Reay 2000; Arnot et al. 2004): communicative competence; emotional maturity; a high level of trust; patience; motivation to learn; and appropriate family support. The discussions we held with lower-achieving pupils, particularly boys often from working-class backgrounds, revealed just how tense and vulnerable they felt in the classroom and how they tried to find ways of learning but had difficulty with so many aspects of classroom life. They did not feel trusted by teachers and were therefore not confident about their learning. The notion of independent learning represented for them a form of regulation rather than an aid to learning. Once pedagogic communication had broken down, the main source of support in learning were their friendships and peer group cultures. Paradoxically, therefore, the assumptions of the independent learner with its expectations of communicative competence appeared to reinforce strong male peer-group cultures and male dominance in the classroom.

The data from these two secondary-school settings suggest that we need to examine the extent to which a positive pedagogic identity is achievable for, in particular, working-class boys and girls in the current learning environment. Bernstein writes about how socialisation within schooling can be "deeply wounding" either for those who wish for, but do not achieve a pedagogic identity, or for the majority for whom the pursuit of an identity is early made irrelevant (Bernstein 1975: 250). An increase in individualisation means that the images, voices and practices that the school provides may make it even more difficult for working-class children to recognise themselves in schooling. It may be particularly problematic for white and minority ethnic working-class boys who already experience daily the strong regulative culture of the classroom and confrontational relations with teachers. This clearly has profound consequences for the production of positive pedagogic identities so desired by the new goals of lifelong learning.

We turn now to the second major theme – that of learners as citizens. Here the narrative takes a different turn. Contemporary discussions about citizenship education – education *for* citizenship – appear precisely to suppress individualisation (and yet again to mask social inequalities) in the name of social solidarity and order.

The Learner as Citizen

> Pupils as citizens should be autonomous, knowing, responsible and aware of their culture, but the emphasis is on future citizenship (Gordon et al. 2000: 199).

Preparation for adult citizenship now represents a strong strand within Western European nations, especially in the light of calls to use citizenship education to recreate the forms of moral solidarity threatened by aggressive individualism and materialism. Citizenship education has been introduced, amended and developed in various national and global contexts (Cogan and Derricott 2000). For example, curricular initiatives have been set up by the Asian Centre for Citizenship Education networks, the Council of Europe, and the Commonwealth Secretariat. Eastern European countries are reforming their communist-inflected models of citizenship education in order to democratise in the Western way. African countries are developing civic programmes as part of their response to international aid agendas, and citizenship-education courses are designed by the American agency Civitas in post-conflict societies (Mustagrudic 2000).

"The good citizen" rather than the critical or protesting citizen is the model being used in neoliberal contexts, although in the United Kingdom there is an attempt to combine such a moral goal with that of civic republicanism (Arnot 2004). However, in neither case are the goals those of challenging social inequality and/or promoting egalitarianism as a democratic ideal (Garmarnikow and Green 1999). In citizenship education we can find an idealised return to the forms of mechanical solidarity which Emile Durkheim (1933) associated with preindustrialisation, where punishment and shame are the basis of the social order rather than societies based on contract (organic societies). Citizenship education now appears to have more to do with establishing nationalist identities and conservative hierarchical social orders than addressing refashioned social relations which are associated with a globalising and individualising society. One example of this paradoxical response is evidenced in the ways in which this political education agenda manages to ignore the very processes of individualisation to be found in liberal democratic Western economies – those associated with gender relations.

Social theorists of globalisation often use as their primary example the transformation of gender relations associated with the 20th century and with predicted changes in the 21st century. The education of girls over the last century is symbolic of the struggle for greater autonomy and freedom (Beck 1992; Sen 1999; Beck and Beck-Gernsheim 2002). Women have fought for the opportunity to become full autonomous citizens in their own right, precisely to become "I am I". Evidence of the impact of individualisation on women can be found in the range of youth cultural studies which identify the individualistic, hedonistic life – values amongst young women today. We talk now in the United Kingdom about the "Can Do" girls, girls who think that the world is at their feet – at least in their teenage years. The extraordinary transformation of white working-class girls' discourse to one of possibility and the language of choice is mapped in Arnot et al. (1999). Here we see the key role which education has come to play in so many young women's lives, with many now achieving higher-level qualifications and higher education. The shift in gender values, about whether women have a right to work, to be independent earners, to share childcare with their partners, has been found to be one of the strongest generational gaps in modern society (Wilkinson 1994). Grandparents and grandchildren disagree most over gender issues – over and above politics, environment, and health.

Drawing on German experiences, Ulrich Beck and Elizabeth Beck-Gernsheim argue that these "irreversible shifts" in gender relations interntionally mark the beginning of a liberation of a new generation from feudally ascribed roles for the sexes, with all their associated antagonisms. Young women are uncoupling themselves from "the clutches of family life" and a life of caring service to take control over their own lives. Freedom's Children at the moment appear to be largely female. Men, in contrast, have appeared to be deeply committed to traditional identities in work and domestic spheres – a strategy that might well be in itself a response to turbulent social change (Beck 1992: 112):

> All the factors which dislodge women from their traditional role are missing on the male side. In the context of male life, fatherhood and career, economic independence and familial life are not contradictions that have to be fought for and held together against the conditions in the family and society: instead their compatibility with the traditional male role is prescribed and protected. But this meant that individualisation ... strengthens masculine role behaviour.

If this continues, it is likely that the position of men and women will become "increasingly unequal, more conscious and less legitimated" (p. 104). There are limited signs in the United Kingdom that young working-class men might be displaying signs of individualisation, although as Miles (2004) points out, this may only reflect what he calls a "mezzanine" condition – of wanting to acquire some of the accoutrements of a middle-class status without rejecting a working-class collective culture. The experience for many women in Western industrialised societies is one of greatest contradiction – never have they been so qualified and never has the gap between educational success and access to high-status decision-making positions in the labour market and political life been so great. Male educational underachievement contrasts with men's success in civic and economic spheres and dominance of different forms of privilege (Arnot et al. 1999). The gender story, therefore, is getting more, not less, complex as we progress into the future. The challenge for citizenship education is to engage with this constantly shifting and contested terrain. Can schools address these unequal processes of individualisation and the complex gender relations which result? How do schools see their contribution to these spiralling gender differences? How do schools prepare boys and girls for social change?

Traditionally, schools have promoted not just a notion of the "abstract pupil" but also an abstract notion of citizenship which all could ascribe to. However, the more developed the women's movement, the more this abstract concept of citizenship has been shown to be gendered and one of the main devices for the exclusion of women from power. Studies have exposed in many different ways how this abstraction becomes the means of containing gender in traditional masculine notions of polity and political power (Arnot and Dillabough 2000).

What is now clear is that, often without realising the significance, Western European educational systems (particularly Anglo-Saxon educational models) promote and export through colonial structures a notion of citizenship that is premised upon what Carol Pateman (1988) called a "civic brotherhood" (see Arnot 2004). Critical feminist analyses have revealed that because of the sexual contract which lies behind this fraternal pact and which subordinates women to men's control, women are often marginalised from the formal public realm and the project of citizenship. State education systems supported these social contracts by differentiating the education of girls and boys and providing forms of education that reproduced the superiority and authority of the white European male. These gendered notions of citizenship which tend to be premised upon notions of the male warrior, soldier, worker and voter demonstrably represent major obstacles to female citizenship. Underlying liberal and even civic republican traditions is the separation of public and private spheres on the basis of alleged biological difference. Essentialist thinking places men, as the main breadwinners, in masculinised public/civic sphere and women are represented as symbolic of family and private life (Arnot and Dillabough 1999). Although there have been many attempts to redesign education to value such female roles it is a matter of concern that teachers may still be assuming such gendered spheres and gender difference.

The findings of a European research project *Promoting Equality Awareness: Women as Citizens*, funded by the European Commission, recently illustrated the relevance of this point (Arnot et al. 1996). The project suggested that male and female teachers employ and position themselves in different political discourses. Whilst male teachers were found to work with strong political discourses of duty based on civic republicanism and classical Greek theory, female teachers in Portugal, Spain, Greece and the United Kingdom appeared neither to use the discourses of civic republicanism nor to find a position for themselves in it. Female teachers in all national samples were more likely to employ the Judaeo-Christian discourses of morality, emphasising the ethics of care and community involvement or contemporary egalitarian discourses around state-provided social rights and social justice. The "good citizen" for them was more often than not the grandmother, the mother, or the carer in the private sphere, instead of the civic leader, representative or voter.

The dominance of men in the public sphere was central to the view of citizenship held by most of the student-teachers in each of the countries involved. It appeared hard to conjure up any positive recent involvement of women within the public sphere. Men were perceived to have the most control over policy decisions and public appointments and an especially strong influence over economic and foreign policy. Women, on the whole, were perceived to have negligible influence on policy and public appointments. Gender and generational differences were noticeable in the United Kingdom– *it seems that young student-teachers were less likely than their college* lecturers to see it as important that women should occupy public positions.

In this cross-national research, there were few indications amongst student teachers that the masculinisation of public life and citizenship could be changed and that women would be needed to help transform such structures. The source of male power in the public realm was partially taken for granted despite a strong awareness of sex discrimination. Male student-teachers in the different European countries studied appeared to agree with differentiated gender roles and expressed little personal commitment to challenge masculine associations surrounding the public realm. There was a seeming naturalness of male power based on gender–role difference. The juxtaposition of power and femininity represented by women in public life disturbed traditional notions of femininity and was expressed as a kind of corruption in which women in public life were either over-assertive (autocrats) or sexually predatory. Men, for example, used the distinction between reproduction and sexuality to categorise women in public domains as either "mothers and madonnas" or as "whores/sluts/bimbos" (Arnot et al. 2000). Women, therefore, were not represented as legitimately successful and autonomous in the public arena.

These issues are particularly relevant critiques of a liberal democratic model of citizenship with its emphasis on the individual over and above the importance of community and social/collective groups and the centrality of individual choice over social intervention in the name of the common good (Nussbaum 1999). Here the communality of women's experience and women's concerns as a social group have been marginalised. The abstract notion of the individual citizen cannot easily recognise pluralism – the differences between men and women in terms of life situations and experiences and the differences between women and between men in terms of ethnicity and social class and in relation to unequal distributions of power. Yet recognition of the particular circumstances which have shaped women's lives and the contributions they have made to the development of society is central to the achievement of gender justice. Without such recognition, it is unclear how learners learning how to become citizens could address the shifting nature of gender relations in society.

The absence or marginalisation of the private sphere from definitions of citizenship is a particularly important aspect of this marginalisation of gender concerns. The failure of citizenship education to engage with the private sphere – "the affective domain" (Nussbaum 1995) – is linked to deeper notions about the rationality of citizenship and the irrelevance of personal/emotional relationships from civic discourse. This in turn results in the failure to value "the caring ethos" and maternal values (Noddings 1998) found in the private and familial sphere which might have provided alternative models of citizenship education and civic virtues. Also, although excluding the private sphere from state control, surveillance and intervention can have benefits in terms of an autonomous space in which women can have agency, it has also the disadvantageous effect of marginalising and discursively subordinating women as non-rational beings and as "non-citizens".

Sue Lees (2000) argued that the ways in which the "personal" is divorced from the "political" in the new English citizenship-education programme mean that this new curricular subject fails to address complex changes in gender relations in the private sphere. Individualising processes have led to the uncoupling of women from traditional family structures and a search for alternative sexualities and life-styles. By the early 1990s, for example, 27% of births in England and Wales were to unmarried mothers; women were marrying later and getting divorced earlier. Divorce has increased sixfold over the last 30 years. Citizenship rights for women as head of household and single parents nevertheless are limited. Indeed, female single parents are now classified as "an excluded group" (Lees 2000: 261–262). Such change in gender relations should surely be central to the education of young future citizens.

Similarly, tolerance of gay and lesbian groups is often only on the condition that they remain within the boundaries defined by society (Richardson 1998). Lesbians and gay men are only "partial citizens" since they are often excluded from civil, political and social rights, left unprotected from discrimination and harassment on grounds of sexuality by the law and the police, and experience prejudicial treatment in relation to social rights of welfare. Lesbian and gay men are "dehumanised" by a "disembodied" concept of citizenship (Richardson 1998). Yet such contemporary debates about sexuality and citizenship, whilst often openly discussed in government, have not challenged the conventional political view of citizenship reproduced in new citizenship curriculum. Citizenship education courses can sustain a conventional model of heterosexuality.

The international human rights community, according to Bunch (1995: 17) has begun to recognise "gender-based violations as pervasive and insidious forms of human rights abuse". However, the mass violation of women's human rights through such gender-based violence is also not generally considered an appropriate topic for citizenship education in schools. Such violations include: the battery of women; their physical and psychological imprisonment in the home; the violent entrapment of women in prostitution; pornography; domestic service; compulsory pregnancy; rape; female infanticide; and the malnutrition of girls. Further, as Sunnari et al. (2002) have demonstrated, gendered and sexualised violence are also part of educational environments. There is clearly much work to be done to address such violence and its associations with masculinity, particularly in relation to the education of boys (Breines et al. 2000). It needs to be stressed that even the most critical models of liberal education are simply not sufficient to address such issues. Citizenship education itself would require far more extensive politicisation in order to address such real but usually hidden gender violence in the public and private spheres.

In sum, the women's movement has fundamentally changed the civic agenda. The processes of individualisation are expressed in the struggle by women globally for autonomy and agency, the expansion of education and the resulting growth in female credentials and women's contribution to the economy (UNESCO 2003). The family structure has also been transformed by the diversity of life-styles in contemporary society. Young women have started to uncouple themselves from economic and social dependency upon men. In the future, women may no longer rely on men to offer support for childrearing and family income. They may wish to focus on their own life plans irrespective of heterosexual relationships. The masculine notions of citizenship associated with liberal democracy (also with civic republicanism) which are promoted through education would seem to be no longer appropriate for such changing gender relations and gender ethics.

Evaluation

Educating the learner-citizen is a complex phenomenon. It involves educating children to be fully participatory citizens. This means looking critically at both the education *of* citizens and education *for* citizenship (Beck 1998), at the ways in which citizens are learners, and learners are prepared to be future citizens. These two projects are not always linked, yet what they share is that aspects of education are being challenged by the same processes of individualisation and in both contexts, existing social divisions have an impact. On one hand, we have new discourses around the independent learner encouraging full participation but no control over learning, while, on the other, we have the struggle by women to achieve autonomy whilst a gendered form of citizenship is offered to young people. From this perspective, schools appear to be addressing the issue of individualisation in complex, contradictory and confused ways.

It seems as if the positive aspects of individualisation described by Ulrich Beck and Elizabeth Beck-Gernsheim can only be mobilised in a context where pedagogic communication is not premised on, or masks, social hierarchies and difference. The independent self-managing learner appears, at the moment, to be the mechanism for the reproduction rather than the erasure of social inequalities. In this context, social-class inequalities mediate gender relations, and the tensions between the sexes are constructed through particular class-based forms of pedagogy. The potential of Freedom's Children is therefore not being harnessed within schools. Neo-liberal government has tended to be more concerned with sustaining an aggressive competitive individualism and/or reasserting the moral order than capturing the knowledge, the energy and the coping strategies of the children they intend to teach. Young people are not treated as citizens in their own right, nor indeed are they recognised to be familiar already with the challenges which the world offers to them in their daily lives and through the media. Further, the models of citizenship taught to children in citizenship education courses and by teachers are equally problematic. We cannot assume that citizen-education courses are designed to challenge gender-dualistic thinking, the separation of public and private spheres, homophobia or violence.

Conclusion

If, as Per Schultz Jorgensen (2004) argues, the notion of character formation is now very different from what it was 50 years ago, then we will have to think carefully about what sort of education we want to achieve. Conformity in the sense of traditional identities and values may be a hindrance to adaptation and growth in a globalising world. But if we abandon traditional identities, how do we then design an education system in which every individual achieves an inner stability and self-understanding in a fragmented, constantly changing world? Should we as educators seek to retain rites and rituals to mark their passages into adulthood? Or should we create new links between the self-culture of individuals and social change? What sort of links between schooling and social change should these be? Amartya Sen (1999: 288) leaves us with the thought that any enhancement of political and civil freedoms should not be taken for granted:

> The general enhancement of political and civil freedoms is central to the process of (economic) development itself. The relevant freedoms include the liberty of acting as citizens who matter and whose voices count, rather than living as well fed well clothed and well entertained vassals.

References

Arnot, Madeleine. 2004. Gender and Citizenship Education. In: *Education for Democratic Citizenship: Issues of Theory and Practice*, ed. by Andrew Lockyer, Bernard Crick and John Annette, 103–119. Aldershot: Ashgate.

———, Helena Araujo, Kiki Deliyanni, and Gabrielle Ivinson. 2000. Changing Femininity, Changing Concepts of Citizenship in Public and Private Spheres. *The European Journal of Women's Studies* 7: 149–168.

———, Helena Araujo, Kiki Deliyanni-Kouimtzi, Gabrielle Rowe, and Tome Amparo. 1996. Teachers, Gender and the Discourses of Citizenship. *International Studies in Sociology of Education* 6(1): 3–35.

———, Miriam David, and Gaby Weiner. 1999. *Closing the Gender Gap: Post-War Education and Social Change*. Cambridge: Polity Press.

———, and Jo-Anne Dillabough. 1999. Feminist Politics and Democratic Values in Education and Citizenship. *Curriculum Inquiry* 29(2): 149–158.

——— (eds.). 2000. *Challenging Democracy: International Perspectives on Gender, Education and Citizenship*. London: Routledge–Falmer Press.

———, David Peddar, Donald McIntyre, and Diane Reay. 2004. *Consultation in the Classroom: Developing Dialogue about Teaching and Learning*. Pearson Books: Cambridge.

———, and Diane Reay. 2004. The Framing of Pedagogic Encounters: Regulating the Social Order in Classroom Learning. In: *Reading Bernstein, Researching Bernstein*, ed. by Johan Muller, Brian Davies and Ana Morais, 137–152. London: Routledge–Falmer.

Bauman, Zigmund. 2002. Individually, Together. Foreword. In: *Individualisation: Institutionalised Individualism and its Social and Political Consequences*, ed. by Ulrich Beck and Elizabeth Beck-Gernsheim, xiv–xix. London: Sage.

Beck, John. 1992. *Risk Society: Towards a New Modernity*. London: Sage.

———. 1998. *Morality and Citizenship in Education*. London: Cassell.

———, and Elizabeth Beck-Gernsheim. 2002. *Individualisation: Institutionalised Individualism and its Social and Political Consequences*. London: Sage.

Bernstein, Basil. 1975. *Class, Codes and Control*, 2nd ed., Vol. 2. London: Routledge and Kegan Paul.

———. 2000. *Pedagogy, Symbolic Control and Identity: Theory, Research and Critique*. Rowman and Littlefield: Lanham.

Breines, Ingeborg, Robert Connell, and Ingrid Eide (eds.). 2000. *Male Roles, Masculinities and Violence: A Culture of Peace Perspective*. Paris: UNESCO.

Bunch, Charlotte. 1995. Transforming Human Rights from a Feminist Perspective. In: *Women Rights, Human Rights: International Feminist Perspectives*, ed. by Julie Peters and Andrea Wolper, 11–17. New York: Routledge.

Cogan, John J., and Ray Derricott. 2000. *Citizenship for the 21st Century*. London: Kogan Page Ltd.

Dillabough, Jo-Anne, and Madeleine Arnot. 2002. Recasting Educational Debates about Female Citizenship, Agency and Identity. *The School Field* 13(3/4): 61–90.

Durkheim, Emile. 1964. (transl. 1933). *The Division of Labour in Society*. London: MacMillan.

Ekholm, Mats. 2004. Learning Democracy by Sharing Power: The Student Role in Effectiveness and Improvement. In: *Democratic Learning: The Challenge to School Effectiveness*, ed. by John MacBeath and Leif Moos, 95–112. London: Routledge–Falmer Press.

Fielding, Michael. 2001. Beyond the Rhetoric of Student Voice: New Departures or New Constraints in the Transformation of 21st Century Schooling? *Forum* (Summer): 100–109.

Garmarnikow, Eva, and Anthony Green. 1999. Social Capital and the Educated Citizen. *The School Field* 10(3–4): 103–126.

Gordon, Tuula, Janet Holland, and Elina Lahelma. 2000. *Making Spaces: Citizenship and Difference in Schools*. London: MacMillan.

Habermas, Jürgen. 2001. In: *Zeit der Übergänge*, ed. by Jürgen Habermas, 104–129. Frankfurt a. M.: Suhrkamp.

Lasch, Stuart. 2002. Individualisation in a Non-linear Mode: Introduction. In: *Individualisation: Institutionalised Individualism and its Social and Political Consequences*, ed. by Ulrich Beck and Elizabeth Beck-Gernsheim, vii–xii. London: Sage.

Lees, Sue. 2000. Sexuality and Citizenship. In: *Challenging Democracy: International Perspectives on Gender, Education and Citizenship*, ed. by Madeleine Arnot and Jo-Anne Dillabough, 259–276. London: Routledge–Falmer Press.

MacBeath, John. 2004. Democratic Learning and School Effectiveness: Are They By Any Chance Related? In: *Democratic Learning: The Challenge to School Effectiveness*, ed. by John MacBeath and Leif Moos, 19–51. London: Routledge–Falmer Press.

———, and Leif Moos (eds.). 2004. *Democratic Learning: The Challenge to School Effectiveness*. London: Routledge–Falmer Press.

Miles, Philip. 2004. *Educational Transitions and Late-modern Anxiety: The Impact of Credentialism and Individualisation on Working Class Youth*. PhD thesis, University of Cambridge.

Moos, Leif. 2004. Introduction. In: *Democratic Learning: The Challenge to School Effectiveness*, ed. by John MacBeath and Leif Moos, 1–18. London: Routledge–Falmer Press.

Mustagrudic, Andrea. 2000. *Education for Citizenship: The Case of Bosnia and Herzegovina*. MPhil thesis, University of Cambridge.

Noddings, Nell. 1988. An Ethic of Caring and its Implications for Instructional Arrangements. *American Journal of Education* 96(2): 215–230.

Nussbaum, Martha C. 1995. Emotions and Women's Capabilities. In: *Women, Culture and Development: A Study of Human Capabilities*, ed. by Martha Nussbaum and Jonathan Glover, 360–395. Oxford: Oxford University Press.

———. 1999. *Sex and Social Justice*. Oxford: Oxford University Press.

Pateman, Carole. 1988. *The Sexual Contract*. Cambridge: Polity Press.

Peters, Michael, James Marshall, and Patrick Fitzsimons. 2000. Managerialism and Educational Policy in a Global Context: Foucault, Neo-liberalism and the Doctrine of Self Management. In: *Globalisation and Education: Critical Perspectives*, ed. by Nicholas C. Burbules and Carlos A. Torres, 109–132. New York: Routledge.

Reay, Diane, and Madeleine Arnot. 2004. Participation and Control in Learning: A Pedagogic Democratic Right? In: *Learning to Read Critically in Teaching and Learning*, ed. by Louise Poulson and Mike Wallace, 151–172. London: Sage.

Richardson, Diana. 1998. Sexuality and Citizenship. *Sociology* 32(1): 83–100.

Rowan, Leonie, Michele Knobel, Chris Bigum, and Colin Lankshear. 2002. *Boys, Literacies and Schooling*. Buckingham: Open University Press.

Rudduck, Jean, and Julia Flutter. 2004. *How to Improve your School*. London: Continuum.

Schultz Jorgensen, Per. 2004. Children's Participation in a Democratic Learning Environment. In: *Democratic Learning: The Challenge to School Effectiveness*, ed. by John MacBeath and Leif Moos, 113–131. London: Routledge–Falmer Press.

Sen, Amartya. 1999. *Development as Freedom*. Oxford: Oxford University Press.

Sunnari, Vappu, Jenny Kangasvuo, and Mervi Heikkinen (eds.). 2002. *Gendered and Sexualised Violence in Educational Environments*. Oulu, Sweden: Oulu University Press.

UNESCO. 2003. *Gender and Education for All: The Leap to Equality. EFA Global Monitoring Report*. Paris: UNESCO.

United Nations Convention of the Rights of the Child. 1989. UN General Assembly Resolution 44, 25.

Wilkinson, Helen. 1994. *No Turning Back: Generations and the Genderquake*. London: Demos.

The Author

Madeleine Arnot received her MA from Edinburgh University and PhD from the Open University. She is Professor in Sociology of Education and is Professorial Fellow at Jesus College at Cambridge University. She has acted as a gender expert for the Council of Europe, an international consultant for the UNESCO *Education for All: Gender Monitoring Project* and on equal opportunities policies. Her work has involved projects on women and citizenship, pupil consultation, gender-education policy and refugee and asylum-seeker children's education.

Contact address: Faculty of Education, University of Cambridge, 184 Hills Road, Cambridge CB2 2PQ, UK. E-mail: mma1000@cam.ac.uk.

CULTURAL DIVERSITY AS RESISTANCE TO NEOLIBERAL GLOBALIZATION: THE EMERGENCE OF A GLOBAL MOVEMENT AND CONVENTION

JENNIFER CHAN-TIBERGIEN

Abstract – While there have been numerous discussions of the impact on educational services made by trade liberalization through the World Trade Organization (WTO), this study looks at the emergence of global resistance to the commodification of culture through the General Agreement on Trade in Services (GATS) within the WTO. In line with the Council of Europe Declaration on Cultural Diversity in 2000 and the UNESCO Declaration on Cultural Diversity in 2001, a global movement has been fighting for a legally binding global convention on cultural diversity under the auspices of UNESCO. The author examines how 'cultural diversity' is defined by various groups and nations. She also discusses the potential implications of such a global convention on cultural diversity for 'cognitive justice', that is, for affirming the validity of diverse knowledge systems over against the dominance of neoliberal ideology. Finally, she argues that the leading definition of cultural diversity, contrary to its stated intention, actually serves to re-assert the cultural hegemony of the North rather than benefit subjugated knowledges of the South.

Zusammenfassung – KULTURELLE VERSCHIEDENHEIT ALS WIDERSTAND GEGEN DIE NEOLIBERALE GLOBALISIERUNG: DIE ENTSTEHUNG EINER GLOBALEN BEWEGUNG UND ÜBEREINKUNFT – Während es zahlreiche Diskussionen über die Wirkung der Dienstleistungen im Bildungsbereich gegeben hat, welche durch die Liberalisierung des Handels seitens der Welthandelsorganisation (WTO) erzielt worden sind, wirft diese Untersuchung einen Blick auf die Herausbildung eines weltweiten Widerstandes gegen die Instrumentalisierung der Kultur durch das General Agreement on Trade in Services (GATS) innerhalb der WTO. In einer Linie mit der Erklärung über kulturelle Vielfalt des Europarates im Jahre 2000 und der Allgemeinen Erklärung zur kulturellen Vielfalt der UNESCO im Jahre 2001 kämpft seitdem eine weltweite Bewegung für eine gesetzlich bindende weltweite Übereinkunft zur kulturellen Vielfalt unter der Aufsicht der UNESCO. Die Autorin untersucht, wie ‚kulturelle Vielfalt' von verschiedenen Gruppen und Nationen definiert wird. Sie diskutiert auch die möglichen Implikationen einer solchen weltweiten Übereinkunft über kulturelle Vielfalt für ‚kognitive Gerechtigkeit', d. h. dafür, die Gültigkeit unterschiedlicher Wissenssysteme gegen die Vorherrschaft der neoliberalen Ideologie zu bestätigen. Zum Schluss stellt sie dar, dass die gängige Definition der kulturellen Vielfalt im Gegensatz zu ihrer eigentlichen Absicht tatsächlich eher dazu dient, die kulturelle Hegemonie des Nordens erneut zur Geltung zu bringen, anstatt das unterdrückte Wissen des Südens zu begünstigen.

Résumé – LA DIVERSITÉ CULTURELLE COMME RÉSISTANCE À LA GLOBALISATION NEO-LIBÉRALE: L'ÉMERGENCE D'UN MOUVEMENT ET D'UN ACCORD GLOBAL – Alors qu'il y a eu de nombreuses discussions sur l'impact des services éducatifs réalisés par la libéralisation du commerce par l'Organisation Mondiale du Commerce (OMC), cette étude se tourne vers l'émergence de la résistance globale à l'uniformisation de la culture à travers l'Accord Général sur le commerce et les

J. Zajda (ed.), Education and Social Justice, 79-95.

services (AGCS) au sein de l'OMC. En accord avec la Déclaration du Conseil de l'Europe sur la Diversité Culturelle en 2000 et la Déclaration de l'UNESCO sur la Diversité Culturelle en 2001, un mouvement global a combattu pour un accord global légalement obligatoire sur la diversité culturelle sous les auspices de l'UNESCO. L'auteur examine comment la 'diversité culturelle' est définie par des groupes et des nations variés. Elle discute également des implications potentielles d'un tel accord global sur la diversité culturelle pour la 'justice cognitive', c'est-à-dire pour l'affirmation plus forte de la validité des divers systèmes de connaissance face à la domination de l'idéologie néo-libérale. Enfin, elle soutient que la définition phare de la diversité culturelle, contrairement à son intention affirmée, sert en réalité à réaffirmer l'hégémonie culturelle du Nord, plutôt qu'elle ne bénéficie aux savoirs subordonnés du Sud.

Resumen – LA DIVERSIDAD CULTURAL COMO RESISTENCIA FRENTE A LA GLOBALIZACIÓN NEOLIBERAL: EL SURGIMIENTO DE UN MOVIMIENTO Y CONVENCIÓN GLOBAL – Mientras ya se han realizado numerosos debates sobre el impacto que la liberalización del comercio a través de la Organización Mundial del Comercio (OMC) tiene sobre los servicios de educación, este estudio enfoca el surgimiento de una resistencia global contra la mercantilización de la cultura a través del Acuerdo General sobre el Comercio de Servicios (GATS) dentro de la OMC. De conformidad con la Declaración sobre Diversidad Cultural del Consejo de Europa de 2000 y la Declaración universal de la UNESCO sobre la diversidad cultural de 2001, un movimiento global ha estado luchando por una convención global y vinculante sobre la diversidad cultural, bajo los auspicios de la UNESCO. La autora analiza cómo diferentes grupos y naciones definen la 'diversidad cultural'. También describe los posibles efectos que una tal convención global sobre diversidad cultural podría tener sobre una 'justicia congitiva', al afirmar la validez de diferentes sistemas de conocimiento por encima de la dominación de una ideología neoliberal. Al finalizar, la autora argumenta que, contrariamente a su intención declarada, la definición más difundida de diversidad cultural en realidad se presta más a una reafirmación de la hegemonía del Norte que al beneficio de los conocimientos subyugados del Sur.

Резюме – КУЛЬТУРНОЕ МНОГООБРАЗИЕ КАК СОПРОТИВЛЕНИЕ НЕОЛИБЕРАЛЬНОЙ ГЛОБАЛИЗАЦИИ: ВОЗНИКНОВЕНИЕ ГЛОБАЛЬНОГО ДВИЖЕНИЯ И КОНВЕНЦИИ – В то время когда ведется множество дискуссий о влиянии либерализации торговли через Всемирную Торговую Организацию (ВТО) на образовательные услуги, данное исследование рассматривает возникновение глобального сопротивления коммодификации культуры в свете Генерального соглашения по торговле в сфере услуг (GATS) внутри ВТО. Согласно Декларации Совета Европы о культурном многообразии 2000 года и Декларации ЮНЕСКО о культурном многообразии 2001 года, глобальное движение борется за глобальную конвенцию о культурном многообразии под эгидой ЮНЕСКО, которая имела бы обязательную юридическую силу. Автор статьи рассматривает определение «культурного многообразия», предлагаемое разными национальными группами и народами. Автор также обсуждает потенциальное влияние такой глобальной конвенции на культурное многообразие для «когнитивной справедливости»», т.е. для укрепления законности разнообразных систем знаний над доминирующей неолиберальной идеологией. В конечном итоге автор статьи утверждает, что лидирующее определение культурного многообразия, в отличие от первоначального, в действительности служит утверждению культурной гегемонии севера над народами юга.

The late 1990s saw a dramatic cultural turn in the international political economy. The incursion of the World Trade Organization (WTO) into culture through the General Agreement on Trade in Services (GATS) since 1995 has raised alarms among cultural communities and nations. Behind the immediate question of whether cultural goods and services are different from other goods and hence merit protective measures in world trade lurks a more complex questioning of what culture signifies in the age of global capitalism. Is culture, by nature or application, capitalistic? Or can culture ground and redeem capitalism from its inherent crises? The tension between 'cultural capitalism' and 'cultural counter-hegemony' not only ignites but also divides a worldwide cultural diversity movement.

This study raises two questions. Firstly, what is the "home discourse" (Bannerji 2000: 53) of "cultural diversity" as a response to neoliberal globalization? Secondly, in what ways can cultural diversity be re-imagined as narrative knowledges that re-territorialize and embed capitalism in a radically more pluralistic social space? It is argued that the culturalization of world-trade politics through the proposed international instrument on cultural diversity does not necessarily challenge existing global capitalist hegemony. Indeed, such a new instrument, which is essentially centred on the state, might only reinforce the cultural hegemony of dominant states and capitalist hegemony through the use of culture as a tool of capitalism.

To go beyond cultural capitalism – another "gigantism" (Roy, quoted in Bello 2002: 115) – that is, for culture to assert its counter-hegemonic role against neoliberal globalization, a new cosmopolitan culturalism, in the form of a multiplicity of narratives, can act as a living, "decolonizing methodology" (Smith 1999) and political resource (Young 2000) for individuals, communities, and nations to negotiate not only the terms of capitalism, but alternative livelihoods (cf. the concept of "social difference as political resource" in Young 2000 as well as the notion of community in Chatterjee 1993 as a cultural resource for people to negotiate the terms against the grand narrative of history). The purpose of such methodologies and resources is to provincialize neoliberal capitalism through an "insurrection of subjugated knowledges" (Foucault 1980) so that "the economy did not have to be thought of as a bounded and unified space with a fixed capitalist identity. Perhaps the totality of the economic could be seen as a site of multiple forms of economy whose relations to each other are only ever partially fixed and always under subversion" (Gibson-Graham 1996: 12).

This study proceeds in three parts. Part I outlines the movement for an international convention on cultural diversity. Through a discursive analysis of the 2001 UNESCO Universal Declaration on Cultural Diversity and a draft convention on cultural diversity by the nongovernmental International Network on Cultural Diversity, Part II deconstructs 'cultural diversity' as a new global ideology where the state remains the predominant representative embodiment of culture. Part III presents my argument on the role of cultural narratives as a living methodology and political resources in the construction of a "heterogeneous public" (Young 1990) in overlapping levels of governance.

Cultural Paradox, Dilemma and Exception

It would not be an exaggeration to say that the cultural worlds we live in today are dramatically different from the one experienced by our parents. Whether in visual arts, performing arts, or popular culture, cultural expression seems to have witnessed a global explosion. Displacement, migration, tourism, and the ever-expeditious exchange of ideas, aided by technology, have helped create an enormous global market for the "creative industries" (Caves 2000) estimated to be around US-$ 800 billion per year. The curious paradox, though, as Grant and Wood (2004) point out, is that this expansion has led to more cultural homogenization rather than pluralism. Whether it is in the business of book publishing, film, music, or media in general, between five and ten firms, mostly US-based, usually dominate the world market (McChesney 2000; Grant and Wood 2004). The corporatization and concentration of ownership through mega-mergers in the past two decades have made small productions within dominant states or most cultural industries in countries without a large domestic market economically non-viable. Hence, we have can be called a "cultural dilemma". For instance, Canada practices an open cultural market. But it is also the always-threatened neighbor of the largest producer of cultural goods. Despite government cultural-policy measures such as limits on foreign ownership, content regulation, preferential treatment of Canadian rights holders, funding programs, and government cultural agencies, foreign firms and products dominate the Canadian cultural market: 97% in films, 81% in English-language magazines, 79% in music, and 45% in books (Canadian Cultural Industries Sectoral Advisory Group on International Trade 1999). Should culture then be exempt from agreements on trade liberalization?

Some have argued that several characteristics of cultural products distinguish them from other goods (Grant and Wood 2004). First, they are public goods whose production cost is independent of the number of consumers. Hence, market prices often far exceed marginal cost. Second, since they are 'experience' goods, they are not as substitutable as regular goods, and both information and competition are far from being perfect, as is assumed in the traditional efficient market equilibrium. Third, the high fixed costs of these industries favors large, established firms, making the entry of individual or small competitors extremely difficult. To these 'curious economics' of cultural goods, one can add the more fundamental opposition between the principle of comparative advantage, emphasizing efficiency, and that of cultural diversity, centred on the fundamental freedom of expression.

The issue of cultural exemption in world trade is not new. In the 1988 Canada/US Free Trade Agreement (FTA), for example, Canadian cultural industries are exempt from the Agreement except those inconsistent with the Agreement. A similar cultural-exemption approach is used in the North American Free Trade Agreement (NAFTA), whereby Canada has negotiated the right to exempt the cultural industries from most terms of the agreement and "continue to support its cultural industries as long as the measures it uses are otherwise consistent with the pre-existing Canada/US Free Trade Agreement" (Canadian Cultural Industries Sectoral Advisory Group on International Trade 1999). Since 1995, however, negotiations on cultural trade have returned through GATS within the WTO. GATS is a framework of rules that lays out the general obligations of member states in trade in services. It summarizes four modes of supply through which services can be traded: cross-border supply, consumption abroad, commercial presence, and movement of natural persons. During GATS negotiations, member states did not agree to exempt culture from the agreement but they did allow countries to opt out of the Most Favored Nation (MFN) obligations (i.e., countries that are partners to the agreement agree to treat all equally) or national treatment obligations (i.e., no discrimination can be made in favor of national providers). Thus, Canada took an MFN exemption for its film and television co-productions and did not include any commitments for national treatment in the cultural sector, effectively withholding its cultural policies from the GATS disciplines (Canadian Cultural Industries Sectoral Advisory Group on International Trade 1999).

Unlike the earlier near-blanket cultural exemption approach in FTA and NAFTA, however, the Canadian Cultural Industries Sectoral Advisory Group on International Trade (SAGIT) felt that this country- and sector-specific approach was insufficient. Member states that wish to maintain any limitation on market access or the principle of non-discrimination have the onus to schedule the limitations, "subject to the continued international pressures to change domestic cultural policies" (Canadian Cultural Industries Sectoral Advisory Group on International Trade 1999). Led by the Canadian government and supported by an emerging global non-governmental movement for cultural diversity, there was an increasing consensus by the late 1990s that only a new international convention would provide a broad consensus on the importance of cultural diversity and clarify the relationships between global trade agreements and domestic cultural measures.

In 1998, an informal group of over 40 culture ministers formed the International Network on Cultural Policy (INCP) at a meeting in Ottawa under the leadership of the Canadian Minister of Heritage, Sheila Copps. The meeting rode on the groundbreaking UNESCO conference earlier that year in Stockholm on linking culture to development, emphasizing that "culture then is not a means to material progress; it is the end and aim of 'development' seen as the flourishing of human existence in all its forms and as a whole" (International Network for Cultural Diversity 2004). A non-governmental International Network for Cultural Diversity (INCD) was also created in 1999, now encompassing non-governmental organizations (NGOs) in 70 countries and cultural ministers in 53 countries. In 2000, members of INCD met in parallel at the

INCP annual conference in Santorini, Greece and concluded that "market forces alone cannot ensure cultural diversity at the national and international levels"; "states have a right and responsibility to implement policies and programs that support diverse artistic and cultural activities"; and that only a new international instrument could "give a permanent legal foundation for cultural diversity" (Neil 2003: 107). That same year, the Council of Europe issued the first Declaration on Cultural Diversity. In 2001, UNESCO announced the Universal Declaration on Cultural Diversity. Since then, both INCP and INCD have worked in tandem around a new international convention on cultural diversity under the auspices of UNESCO.

Cultural Diversity as a Global Ideology

If ideology is defined as "an interpretive frame of references which seeks to describe social, economic, and moral conditions in society in order to direct and mobilize groups towards specific political ends" (Hazareesingh 1994: 6), both the UNESCO Universal Declaration on Cultural Diversity (UDCD) and the proposed convention on cultural diversity by INCD can be seen as new global ideologies in the making. To understand the novelty of a cultural-diversity frame at the international level, one needs to contrast the definitions of culture by UNESCO over time. Until the early 1980s, culture was no more than traditional "arts and literature" (UNESCO 2002: 18). After the 1982 World Conference on Cultural Policies in Mexico City, culture took on a larger anthropological meaning: "culture should be regarded as the set of distinctive spiritual, material, intellectual and emotional features of a society or social group, and ... encompasses, in addition to art and literature, lifestyles, ways of living together, value systems, traditions and beliefs" (UNESCO 2002: 18). It was not until 2001, in the UDCD, that culture ceased to be defined in isolated terms: cultural diversity is a "source of exchange, innovation and creativity". Culture is no longer merely arts, literature and lifestyles, but cultural diversity is a heritage of humanity (Art. 1), indissoluble from democracy (Art. 2), a root of development (Art. 3), human rights (Art. 4), cultural rights (Art. 5), accessible to all (Art. 6), fosters creativity and dialogue among cultures (Art. 7), vectors of identity, values, and meaning (Art. 8), a state prerogative (Art. 9), in need of international solidarity (Art. 10), sustained through public-private-civil-society partnership (Art. 11), and a mandate for UNESCO (Art. 12) (UNESCO 2001).

Taking these general principles a significant step further, the proposed convention on cultural diversity by INCD consists of objectives and definitions, general commitments, measures to preserve and enhance cultural diversity, and mechanisms to settle disputes. While the convention clearly aims to establish a "multilateral framework of principles" to preserve and enhance cultural diversity, "culture" is consciously left undefined: "nothing in this Convention shall be construed to limit the sovereign authority of a Party to define such terms and concepts as 'culture', 'cultural diversity', and 'indigenous or national culture' in a manner it considers appropriate to the characteristics of its particular society" (Art. II. 1). Signatory states shall positively "develop policies" and "integrate ... the preservation and enhancement of cultural diversity into relevant economic, international, trade, social and environmental policies and programs" (Art. III. 1). In particular, states party undertake to provide direct or indirect financial support and preferential treatment to individuals, institutions, state enterprises, associations, nongovernmental organizations or cultural enterprises (Art. VII). States party may also prohibit or limit foreign investment through the control of domestic content, co-production or co-distribution, nationality requirement of senior management, qualification requirements, limitations on the number of cultural service suppliers, total value of transactions or natural persons employed in a particular cultural service sector etc. (Art. X and XI). Last but not least, unlike many other international instruments concerning culture, this proposed convention will, a year after ratification, provide for a dispute-settlement regime that is multilateral, transparent, and binding and that protects the rights of both individuals and corporations in their freedom of expression, and allows for intervention by NGOs (Art. XIV).

Though the proposed convention links cultural diversity to humanity, identity, human rights, and sustainable development, 'cultural diversity' in this new global project is primarily, if not exclusively, defined in parameters of capitalism. As the preamble attests, the convention desires to strengthen the capacity of "all sovereign states to ... develop and implement measures to support diversity of artistic, linguistic and cultural expression ... taking into account the potential *impediments to these goals that may arise from international trade, investment, and services disciplines*" (my emphasis). While pluralism and creativity are extolled in the preamble, the meat of the convention refers to the specific measures and limitations a nation-state can impose in its cultural market, and when all else fails, its ability to file grievance in some form of international cultural trade tribunal. To justify those measures, a state will have to define the 'diverse' according to four grounds:

(a) distinct indigenous and national forms of cultural expression
(b) country of origin of the artist
(c) character, content, language or informational characteristics of such goods or services
(d) any other qualities or features that are relevant to preserving and enhancing diverse forms of cultural expression (Art II. 2).

Hence, we run into a central paradox built into the proposed new instrument: This thing called 'cultural diversity' which is not meant to be foreclosed will always need to be defined in order to justify its existence. Though the definition of 'culture' and 'cultural diversity' is deliberately and strategically left open, the *raison d'être* of the new instrument may reinforce state definitions of culture. Will an international instrument designed to promote cultural pluralism end up legitimizing cultural nationalism? Culture becomes the extension, albeit in honorific language, of both the state and global capitalism. To see the proposed convention on cultural diversity as an ideological construction is not only to question its (capitalistic) frames of reference and political ends, but also to expose what it masks/silences. When Ministers of Culture met in Ottawa in 1998, the cultural priorities of the developing world were not at the top of their agenda. At the 2002 INCP meeting in Cape Town, South Africa, largely at the insistence of the South African delegate, the ministers concluded that the needs of developing countries should be reflected in the new international instrument on cultural diversity; gender should be infused in all aspects of the instruments; and the cultural sector should be linked to social and economic development (INCD 2002). Artists in the South pinpointed the danger of silencing racism in the name of cultural diversity. At the fourth INCD annual conference in Croatia in 2003, Mike van Graan (2003) cautioned:

> What we have learned is that while the current hegemony around the language of cultural diversity describes the sphere of global trade and its potentially adverse impact on cultural industries and cultures generally, we need to be sensitive to and acknowledge the negative baggage that the concept carries, for we attach different experiential, historical and intellectual meanings to the same words and concepts.

Though he was specifically referring to the historical situation in South Africa, where "cultural diversity" was mobilized to institutionalize apartheid, the issue of "cultural equity" (Wyman 2004) remains inadequately addressed in the proposed convention. Beyond the mentioning of indigenous cultures (Art. V), although it is unclear whether the term "indigenous" here means aboriginal or local, and assistance for less-developed countries (Art. VIII), one needs to ask whether an eventual convention will help promote the cultural industries in the South or small, independent artists and cultural communities in the North. African countries, for example, have so little leeway in the global cultural trade that the concept of cultural diversity and the proposed convention might have little relevance to them. The idea of a Global Fund to promote the development of cultural industries in the South was once raised but was never taken up (van Graan 2003).

Other artists have also raised their flags against having a new instrument that would reinforce big cultural industries. Ludwig Laher (2003), a poet and vice-president of the European Council of Artists – an European umbrella organization of artists councils in 24 European countries – cautioned in his keynote address at the Croatia conference that "the [European] Commission had very clear, though disputed perspectives for cultural goods and services, but hardly any for the artists" (INCD 2003). At the first hearing of the European parliament on cultural industries in early 2003, he recalled:

> On this occasion Mr. Reinhard Büscher, the representative of the European Commission, gave an outline of what the positions of the Commission on art and culture are. Cultural industries are a sector of economy just like all the other ones, Mr. Büscher said. They are no longer of marginal importance, but big business worth 100 billion Euros turnover per year. Mr. Büscher regretted productivity deficiencies as one big obstacle for even more success in the field of cultural industries ... Competitiveness is the key to economic success that need not contradict cultural development, because the taste of the majority of the general public is the main criterion for the free market. Mr. Büscher was convinced that a flourishing culture goes hand in hand with a flourishing economy.

Artists from both the North and the South are fully aware of the fact that while 'cultural diversity' has become 'everybody's darling', "endless commercialization is definitely a cultural phenomenon, but not necessarily an artistic one" and "it is no longer mainly a body of cultural experts developing the draft of a convention on cultural diversity, but an international network in the midst of political process" (Laher 2003). Human creativity is not synonymous with cultural industries. If sovereign states and cultural industries represent the homes from which cultural claims are made, the class, racial, and gender assumptions of an emergent global discourse on cultural diversity must be deconstructed. As Bannerji (2000: 51) puts it, "by obscuring or deflecting from historical and present power relations, perceptions and systematized ideologies, the deployment of diversity reduces to and manages difference as ethnic cultural issues ... That is, diversity discourse tries to set up a sphere which claims to be outside of hegemony." Table 1 summarizes the various approaches linking culturalism and capitalism in the discussion thus far on a proposed international convention on cultural diversity.

As a response to US-dominated capitalism embodied in the WTO (quadrant I), the current proposed convention led by the Canadian government, supported by the European Union, especially France, risks being only a tool to further cultural capitalism (quadrant II). The UNESCO UDCD, conceived in much broader terms, holds out the potential of not restricting

Table 1. Culturalism as capitalism or counter-hegemony

Primary/ Secondary	Capital	Culture
Capital	I Capitalism – US, Japan etc.	IV Cultural counter-hegemony – Individual artists, artist associations, some nongovernmental organizations
Culture	II Cultural capitalism – Canada, France/EU, etc.	III Culturalism – UNESCO Universal Declaration on Cultural Diversity

culturalism only as a bedfellow of capitalism (quadrant IV). To the extent that culture does not really exist outside of capitalism and that the culture/capital opposition is unrealistic, however, the crucial question becomes: How does one utilize a new global discourse on cultural diversity to promote a cultural counter-hegemony in which capitalism will not be allowed to take up all social space (quadrant IV)? It is to this central role of culture as counter-hegemony to neoliberal capitalism that I now turn.

Cosmopolitan Culturalism as Living Methodology

Despite a flourishing of literature on multiculturalism in the past decade, little research has linked cultural diversity to democracy at the global level. Theorists such as Taylor (1992) and Kymlicka (1996 and 2000), by arguing in favor of the centrality of culture for the definition of one's selfhood and meaningful citizenship, have mostly confined their analysis of culture to national multicultural societies. Going beyond a framework of multicultural citizenship, Benhabib (2002: 8) argues that culture not only helps a narrative constitution of self, but that complex cultural dialogue is a precondition of justice, that is, "the task of *democratic equality* is to create impartial institutions in the public sphere and civil society where this struggle for the recognition of cultural differences and the contestation for cultural narratives can take place without domination". Similarly, Young (2000) argues that the recognition of group difference for self-development (the ability to express oneself culturally) and self-determination (the ability to participate in determining one's action) is an essential condition for inclusive democratic justice. In her words, "this thicker meaning of inclusion highlights the importance of valuing diverse models of communication in democratic discussion ... Narrative is an important means of conveying the situated knowledge of differently positioned people; *without the thick description of needs and problems and consequences that concrete stories can provide*, political judgments may rest on social understandings that are too abstract" (2000: 120, my emphasis). Linking her own work to Held's (1999) concept of cosmopolitan democracy, Young argues that the recognition of distinct peoples within the norms of communicative democracy and public spheres should apply to cosmopolitans' proposal of a global system of regulatory frameworks coupled with local self-determination (conceived as non-domination).

As a critique of the narrow capitalistic conception of culture within the proposed convention on cultural diversity, I build on the works of Held and Young. Held puts forward a model of "cosmopolitan multilateralism" in which people would come to enjoy "multiple citizenships" (1999: 107) in communities which significantly affect them and "would have access to a variety of political engagement on a continuum from the local to the global, with the local marked by direct and participatory processes while larger domains with significant populations are progressively mediated by representative mechanisms" (2003: 175). I argue that cosmopolitan culturalism – defined as a multiplicity of narrative knowledges in overlapping communities from the local to the global – acts as a living, "decolonizing methodology" (Smith 1999) and political resource against neoliberal capitalism. Smith (1999) names 25 of these "projects" including claiming, testimonies, story-telling, celebrating survival, remembering, indigenizing, intervening, revitalizing, connecting, reading, writing, representing, gendering, envisioning, reframing, restoring, returning, democratizing, networking, naming, protecting, creating, negotiating, discovering, and finally sharing. Here I borrow her concept of "decolonizing methodology" to refer to the process of regaining control over knowledge by traditionally marginalized and oppressed groups. I emphasize four aspects of cultural narratives as criteria for inclusive global democracy: existential legitimation, multiplicity and vernacularism, territoriality, and participation in a heterogeneous public.

First and foremost, cultural narratives are legitimate knowledges in their own right, without recourse to the capitalist metanarrative. As Lyotard (1979: 27) argues, the traditional exclusion of narrative knowledges was due to "the entire history of cultural imperialism from the dawn of Western civilization ... governed by the demand for legitimation"; narratives "define what has the right to be said and done in the culture in question, and since they are themselves a part of that culture, they are legitimated by the simple fact that they do what they do" (p. 23). A cultural narrative reframes "the questions being asked, determines the set of instruments and methods to be employed and shapes the analyses" (Smith 1999: 143) against the methodological individualism and singularity of the global market.

Secondly, for culture to act as a counter-hegemony, cultural narratives have to be multiple and vernacular. As Stone-Mediatore (2003: 6) points out, dominant experiences may also have a narrative form, but they are presented as the "general truth". To the extent that the power of current global capitalism rests upon a dominant official growth narrative, manifested within international institutions such as the WTO or state discourses, new vernacular knowledges challenge neoliberalism as the only viable development strategy. The alternative globalization movement has called this emphasis "globalization from below" (Brecher, Costello and Smith 2000; Falk 2003), centred on the principle of subsidiarity which "respects the notion that sovereignty resides in people ... whatever power can reside at the local level should reside there" (International Forum on Globalization 2002: 60).

Third, to counteract the assumptions of abstract individualism and impartiality of the global market, narrative knowledges reterritorialize global capitalism such that capitalism is portrayed less "as a unified entity than as a set of practices scattered over a landscape" (Gibson-Graham 1996: 254). As Young (2000: 261) points out, "governance cannot be divorced from land, its resources, and a sense of place. People dwell somewhere ... Many of the self-determination claims of oppressed minorities, such as those of most indigenous peoples, concern access to land and resources in order to enhance their economic well-being". Cultural narratives, as resistance, re-embedded global capitalism in existing and future social contracts. Finally, if narrative knowledges are legitimate in their own right, they are nonetheless public and accountable. While Habermas (1996) rightly privileges the public sphere – defined as "a network for communicating information and points of view" (Habermas 1996: 360, quoted in Young 2000: 170) – in his theory of democratic communicative actions, critics find his assumption of a single, homogenous public problematic. Young (2000: 11) argues for a heterogeneous public that encourages the expression of group differences, but with a shared commitment to the larger political order:

The public consists of multiple histories and perspectives relatively unfamiliar to one another, connected yet distant and irreducible to one another. A conception of publicity that requires its members to put aside their differences in order to uncover their common good destroys the very meaning of publicity because it aims to turn the many into one.

It is this last Arendtian characteristic and criteria of the plurality and publicity of cultural narratives that guard them against the charges of romanticism and relativism (cf. Arendt 1958). Objections to the validity of narrative knowledges are often based upon the perceived danger of a reification of tradition – that is, "fables, myths, legends, fit only for women and children" in Lyotard's (1979: 27) words – in a permanent slippery slope of cultural relativism. To argue that cultural narratives are resources in democratic deliberations is precisely to assert the open nature of their construction – as insistent cultural "fragments," to borrow Chatterjee's (1993) expression, in dialogue rather than unitary wholes – and their subjection to basic norms of practical discourse ethics: respect ("the right of all beings capable of speech and action to be participants in the moral conversation") and reciprocity ("each should have the same right to various speech acts, to initiate new topics, and to ask for justification of the presuppositions of the conversation, and the like" (Benhabib 2002: 107). Conceived this way, in their independent legitimation, multiplicity and vernacularism, territorialization, and publicity, diverse cultural narratives serve as a living methodology to realize a new democracy. According to the International Forum on Globalization (2002: 56–57), a network of grassroots organizations in the alternative globalization movement, democracy is maintained by active citizens:

> Democracy flourishes when people organize to protect their communities and rights and hold their elected officials accountable ... We use the terms new democracy and living democracy in part because democracy is equated in many minds with elections alone. As vital as fair elections are to democracy, we want to focus more attention on the dynamic processes initiated by civil society organizations around the world to instill new energy and meaning into democratic movements ... The principle of new democracy means creating governance systems that give those who will bear the costs the vote when decisions are being made.

Table 2. Cosmopolitan culturalism as living methodology and resources in a heterogeneous public

	Capitalism	Cosmopolitan Culturalism
Legitimation/Validity	Instrumental/exclusive scientific knowledge	Inclusive/inexhaustible narrative knowledges
Methodology	Methodological individualism and singularity (officialdom)	Multiplicity and vernacularism of narratives and values
Space	Global abstraction and autonomy of economic theory/economy	Reterritorialization
Accountability	Concentration of power in private market space as a system of unity	Participation and dialogue in a heterogeneous public

If participation is a crucial precondition in redesigning a just and democratic global governance system, the re-valuing of diverse cultural narratives becomes key in encouraging maximum participation. These narratives become political resources in the global movement to redefine a new economic democracy, one that is multi-level, pluralist, accountable, and sustainable. Table 2 contrasts the claims of cosmopolitan cultures with those of global capitalism.

Cultural Diversity and Global Governance: An Evaluation

Through an analysis of the proposed international convention on cultural diversity, I have attempted to deconstruct the assumptions behind an emergent global discourse of cultural diversity. I have argued that the prevailing conception of cultural diversity as capitalism within the proposed convention falls short of addressing the full potential of cultural narratives as counter-hegemony to neoliberal capitalism. In the global resistance movement, cultural economics are important, not only in terms of the local and national cultural productions being at stake, but also as a potential precedent for carving out other exemptions from the comprehensive trade agreements within the WTO. Diverse social movements are already using cultural arguments to frame their struggles for food sovereignty, forests, water rights, and indigenous knowledges against intellectual property rights (Shiva 1997; Glipo et al. 2003; International Commission on the Future of Food and Agriculture 2003; International Center for Trade and Sustainable Development 2003). Thus, cultural diversity in the age of global capitalism is not only about creative industries. Symbolized in the inexhaustible energies of music, dance, popular theatre, paintings, photographs, personal testimonies, peoples' tribunals, film festivals, etc. in the new global public spaces of Seattle, Washington, Prague, Quebec City, Cancun, Porto Alegré, and Mumbai, cultural narratives represent a living methodology directed against the neoliberal capitalist hegemony.

If a new global ideology on cultural diversity intends to empty out a politics of difference, cosmopolitan culturalism as a competing ideology precisely aims to rename culture from the position of the postcolonial (Gunew 2004; Bhabha 1994). By the 'postcolonial', I mean a discursive-subject position rather than national origin (Hall 1996). Following Dirlik (1994), I see global capitalism and postcolonialism as mutually discursively constituted. Cultural, racial, class, and gender differences mark the debates about and struggles for global governance (in Goldberg's words, "who counts as in and who is out, who is central to the body politic and who peripheral, who is autonomous and who dependent": 1994: 83, as quoted in Gunew 2004: 21) despite their abstraction and alleged impartiality. The ultimate narrative act – a public suicide – of a 56-year-old Korean farmer, Lee Kyung-hae, former president of the Korean Advanced Farmers Federation, at the anti-WTO demonstration in Cancun in September 2003, is a powerful reminder of the significance of marginalized cultural narratives emerging not only from small-holder peasant communities in Korea but rural farming communities worldwide in resisting the deadly politics of global capitalism.

Conclusion

To take seriously the cosmopolitan conception of cultural diversity sketched in this contribution means to go beyond merely carving out cultural exemptions within the General Agreement on Trade in Services. This band-aid approach, even if successful, fails to address the more fundamental issues of crises of legitimation within global capitalism (Bello 2002). The current WTO methodology, for example, based on the mercantilism of a few powerful states/blocs backed by their domestic interest groups rather than democratic agreement (Kwa 2003), needs to be scrutinized by an open process of deliberation and participation. Whether or not that process results in a throwback to the original Bretton Woods system (in Dani Rodrik's words, quoted in Bello 2002: 98, where "rules left enough space for national development efforts to proceed along successful but divergent paths", that is, in a "regime of peaceful coexistence among national capitalisms") and/or some new multilateral power networks, cosmopolitan culturalism demands the reconstitution of global governance structures as heterogeneous publics where cultural narrative knowledges are not only recognized but determinant of the myriad possibilities of capitalism. To borrow Amin's words (1998: 145):

> Pure economics may appear to be an excellent tool for crisis management from the perspective of the capitalist group that gains from prolongation of the crisis (currently the globalized financial markets), but a way out of the crisis it certainly is not. If society is ever to emerge from its crisis, that can only come about through the establishment of a new balance of social forces.

At stake is much more than the US-$ 800 billion market in cultural goods and services. The cultivation of diversity pertains to our fundamental freedom to develop, self-organize, and self-govern, without which growth and democracy remain only beautiful but empty rhetoric.

References

Amin, Samir. 1998. *Spectres of Capitalism: A Critique of Current Intellectual Fashions.* New York: Monthly Review Press.

Arendt, Hannah. 1958. *The Human Condition.* Chicago: University of Chicago Press.

Bannerji, Himani. 2000. *The Dark Side of the Nation.* Toronto: Canadian Scholars' Press.

Bello, Walden. 2002. *Deglobalization: Ideas for a New World Economy.* London, New York: Zed Books.

Benhabib, Seyla. 2002. *The Claims of Culture: Equality and Diversity in the Global Era.* Princeton: Princeton University Press.

Bhabha, Homi. 1994. *The Location of Culture.* London and New York: Routledge.

Brecher, Jeremy, Tim Costello, and Brendan Smith 2000. *Globalization from Below: The Power of Solidarity.* Boston: South End Press.

Canadian Cultural Industries Sectoral Advisory Group. 1999. Canadian Culture in a Global World. Available at http://www.dfait-maeci.gc.ca/tna-nac/canculture-e.asp, accessed 15 October 2004.

Caves, Richard. 2000. *Creative Industries: Contracts Between Art and Commerce.* Cambridge, MA: Harvard University Press.

Dirlik, Arif. 1994. The Postcolonial Aura: Third World Criticism in the Age of Global Capitalism. *Critical Inquiry* 20(2): 328–356.

Falk, Richard. 2003. Globalization from Below: An Innovative Politics of Resistance. In: *Civilizing Globalization: A Survival Guide*, ed. by Richard Sandbrook, 91–206. Albany: State University of New York.

Foucault Michel. 1980. *Power/Knowledge: Selected Interviews and Other Writings, 1972–1977*, ed. and transl. by Colin Gordon. Brighton: Harvester Press.

Gibson-Graham, J.K. 1996. *The End of Capitalism (as we knew it).* Malden, MA: Blackwell Publishers.

Glipo, Arze, Laura Carlsen, Arza Talat Sayeed, Rita Schwentesius de Rindermann, and Jayson Cainglet. 2003. Agreement on Agriculture and Food Sovereignty. Unpublished paper for the WTO Conference in Cancun.

Goldberg, David Theo. 1994. Introduction: Multicultural Conditions. In: *Multiculturalism: A Critical Reader*, ed. by David Theo Goldberg, 3–18. Oxford: Blackwell.

Grant, Peter, and Chris Wood 2004. *Blockbusters and Trade Wars: Popular Culture in a Globalized World*. Vancouver, Toronto: Douglas and McIntyre.

Gunew, Sneja. 2004. *Haunted Nations: Postcolonial Dimensions of Multiculturalism*. New York, London: Routledge.

Habermas, Jurgen. 1996. *Between Facts and Norms*. Cambridge MA: MIT Press.

Hall, Stuart. 1996. When was 'the Post-Colonial'? Thinking at the Limit. In: *The Post-Colonial Question: Common Skies, Divided Horizons*, ed. by Iain Chambers and Lidia Curti, 242–260. London: Routledge.

Hazareesingh, Sudhir. 1994. *Political Traditions in Modern France*. Oxford: Oxford University Press.

Held, David. 1999. The Transformation of Political Community: Rethinking Democracy in the Context of Globalization. In: *Democracy's Edges*, ed. by Ian Shapiro and Casiano Hacker Cordon, 53–88. Cambridge: Cambridge University Press.

———. 2003. From Executive to Cosmopolitan Multilateralism. In: *Taming Globalization*, ed. by David Held and Mathias Koenig-Archibugi, 160–186. Cambridge: Polity Press.

International Center for and Trade Sustainable Development [ICTSD]. 2003. *Trade and Forests: Why Forest Issues Require Attention in Trade Negotiations. Policy Brief on Trade and Natural Resource Management*. Geneva: ICTSD.

International Forum on Globalization. 2002. *Alternatives to Economic Globalization: A Better World is Possible*. San Francisco: Berrett-Koehler Publishers.

International Network for Cultural Diversity [INCD]. 2002. Cape Town Statement. Available at http://www.incp-ripc.org, accessed 3 May 2004.

———. 2003. Conference Keynote Address. Available at http://www.incd.net/conf2003keynote.htm, accessed 3 May 2004.

Kwa, Aileen. 2003. *Behind the Scenes: Power Politics in the WTO*. New York: Zed Books.

Kymlicka, Will. 1996. *Multicultural Citizenship*. New York: Oxford University Press.

———. 2000. *The Rights of Minority Cultures*. New York: Oxford University Press.

Laher, Ludwig. 2003. Art for Sale? Keynote address at the International Network on Cultural Diversity Fourth Annual Conference in Croatia.

Lyotard, Jean-Francois. 1979. *The Postmodern Condition: A Report on Knowledge*. Minneapolis: University of Minnesota Press.

McChesney, Robert. 2000. *Rich Media, Poor Democracy: Communication Politics in Dubious Times*. New York: The New Press.

Neil, Gary. 2003. Arts and Culture in World Trade: Promoting Cultural Diversity. In: *Civilizing Globalization: A Survival Guide*, ed. by Richard Sanbrook, 99–110. Albany: State University of New York Press.

Rodrik, Dani. 1998. The Global Fix. *New Republic* 219(18): 17–20.

Shiva, Vandana. 1997. *Biopiracy: The Plunder of Nature and Knowledge*. Boston: South End Press.

Smith, Linda Tuhiwai. 1999. *Decolonizing Methodologies: Research and Indigenous Peoples*. London, New York: Zed Books.

Stone-Mediatore, Shari. 2003. *Reading Across Borders: Storytelling and Knowledges of Resistance*. New York: Palgrave Macmillan.

Taylor, Charles. 1992. Multiculturalism and the Politics of Recognition. In: *Multiculturalism*, ed. by Amy Gutmann, 30–66. Princeton: Princeton University Press.

UNESCO. 2002. *Universal Declaration on Cultural Diversity, Cultural Diversity Series No. 1*. Document for the World Summit on Sustainable Development in Johannesburg. Paris: UNESCO.

Van Graan, Mike. 2003. Background to the Debate on Cultural Diversity. Presentation at the International Network on Cultural Diversity Fourth Annual Conference in Croatia.

Wyman, Max. 2004. *The Defiant Imagination: Why Culture Matters*. Vancouver: Douglas and McIntyre.

Young, Iris Marion. 2000. *Inclusion and Democracy*. New York: Oxford University Press.

The Author

Jennifer Chan-Tibergien is Assistant Professor in the Department of Educational Studies, Faculty of Education, as well as a Faculty Associate in the Center for Research in Women's Studies and Gender Relations and in the Centre for Japanese Research at the University of British Columbia, Canada. She is currently a Visiting Scholar in the Reischauer Institute for Japanese Studies at Harvard University.

Contact address: Reischauer Institute for Japanese Studies, Harvard University, 1737 Cambridge Street, Cambridge, MA 02138, USA. E-mail: chan7@fas.harvard.edu; jentiber@interchange.ubc.ca.

L'APPRENTISSAGE PRÉCOCE DES LANGUES: DES PRATIQUES SOCIOLOGIQUEMENT ET POLITIQUEMENT MARQUÉES

DOMINIQUE GROUX

Résumé – Il existe, dans le monde, une grande diversité de curricula qui proposent un apprentissage des langues plus ou moins intensif et plus ou moins tôt dans le cursus. Ces curricula correspondent à des choix pédagogiques différents. Mais ces options pédagogiques ne sont pas neutres. Elles sont le produit de choix politiques. Elles sont aussi sociologiquement discriminantes. L'auteur étudie les différentes formes d'apprentissage des langues dans certains pays (contrastés) et à l'intérieur même de ces pays (corrélation entre enseignements bilingues et écoles privées, par exemple, choix d'une éducation bilingue à des fins politiques). Elle propose une grille de classement de ces formes d'enseignement précoce des langues étrangères en fonction de critères sociologiques et de choix politiques.

Abstract – EARLY LANGUAGE TRAINING: SOCIOLOGICALLY AND POLITICALLY DETERMINED PRACTICES – Throughout the world there is a great diversity of curricula for introducing early foreign language training more or less intensively. These curricula correspond to different pedagogical approaches. But these pedagogical choices are not neutral. They are the result of political choice. They are also sociologically discriminatory. The author studies and contrasts various forms of language training of certain countries and within the same countries (for example, the correlation between bilingual training and private schools, or the choice of bilingual education as a political goal). She proposes a scale for classifying the kinds of early foreign language training, depending on sociological criteria and political choice.

Zusammenfassung – FREMDSPRACHENUNTERRICHT IM FRÜHEN KINDESALTER: SOZIOLOGISCH UND POLITISCH DETERMINIERTE PRAKTIKEN – Weltweit gesehen besteht eine große Diversität in den Lehrplänen für die Einführung von Fremdsprachenunterricht im frühen Kindesalter (in mehr oder weniger intensiver Weise). Solche Lehrpläne entsprechen verschiedenen pädagogischen Zugangsweisen. Aber diese pädagogischen Entscheidungen sind nicht neutral. Sie sind das Ergebnis politischer Entscheidungen. Sie sind auch, soziologisch betrachtet, diskriminierend. Die Autorin untersucht und vergleicht verschiedene Formen von Sprachunterricht in bestimmten Ländern und innerhalb dieser Länder selbst (z. B. das Verhältnis von bilingualem Unterricht und Privatschulen oder die Wahl der bilingualen Erziehung als ein politisches Ziel). Sie schlägt ein Raster vor, mit dem sich die Arten des Fremdsprachenunterrichtes im frühen Kindesalter abhängig von soziologischen Kriterien und politischen Entscheidungen klassifizieren lassen.

Resumen – EL APRENDIZAJE PRECOZ DE LAS LENGUAS LAS PRÀCTICAS SOCIOLOGICA Y POLÍTICAMENTE DETERMINADAS – Alrededor del planeta existe una gran diversidad de planes de estudio para el aprendizaje más o menos intensivo de una lengua extranjera a temprana edad. Estos currículos se corresponden con

J. Zajda (ed.), Education and Social Justice, 97-113.

diferentes enfoques pedagógicos. Sin embargo, la elección de estos enfoques no es neutral; estos enfoques son el resultado de una elección política, y también son discriminantes a nivel sociológico. La autora analiza y contrasta diferentes formas de aprendizaje de lenguas extranjeras de determinados países y dentro de los mismos países (por ejemplo, la correlación existente entre enseñanza bilingüe y escuelas privadas, o la elección de una educación bilingüe como objetivo político). La autora propone que se confeccione una escala, para clasificar las formas de enseñanza precoz de lenguas extranjeras en función de criterios sociológicos y de elecciones políticas.

Резюме – РАННЕЕ ОБУЧЕНИЕ ЯЗЫКАМ: ПОЛИТИЧЕСКИ И СОЦИОЛОГИЧЕСКИ ОБУСЛОВЛЕННАЯ ПРАКТИКА – Во всем мире существует большое разнообразие учебных программ по введению раннего обучения иностранным языкам с большей или меньшей интенсивностью. Эти учебные программы соответствуют различным педагогическим подходам. Но их выбор не является нейтральным. Они являются результатом политического выбора, они также обусловлены социологически. Автор статьи изучает и сравнивает различные формы обучения языкам в некоторых странах и внутри этих стран (например, соотношение между билингвальным обучением и частными школами; или выбор билингвального образования в качестве политической цели). Автор предлагает шкалу для классификации видов раннего обучения иностранным языкам в зависимости от социологических критериев и политического выбора.

La situation de l'enseignement des langues en France : l'exemple de l'Ile de France

Pour les privilégiés

En Ile de France, il existe des possibilités pour les enfants des classes favorisées d'être scolarisés dans un établissement bilingue français-anglais (95% des possibilités) ou français-allemand et français-espagnol (5% des possibilités), exclusivement dans les arrondissements et les banlieues riches.

En effet, l'implantation géographique de ces établissements n'est pas neutre et fonctionne comme un critère discriminant. Si l'on considère le cas de Paris, on note que les établissements bilingues (anglais/allemand/espagnol) sont implantés dans les arrondissements suivants: 7ème arrondissement parisien pour les cycles pré-primaire et primaire de l'école Jeannine Manuel, 15ème arrondissement pour le secondaire de ce même établissement, 8ème arrondissement pour l'École Active Bilingue, 16ème arrondissement pour l'Eurécole et pour l'International School of Paris. Si l'on considère à présent la banlieue, The English Language Montessori School se trouve à Chantilly, le Centre Actif Bilingue à Fontainebleau, l'École Montessori Internationale à Bailly (entre Versailles et Saint-Germain-en-Laye), le Lycée International à Saint-Germain-en-Laye, l'École Internationale Malherbe au Vésinet, deux sections internationales (français-anglais ou français-allemand) de la maternelle à la terminale au Lycée de Sèvres, la British School of Paris à Bougival, la Deutsche Schule Paris à Saint-Cloud, le Lycée Espagnol à Neuilly sur Seine, le Lycée franco-allemand à Buc.

Avec les lieux d'implantation des établissements bilingues, on voit très bien qu'il y a une corrélation entre les trois formes de ségrégation: ségrégation sociale, ségrégation spatiale, ségrégation scolaire. (On a fait la même étude avec les lieux d'implantation des ZEP.)

Il faut noter aussi le coût extrêmement élevé des études dans la plupart de ces établissements, à l'exception de quelques établissements publics (sections publiques du Lycée de Saint-Germain-en-Laye, Lycée de Sèvres). Par exemple, une année de maternelle à l'International School of Paris, coûte 8660 €. Elle est un peu moins chère à l'École Active Bilingue (1100 € par trimestre). À ce coût élevé de la scolarité, il convient bien entendu d'ajouter les frais relatifs aux activités extra-scolaires.

J'ai choisi de présenter deux établissements bilingues qui proposent un cursus bilingue de la maternelle à la fin du secondaire. L'un, le Lycée de Saint-Germain-en-Laye, est un établissement public (toutefois, quelques-unes de ses sections sont privées et les frais de scolarité y sont alors élevés). L'autre, l'École bilingue Jeannine Manuel, est un établissement privé, sous contrat d'association avec l'État.

Le Lycée international de Saint-Germain-en-Laye représente un exemple d'éducation plurilingue qui mériterait d'être généralisé. Avec ses douze sections nationales (allemande, américaine, britannique, danoise, norvégienne, suédoise, espagnole, italienne, japonaise, néerlandaise, portugaise, polonaise), le lycée offre la possibilité, dès l'école maternelle, d'un double enseignement, en langue nationale à raison de 6 heures hebdomadaires (littérature, histoire, langue du pays) et en langue française. En 2001 par exemple, sur 260 élèves présentés au baccalauréat (option internationale du baccalauréat), 183 élèves ont obtenu leur baccalauréat avec mention, 77 sans mention. Aucun élève n'a été ajourné. Les élèves parlent tous couramment au moins trois langues. Ils bénéficient, grâce aux contacts quotidiens avec des enfants d'autres nationalités d'une grande ouverture d'esprit. Le proviseur récemment nommé dans cet établissement signale que ces enfants ont une maturité intellectuelle plus précoce que dans son établissement précédent ; ils sont aussi très curieux culturellement et organisent souvent des manifestations v gdartistiques (théâtre en particulier) qui leur permettent d'aborder des sujets de société sur lesquels ils s'expriment facilement et de manifester leur compréhension du monde.

Un autre établissement prestigieux, l'École active bilingue Jeannine Manuel, accueille depuis 1954 des enfants (1800 élèves en 2003, 66 nationalités différentes) français (70%) et étrangers (30%) qui étudient l'anglais dès la maternelle dans un cursus bilingue (une heure et demie d'anglais par jour en primaire et certains enseignements disciplinaires dans cette langue). Pour les inscriptions en maternelle, il faut prévoir au minimum un an d'attente (si toutefois l'on satisfait à certains critères non explicités). Les élèves sont scolarisés à l'âge de quatre ans. Ils lisent en français dès la maternelle et en anglais dès le cours préparatoire. À partir du CM1, certains élèves peuvent être placés en immersion dans une classe : tous les cours se font en anglais à l'exception d'une heure et demie en français. Ils peuvent aussi, à partir du CM1, suivre un enseignement de japonais qu'ils pourront continuer en secondaire. À partir de la sixième, l'histoire, la géographie et les sciences sont enseignées en anglais par des professeurs anglophones. Les cours de langue anglaise ne sont plus dispensés qu'à raison de quatre heures par semaine. Une troisième langue est alors introduite : l'allemand, l'italien, le russe ou le japonais. À la fin de leurs études secondaires, les élèves qui intègrent une université américaine sont parfois plus performants en anglais que des anglophones natifs.

Pour les enfants des classes moyennes et des classes défavorisés

Dispositif bilingue
On le voit, il existe peu de possibilités pour les enfants des classes moyennes et des classes défavorisées de suivre un enseignement bilingue dans les conditions exposées précédemment (facteurs discriminants de l'implantation géographique, du coût des études et du capital culturel et social des familles rapidement évalué par les responsables lors de l'inscription).

Le seul enseignement bilingue proposé actuellement dans les autres arrondissements parisiens se fait dans trois écoles primaires (cycle maternel et primaire): l'école primaire publique de la rue de Tanger (19ème arrondissement), Le Petit Cours, école privée laïque, sans contrat avec l'éducation nationale, située 104, rue Orderer, dans le 18ème arrondissement et l'école primaire, située au 216bis, rue La Fayette, dans le 10ème arrondissement.

L'école primaire de la rue de Tanger scolarise 300 élèves qui pratiquent un bilinguisme français-arabe. Les mathématiques, l'histoire, la géographie, les sciences naturelles et la gymnastique sont enseignées en arabe. La langue arabe est dispensée par un enseignant arabe à raison de cinq heures hebdomadaires.

Le Petit Cours accueille 60 enfants dès l'âge de deux ans 3 mois et leur propose un enseignement bilingue anglais-français jusqu'à la fin du primaire. Des enseignants natifs du (ou des) pays dont ils enseignent la langue assurent les cours d'anglais à parité avec les cours de français (13 heures d'anglais, 13 heures de français).

L'école primaire de la rue La Fayette propose un enseignement en allemand à une classe par niveau (du cours préparatoire au cours moyen) dans l'établissement. Une institutrice allemande enseigne l'allemand à ces enfants à raison de 3 heures par semaine.

Toutefois les capacités d'accueil de ces établissements sont faibles et cet enseignement se limite au cycle primaire. Les enfants peuvent continuer à développer leurs compétences bilingues dans les sections internationales du Lycée Honoré de Balzac (17ème arrondissement).

En effet, ce lycée propose dans ses sections internationales d'anglais, d'allemand, d'espagnol, de portugais et d'arabe, un enseignement à partir de la sixième de 5 à 6 heures de langue et littérature nationales et de 2 heures d'histoire et de géographie spécifiques à l'aire étudiée. L'objectif de cet enseignement est de donner aux enfants une compétence bilingue et biculturelle. Le lycée accepte en sixième, après un examen d'entrée, les enfants qui ont déjà une compétence dans une langue étrangère. En première, dans la perspective de la préparation de l'option internationale du baccalauréat, une nouvelle sélection des élèves est opérée. Le lycée qui accueille 2900 élèves en scolarise 500 dans ses sections internationales et tous les élèves qui présentent l'option internationale du baccalauréat sont reçus (comme au Lycée de Saint-Germain-en-Laye).

Ce dispositif d'éducation bilingue n'est certes pas aussi développé dans les arrondissements du Nord parisien que dans les établissements de l'Ouest, mais il présente l'avantage d'être mis à la disposition d'une élite intellectuelle (examens discriminants par le mérite, puisqu'il n'y a malheureusement pas de possibilité d'accueil pour tous) et non financière.

Dispositif d'initiation aux langues en primaire

Le seul enseignement qui soit proposé actuellement dans les écoles publiques et dans la plupart des écoles privées est un enseignement précoce des langues à raison d'une séquence quotidienne d'un quart d'heure par jour en CE1 et de deux à trois heures hebdomadaires en CM1 et CM2 (circulaire du 16 mars 1989). Plus tard, la circulaire du 4 novembre 1999 réduira l'horaire hebdomadaire à 1h30.

Il faut signaler aussi que le voeu pieux exprimé dans la circulaire de rentrée n°2001-051 du 21 mars 2001 qui affirmait qu'en 2005, tous les élèves apprendraient une langue vivante en grande section de maternelle, ne tenait pas compte de la réalité. En effet, tous les enseignants du primaire ne sont pas capables d'enseigner une langue étrangère et les villes ne sont pas toutes prêtes à investir dans les salaires de vacataires extérieurs, natifs ou non, ayant obtenu leur habilitation pour enseigner les langues étrangères. Actuellement, la tendance est de former les enseignants titulaires des classes à enseigner une langue étrangère, l'anglais, et de faire de moins en moins appel à des extérieurs. Cela signifie que les enseignants se forment à la didactique des langues étrangères et reçoivent un complément de formation linguistique le plus souvent lors de stages de deux semaines. Il n'est pas prévu de les former à l'étranger ni dans des centres de langue en France.

Remarques sur cette situation

On le voit, si l'on compare l'enseignement qui est proposé aux enfants de certaines élites fortunées à celui qui est proposé à la masse de la population, il y a de toute évidence une différence de traitement. Puisque distinction il doit y avoir entre les élites et les autres, comme nous l'a si bien enseigné Bourdieu, serait-ce à dire que le niveau de maîtrise d'une langue étrangère joue et va jouer de plus en plus un rôle prépondérant dans la détermination de cette distinction ? Aux véritables bilingues, voire trilingues, seront réservés les postes de décision dans les domaines de la politique, de l'économie, des finances etc. C'est déjà souvent le cas actuellement, comme cela l'était jadis. Rappelons-nous l'importance qu'accordaient aux langues Montaigne dans le chapitre De l'Éducation de ses *Essais* ou Rabelais dans sa *Lettre de Gargantua à Pantagruel*. Plus près de nous, au 18ème siècle, les cours européennes étaient plurilingues et les aristocrates de Moscou, de Vienne ou de Berlin avaient tous des gouvernantes françaises ou anglaises pour leurs enfants. Encore plus près de nous, Louis-Philippe avait la réputation de parler toutes les langues de l'Europe.

J'ajouterai donc au fait que, si un véritable enseignement précoce des langues, je veux parler non pas d'un enseignement au rabais, mais d'un enseignement bilingue, apparaît comme le moyen le plus facile pour parvenir à une réelle maîtrise de la langue étrangère, il faut pouvoir le proposer à tous les enfants, quelle que soit leur origine sociale, pour des raisons de justice sociale. La langue est un objet de pouvoir aux mains des classes favorisées comme l'a justement montré Bourdieu (1982) dans son livre *Ce que parler veut dire, L'économie des échanges linguistiques*. La langue étrangère, l'anglais prioritairement, mais les autres langues aussi, confèrent à leurs locuteurs un pouvoir symbolique fort que nous ne devons pas laisser exclusivement à ceux qui ont le pouvoir financier et qui veulent comme toujours rassembler en leurs mains tous les capitaux: économique, culturel (avec sa composante linguistique), et social.

Certes, on me dira que l'enseignement précoce des langues tel qu'il est pratiqué actuellement dans les écoles, ou tel qu'on le pratique dans des expériences inspirées de l'éveil aux langues (*awareness of language*) a des vertus, qu'il développe l'ouverture aux autres, par le biais de la connaissance d'autres codes culturels, de réflexions métalinguistiques grâce à la comparaison de structures linguistiques. Je répondrai qu'au royaume des aveugles, les borgnes sont rois et qu'il vaut mieux faire cela que de ne rien faire du tout. Même si quelques enquêtes ont démontré l'inefficacité de certaines formes d'enseignement précoce des langues (Génelot 1995, 1996).

Il convient, par souci encore une fois je le répète, de justice sociale, de développer l'enseignement bilingue en France car c'est le type d'éducation qui permet le mieux de maîtriser une langue, de s'ouvrir sur le monde extérieur, d'approcher de l'intérieur la culture de l'autre et de véritablement s'éduquer à l'altérité (Groux 1999a, b, 2003a, b). Il serait malhonnête de cautionner le système existant qui est proposé par les décideurs pour répondre à une demande sociale, ces mêmes décideurs ayant recours pour eux-mêmes et leurs enfants, à d'autres stratégies que celles qui sont proposées par l'école : cours de langues proposées par les universités étrangères et séjours linguistiques longs en immersion à l'étranger, étudiants ou jeunes filles au pair, etc.

Que peut-on proposer en matière d'éducation bilingue ?

De la nécessité d'un curriculum d'ensemble

J'ai présenté en d'autres lieux et en particulier dans « Plaidoyer pour une politique linguistique cohérente en matière d'apprentissage précoce des langues » (Groux 1999a) certains curricula d'enseignement bilingue et quelques formations d'enseignants pour la mise en place de ces curricula.

J'ai présenté en particulier le curriculum des écoles bilingues égyptiennes qui propose un enseignement paritaire de la langue française et de la langue arabe à partir de la maternelle. Les enfants apprennent à lire et à écrire en même temps dans les deux langues, c'est-à-dire au niveau de la première année de primaire. Ils ont également un enseignement disciplinaire en français : les mathématiques et les sciences sont enseignées en français. Le français prend alors tout son sens. Il n'est pas une matière de plus, que l'on étudie pour introduire un objet d'étude supplémentaire, mais une langue utile pour comprendre les disciplines et acquérir les savoirs afférents à cette discipline. La seconde langue étrangère, l'anglais, est introduite très rapidement en troisième ou quatrième année de primaire selon les écoles. Evidemment, dès la fin du primaire, les élèves ont acquis des connaissances solides dans les deux langues étrangères. Ils n'ont pas peiné laborieusement pour étudier ces langues comme on le fait souvent quand on étudie la langue pour la langue, qu'on provoque des situations artificielles en classe pour se mettre dans la peau de (jeux de rôle, simulation etc.), alors qu'il est si simple d'utiliser une langue quand on en a besoin pour résoudre un problème mathématique, pour décrire un animal et ses conditions de vie, un phénomène physique etc.

Je rappellerai que le curriculum de français des écoles bilingues est un ensemble cohérent qui présente des progressions rigoureuses dans les quatre domaines constitués par la production et la compréhension écrites, la production et la compréhension orales.

L'acquisition de ces compétences est facilitée par le fait que l'enfant apprend très vite à reproduire des sons, des mots et des phrases par mimétisme quand il est très jeune. Il reproduit parfaitement les sons, sans accent, parce que ses organes phonatoires sont aptes à le faire. Et puis, quand il est très jeune, l'enfant n'a pas de fausse pudeur à parler dans une langue étrangère. Il ne se sent pas ridicule : il a besoin de la langue pour avoir accès à des savoirs, pour jouer, pour chanter, il utilise donc la langue qui lui permet d'agir. Et plus il utilise la langue, plus elle lui permet de réaliser d'actions, plus il acquiert de confiance en lui-même.

L'enfant acquiert aussi des compétences culturelles et des compétences interculturelles. Par le biais de correspondances scolaires classiques ou par internet, il découvre les codes culturels de ses correspondants, la manière dont ils vivent dans leur pays, leur rapport à leur famille, à leurs amis, leurs habitudes gastronomiques, leurs règles de politesse, leur façon de vivre l'intimité etc. L'enfant bilingue compare avec ses propres habitudes. Il se décentre et apprend à relativiser. Les codes de l'autre valent bien les siens ; il ne hiérarchise pas; il compare simplement et il note les différences. Certes, cette approche est possible également dans une école monolingue, où l'on met parfois en place de telles activités mais la scolarisation en établissement bilingue transforme ces démarches de découverte de l'autre en démarches plus nécessaires, plus naturelles et plus faciles.

C'est parce qu'il possède bien la langue et qu'il la maîtrise rapidement que l'enfant peut avoir accès à la culture qui se cache derrière la langue et qu'il peut comprendre la cohérence de cette culture et du même coup percevoir de façon plus claire la cohérence singulière de la sienne. Dans cette découverte de l'altérité, dans cette confrontation de l'*ego* avec l'*alter*, l'enfant va se découvrir lui-même et s'enrichir de la rencontre avec l'autre.

Puisqu'il a plus de facilité qu'un enfant monolingue et monoculturel, à comprendre l'autre dans sa différence, il ne sera pas tenté de le rejeter, mais il va l'accepter, parce qu'il comprend la différence de l'autre et qu'il peut voir que cette différence est mutuellement enrichissante.

Il existe bien d'autres curricula bilingues qui produisent également d'excellents résultats. Il suffit de penser au système éducatif luxembourgeois où les enfants qui parlent le luxembourgeois en maternelle, commencent l'apprentissage de l'allemand en première année de primaire pour continuer en deuxième année avec l'apprentissage du français et pour poursuivre avec celui de l'anglais en première année de collège. Là aussi, les langues sont des vecteurs disciplinaires et elles ne sont pas étudiées uniquement pour elles-mêmes, ce qui leur confère du sens. On ne les utilise pas seulement à des fins de communication artificielle dans la classe.

En ce qui concerne les objectifs d'apprentissage, ils sont ambitieux et, on le sait, plus l'enseignement est exigeant, plus l'élève acquiert de compétences. L'enfant est capable d'assimiler beaucoup de choses et il faut profiter de ses grandes capacités d'apprentissage. À 3 ans, on peut apprendre une langue étrangère sans souffrir, en jouant, en chantant, en imitant des sons, en répétant des comptines, choses que l'on fera beaucoup plus difficilement vers l'âge de dix ans.

De la nécessité d'un dispositif de formation

Que dire à présent de la formation des enseignants qui auront à pratiquer la langue et à enseigner dans la langue? Certes, l'enseignant doit avoir une bonne compétence linguistique s'il veut que l'enfant maîtrise lui aussi la langue, de façon fluide et sans accent. C'est la raison pour laquelle il me semble qu'un enseignant originaire du (ou des) pays dont il enseigne la langue aura plus de chances qu'un enseignant français d'amener l'enfant à s'exprimer comme lui, par mimétisme, sans accent, de façon courante. De plus, l'enseignant natif véhicule des valeurs que l'enfant va découvrir derrière la langue. Celle-ci ne sera pas seulement un habillage vide de sens, vide de culture. Bien que certains travaux universitaires (Derivry-Plard 2003), à mon avis complètement biaisés, aient réussi à prouver qu'un enseignant de langue non natif obtient de meilleurs résultats avec ses élèves qu'un enseignant natif, il n'a pas la même compétence linguistique ni culturelle que le natif. Il est certainement capable de faire réussir ses élèves aux examens parce qu'il en connaît mieux que le non natif les arcanes et les présupposés, les règles en quelque sorte.

Pour obtenir de bons résultats, l'enseignant doit évidemment comprendre les enjeux et les objectifs de son enseignement, et réfléchir sur les méthodes à utiliser pour les atteindre. Il doit aussi être inventif et créatif. Il va imaginer des jeux et des séquences d'apprentissage. Il va créer ses propres outils pour parvenir à ses fins : l'acquisition de compétences et de connaissances par les élèves.

Évidemment, cela suppose que l'enseignant ait un bon niveau linguistique pour enseigner la discipline dans la langue étrangère, des compétences dans la discipline qu'il va enseigner et des compétences pédagogiques pour enseigner à la fois la langue et la discipline.

Le dispositif bilingue mis en place dans l'académie de Strasbourg peut-il s'étendre et se généraliser à l'ensemble de la France ?

Le dispositif bilingue de l'académie de Strasbourg

L'Académie de Strasbourg a mis en place très tôt, dès 1970, un enseignement de l'allemand dans des conditions équivalentes à celles qui sont actuellement proposées par l'EILE depuis 1989 sur l'ensemble de la France, c'est-à-dire que l'on enseignait l'allemand à raison de 3 heures par semaine en CM2. (À l'initiative de l'inspecteur général Holderith, l'allemand est implanté en 1970 au cours moyen. L'expérience est amplifiée en 1982 par le recteur Pierre Dayon et à partir de 1984, grâce au concours de la Région Alsace et des départements du Haut-Rhin et du Bas-Rhin.) Puis on s'est orienté vers le bilinguisme dès 1991 et on a alors mis en place des sites à six heures en CE2, CM1 et CM2. Il ne s'agissait plus d'enseigner la langue pour elle-même mais de l'utiliser pour avoir accès à des savoirs disciplinaires. Avec cette nouvelle finalité, la langue devient nécessaire pour comprendre les disciplines et l'élève n'a plus besoin de se créer des motivations artificielles. La langue est indispensable et elle doit être maîtrisée si l'on ne veut pas être en situation d'échec dans les différents apprentissages. C'est le facteur essentiel de réussite de l'éducation bilingue. Enfin, le dispositif a été encore amélioré à partir de 1994 puisqu'on est passé à un enseignement paritaire: 13 heures de français assurées par un maître français et treize heures d'allemand assurées par un enseignant allemand durant la semaine. C'est alors le bilinguisme équilibré qui est recherché, l'enfant devant pouvoir idéalement s'exprimer aussi bien en français qu'en allemand. En maternelle, les activités sont réparties entre les deux langues. L'apprentissage de la lecture se fait en français et en allemand dès la maternelle. À partir du CP, la géographie, les sciences et technologies, les mathématiques sont enseignées en allemand ; l'histoire, l'éducation physique et la géométrie en français.

Comme au Luxembourg, l'élève va étudier l'anglais dans des sections trilingues en sixième. Ce n'est donc pas seulement le bilinguisme français-allemand que l'on veut atteindre, mais le trilinguisme dès le début du collège (anglais, espagnol, arabe, portugais, italien), puis l'apprentissage d'une quatrième langue en seconde. Nous retrouvons là les conditions idéales d'apprentissage d'une langue que nous avons évoquées au début de notre exposé à propos du Lycée de Saint-Germain-en-Laye ou de l'École Jeannine Manuel.

Cette fois, le public visé n'est pas seulement, comme dans ces établissements prestigieux, un public d'enfants de milieux favorisés. Cet enseignement concerne tous les élèves, à condition qu'ils aient été inscrits dans ces sites bilingues au début de leur scolarité. On ne peut pas intégrer, pour les raisons que l'on comprend aisément, le cursus en cours de route.

Actuellement, environ 50% des enfants de cette région bénéficient de cet enseignement bilingue et l'objectif des responsables politiques est de le proposer à tous les enfants. On est bien, cette fois, dans une logique démocratique. Il n'est plus question de ségrégation éducative et de discrimination par l'argent. Chaque collège propose une section trilingue allemand-anglais par niveau, de la sixième à la troisième, et certains collèges disposent de plusieurs sections par niveau.

À l'entrée en seconde, les élèves sont accueillis dans des sections européennes qui offrent un enseignement renforcé des langues vivantes et l'enseignement d'une discipline dans les langues étudiées. Ces sections existent pour l'allemand, l'anglais, l'espagnol, l'italien et le portugais. En général, les élèves choisissent une troisième langue étrangère et reçoivent donc un enseignement disciplinaire dans cette troisième langue.

Comme je le disais précédemment, pour qu'une réforme de cette ampleur réussisse, il faut d'abord avoir opéré un choix politique. Dans ce cas, on a voulu faire de tous les enfants alsaciens de véritables bilingues dans une perspective politique claire, celle de la construction européenne: « C'est sur cette démarche en profondeur, commencée dès l'âge des apprentissages fondamentaux et poursuivie dans la durée du parcours éducatif, que pourra s'édifier une Europe harmonieuse, ... une Europe non imposée de l'extérieur mais assumée de l'intérieur » (De Gaudemar 1996). Ensuite, il faut prendre les moyens de mettre en œuvre cette politique linguistique. Il faut au préalable avoir conçu un plan de formation pour les enseignants qui vont être engagés dans le processus. Il faut aussi avoir prévu des progressions d'apprentissage sérieuses de la maternelle au collège, avoir mis en place des matériels pédagogiques et avoir modifié les programmes du collège, contrairement à ce qui se passe actuellement dans le reste de la France pour l'EILE. Il faut aussi avoir prévu un dispositif d'évaluation de l'expérimentation.

Que disent les évaluations qui ont été menées jusqu'à présent ? Elles montrent que les élèves scolarisés dans ce système acquièrent les compétences linguistiques et culturelles d'enfants plurilingues, puisque l'apprentissage de l'anglais, à partir du collège, et celui d'une autre langue, à partir du lycée, sont facilités par l'apprentissage précoce de la première langue étrangère, l'allemand.

Ce dispositif peut-il se généraliser à l'ensemble de la France ?

Lorsque je présente, lors de mes conférences, les dispositifs d'éducation bilingue canadien ou luxembourgeois, ou encore égyptien, mes interlocuteurs manifestent une grande admiration pour ces réalisations et ils déplorent que la situation française ne permette pas d'acquérir des compétences plurilingues au sein de l'école. Si je leur dis qu'ils se trompent en me référant à la situation alsacienne, ils sont tout d'abord surpris de découvrir que ce qu'ils pensaient irréalisable dans le contexte français existe bel et bien, et puis, après réflexion, ils me répondent que l'Alsace a une histoire bien particulière, que sa proximité géographique et économique avec l'Allemagne explique la réussite de cette expérience, mais que cela n'est pas généralisable au reste de la France.

Que penser de cela ? L'expérience alsacienne ne pourrait-elle pas s'étendre à d'autres régions comme l'Aquitaine, le Midi-Pyrénées, le Nord Pas-de-Calais, la région Provence-Alpes-Côte d'Azur ? Si le fait d'appartenir à une région frontalière avec des intérêts économiques et culturels communs avec le pays étranger tout proche peut expliquer la réussite du dispositif, pourquoi ne pas tenter de l'étendre au moins à ces régions ? On me répondra que même dans ces régions frontalières, on a fait, pour la langue enseignée en primaire, prioritairement le choix de l'anglais et non celui de la langue du pays voisin. Et dans le reste de la France? Là aussi bien évidemment, on choisit majoritairement l'anglais, parce que les parents ont peur que leur enfant ne maîtrise pas bien l'anglais et ils ne veulent pas qu'il consacre du temps à une autre langue. – Pour l'année 2002–2003, 78,6% des classes du public et 89,1% des classes du privé sous contrat bénéficient de l'enseignement de l'anglais. Dans trois académies, cette proportion dépasse 90% (Caen, Limoges, Poitiers) et se situe au-dessous de 70% dans trois autres (Strasbourg, Nancy-Metz et Paris). Ces académies choisissent respectivement l'allemand à 96%, 43,2% et 20,5%. Signalons aussi que l'académie de Toulouse choisit l'espagnol à 16,5% (Bordeaux: 8,4% seulement) et que l'académie de Corse choisit l'italien à 16,3% (Grenoble: 6,5% et Nice: 9,4%) (DESCO A1 2003).

Or, on le sait, il est facile d'apprendre l'anglais en seconde langue parce que les mécanismes de pensée sont assez similaires en français et en anglais. Ils le sont beaucoup moins en français et en allemand, en japonais ou en arabe. L'effort que va faire l'enfant dans une langue étrangère, vraiment étrangère à la sienne, développe ses compétences cognitives et ses capacités métalinguistiques beaucoup plus que lors de l'apprentissage de l'anglais. Et cette souplesse intellectuelle acquise grâce au va-et-vient entre deux codes linguistiques très différents facilite l'apprentissage de la seconde langue étrangère. L'apprentissage de l'anglais sera alors un jeu d'enfant. D'ailleurs, des écoles prestigieuses comme l'École Alsacienne ou l'École Jeannine Manuel proposent l'apprentissage du japonais et du chinois en primaire.

Alors, est-ce un combat perdu que de vouloir persuader les parents qu'il ne faut pas que leur enfant apprenne l'anglais en première langue parce que de toute façon, il s'investira dans l'apprentissage de l'anglais pour toutes sortes de raisons (proximité culturelle, nécessité professionnelle etc.), quel que soit le moment où il va commencer à l'apprendre, alors que pour une autre langue, l'investissement ne sera certainement pas similaire? Cela semble pourtant évident. Le bilinguisme français-anglais vers lequel on est en train de s'orienter va nuire au trilinguisme ou au moins ne va pas le favoriser, alors qu'un autre bilinguisme se serait logiquement transformé en trilinguisme.

Faut-il se résigner et accepter d'avoir perdu ce combat? L'anglais va certainement s'imposer bientôt dans toutes les écoles primaires. D'ailleurs, le signe avant-coureur de cet état de fait est bien qu'actuellement, les formations des enseignants de primaire ne se font, dans l'académie de Paris par exemple, qu'en anglais. Une seconde langue étrangère sera donc introduite au collège.

Le fait qu'il n'y ait plus qu'une langue enseignée en primaire peut-il favoriser la mise en place d'un dispositif bilingue? Quels sont les problemes qui se posent et qui font qu'il est encore prématuré d'imaginer une telle possibilité?

Je dirais tout d'abord qu'il y a un problème de ressources humaines. Les enseignants français ne sont pas, dans l'état actuel des choses, bilingues comme au Canada, au Luxembourg ou en Égypte. Il va falloir, si l'on ne veut pas faire appel à des intervenants extérieurs, natifs de préférence, former ces enseignants sur le plan linguistique et pédagogique (cela semble être malheureusement la tendance actuelle). Ne parlons pas d'un enseignement disciplinaire dans la langue étrangère, nous en reparlerons dans quelques siècles ... Donc si l'enseignement disciplinaire ne se fait pas dans la langue étrangère, il n'est pas question d'éducation bilingue.

La seule manière de mettre en place une éducation bilingue dans le système éducatif public français serait de faire appel à des enseignants étrangers, qui enseigneraient certaines disciplines dans leur langue en attendant que les enseignants titulaires des classes soient aptes à le faire. (Comme dans la plupart des établissements bilingues cités en dans le premier paragraphe du texte.)

On pourrait faire appel aussi à des étudiants Erasmus, à des étrangers vivant en France à qui on donnerait une formation pédagogique ou à des étudiants français qui préparent leur CAPES en langue. Il est plus aisé et plus rapide de donner une formation pédagogique qu'une formation linguistique. Mais peut-on imaginer la réaction des syndicats d'enseignants à de telles propositions? Et puis les politiques sont-ils réellement prevues pour investir dans une réelle et sérieuse politique linguistique qui aurait pour but de promouvoir le bilinguisme, voire le trilinguisme? Pourquoi n'impose-t-on pas une épreuve obligatoire de langue au concours d'entrée à l'IUFM ? Puisque les parents semblent se satisfaire de ce qu'on leur donne, il est inutile d'investir davantage dans un enseignement des langues efficace pour tous, puisque de toute façon, les élites ont les moyens de l'acquérir par ellesmêmes, sans l'aide de l'école.

La boucle est bouclée. Les errances actuelles de l'apprentissage précoce des langues ne sont pas prêtes de prendre fin. L'horizon semble bien bouché. Les classes moyennes tenteront de mettre en place, à l'instar des classes favorisées, des stratégies pour combler les lacunes de l'enseignement public. (Le privé va continuer à vivre sur ces lacunes et à proposer un enseignement des langues qu'il dira performant, ce qui n'est la plupart du temps qu'un leurre.) Les classes défavorisées continueront à se contenter de ce qu'elles ont.

Si l'on constate lors de manifestations comme Expolangues, le succès des séjours linguistiques à l'étranger, qui s'effectuent de plus en plus tôt, c'est certainement parce que les parents commencent à accepter les insuffisances de l'école primaire en matière de langue. (Jusqu'à présent, les échecs se manifestaient dans le secondaire.) Et les familles compensent avec des séjours linguistiques. Mais peut-être aussi continue-t-on à vivre avec l'idée, fausse de toute évidence, qu'une langue ne peut pas s'apprendre à l'école. Les écoles bilingues et leur succès sont là pour témoigner du contraire.

Ce qu'apprendre une langue étrangère veut dire. Tentative de classification

Des pratiques sociologiquement discriminantes en France

– des écoles bilingues pour l'élite, situées dans les quartiers favorisés

  Des langues reconnues socialement. Pas d'arabe en particulier au lycée de Saint-Germain-en-Laye (pourtant existence de 12 sections). Bilinguisme positif, additif. Type sociologique de population: milieux très aisés, diplomates, couples mixtes ayant vécu à l'étranger, enfants d'origine française ayant un bon dossier (pour l'entrée en maternelle, enfants dont les parents ont un fort capital culturel, social et économique).

  Projet de l'école: former une *élite* possédant une parfaite maîtrise des langues et lui constituer un important capital linguistique, culturel et social (importance du réseau des parents: APELI Association des parents d'élèves du Lycée de Saint-Germain-en-Laye).

– une école bilingue pour une population d'origine étrangère, située dans le 19ème arrondissement, créée sous l'impulsion de militants. L'expérience ne s'est jamais étendue. Elle a rencontré beaucoup de résistance. L'arabe, langue non reconnue socialement. Bilinguisme négatif, soustractif. Type sociologique de population: enfants du quartier, milieu très modeste.

Projet de l'école: *lutter contre l'échec* scolaire par l'apprentissage d'une langue étrangère, réconcilier les enfants avec leurs origines, transformer le bilinguisme soustractif en bilinguisme additif.

- des écoles primaires bilingues dans les quartiers défavorisés de Paris avec un enseignement d'anglais (école privée hors contrat: 60 élèves) et un enseignement d'allemand (école publique: 3h par semaine à partir de la maternelle par une enseignante allemande) et possibilité réservée aux *élèves les plus compétents* de poursuivre cet enseignement dans les sections européennes du lycée Balzac.
- des écoles bilingues : langue régionale-français en Bretagne, Corse, Pays Basque, etc. Volonté politique, militantisme. Volonté de *distinction* politique.
- des écoles privées pas nécessairement prestigieuses mais qui proposent un enseignement précoce des langues qu'elles disent plus performants que celui des écoles publiques: langue = produit d'appel (*discriminant* pour échapper à la mixité sociale de l'école publique)
- des écoles publiques bilingues en Alsace désireuses de proposer à tous les élèves un enseignement plurilingue dans une perspective de construction européenne.
- des écoles publiques plus ou moins performantes dans le domaine de l'apprentissage des langues. Cela dépend des compétences linguistiques des enseignants sur place, de la motivation des parents qui peuvent faire pression sur les municipalités pour avoir des postes de vacataires chargés des langues. Pénurie de moyens. Horaire peu important. Enseignants en poste peu formés en langue. D'où un enseignement peu performant. Des parents qui adoptent des stratégies pour combler les lacunes en fonction de leur prise de conscience de la place des langues dans la constitution du capital culturel en vue d'accroître le capital économique.

Cette grille valable pour la France fonctionne-t-elle pour l'étranger?

Trois exemples:

- les écoles francophones du Québec

  Projet: remédier à la *discrimination* sociale des familles anglophones au Québec. D'où volonté des parents que leurs enfants maîtrisent parfaitement le français.
- les écoles bilingues égyptiennes

  Projet: *Distinction* sociale liée à la maîtrise du français et de l'anglais. Capital linguistique et culturel liés au capital économique (travail facilement accessible quand on est issu d'une école bilingue). Semblable au fonctionnement des établissements d'élite français.

– les écoles luxembourgeoises

Nécessité pour tous les Luxembourgeois de s'ouvrir sur les pays limitrophes. D'où nécessité d'apprendre le français, l'allemand et l'anglais, langue de communication internationale. La plus ou moins grande maîtrise des langues internationales par les Luxembourgeois peut être également un *facteur de distinction discriminant*.

Conclusion

Lorsqu'on étudie attentivement cette grille présentant quelques choix d'éducation bilingue en France et dans le monde, on arrive à la conclusion que, dans tous les cas, l'excellente maîtrise d'une langue, voire de deux langues étrangères, permet la distinction sociale. C'est le cas des écoles bilingues de l'ouest parisien et de la banlieue riche qui proposent un enseignement discriminant à une élite sur des critères financiers et culturels (culture de classe). C'est le cas de nombreuses écoles privées qui s'appuient sur l'offre de langue pour asseoir leur réputation, conscientes du pouvoir symbolique que les langues représentent. C'est le cas des établissements du nord parisien qui proposent également un enseignement discriminant à une élite, par le biais de la méritocratie. C'est le cas des écoles francophones du Québec qui forment des anglophones capables de maîtriser parfaitement le français pour éviter la discrimination sociale. C'est le cas des écoles bilingues égyptiennes qui confèrent à leurs élèves un fort capital culturel et linguistique, préalable à leur réussite sociale.

Seules, les écoles bilingues alsaciennes et les écoles luxembourgeoises ne sont pas conçues à partir de cette volonté discriminante, puisqu'en Alsace comme au Luxembourg, elles ont été conçues pour former tous les élèves alsaciens et luxembourgeois. Certes, tous les élèves n'auront pas à l'issue de leur cursus, le même niveau linguistique et culturel. Certains se distingueront par leur plus grande maîtrise des langues et des cultures étudiées.

Enfin, les écoles bilingues dans lesquelles les langues régionales sont enseignées expriment un projet politique fort et les parents manifestent ainsi leur différence politique et leur attachement aux valeurs patrimoniales. Quant aux écoles où l'arabe est enseigné, le projet politique qui a permis leur mise en place est clair: il s'agit d'offrir aux enfants d'origine étrangère l'accès à une double culture (celle du pays d'accueil et celle de leurs parents) et de faciliter ainsi leur intégration.

La France n'a pas fait le choix du bilinguisme pour tous. Si nous étions cyniques, nous dirions que c'est parce qu'il faut bien conserver certains critères de distinction sociale. Nous dirons seulement qu'elle n'en pas, actuellement, les moyens. Elle a fait le choix, dans 95% de ses établissements publics, d'un enseignement des langues étrangères à dose homéopathique et, on le sait à présent, les effets de cet enseignement sont pratiquement nuls. Il reste à souhaiter que la réussite de certains dispositifs comme les prestigieuses écoles bilingues françaises, les écoles bilingues de Strasbourg, ou les écoles bilingues étrangères, vont finir par convaincre nos responsables de l'urgence des choix politiques à faire. C'est évidemment vers le bilinguisme et le plurilinguisme qu'il faut aller comme l'a fait l'Académie de Strasbourg. Nos responsables politiques sont déjà conscients, pour eux et pour les classes dominantes, des enjeux formidables du plurilinguisme acquis dans le cadre de l'institution scolaire. S'ils souhaitent construire un jour un monde respectueux des identités culturelles, un monde à la recherche de l'altérité structurante, alors ils mettront à la portée de tous ce formidable dispositif que représente l'éducation bilingue et plurilingue.

Références

Bourdieu, Pierre. 1982. *Ce que parler veut dire. L'économie des échanges linguistiques.* Paris: Fayard.

Byram, Michael, et Manuel Tost Planet 1999. *Identité sociale et dimension européenne: la compétence interculturelle par l'apprentissage des langues vivantes.* Strasbourg: Conseil de l'Europe.

Calvet, Louis-Jean. 2002. *Un marché aux langues : essai de politologie linguistique sur la mondialisation.* Paris: Plon.

De Gaudemar, Jean-Paul. 1996. «Circulaire rectorale due 20 septembre 1991: Programme à moyen terme de développement de l'allemand à l'école». Dans: *Le programme 'Langue et culture régionales' en Alsace. Textes de référence 1991–1996*, 45–58. Strasbourg: Académie de Strasbourg, Ministère de l'Éducation Natinale, de l'enseignement supérieur et de la Recherche.

Derivry-Plard, Martine. 2003. *Les enseignants d'anglais « natifs » et « non-natifs ». Concurrence ou complémentarité de deux légitimités.* Thèse de doctorat présentée à l'Université de Paris III Sorbonne.

DESCO A1 Ministère de l'Éducation Nationale [MEN]. 2003. *Enquête effectuée auprès des inspections académiques, Repères et références statistiques.* Paris: MEN.

Eurydice. 2001. *L'enseignement des langues étrangères en milieu scolaire en Europe.* Bruxelles: Commission européenne.

Garabédian, Michèle. 1993. Quels modèles didactiques pour enseigner apprendre une langue étrangère à de jeunes scolaires? *Études de linguistique appliquée* 89 : 34–89.

Génelot, Sophie. 1995. *Note sur l'enseignement des langues vivantes à l'ecole elementaire: éléments d'évaluation des effets au collège.* Dijon: IREDU.

———. 1996. *Note sur l'enseignement des langues vivantes à l'école élémentaire : éléments d'évaluation des effets au collège.* Dijon: IREDU.

Girard, Denis. 1991. Bilan didactique qualitatif des expériences d'enseignement précoce d'une langue étrangère (1960–1980). Dans: *Les langues vivantes à l'ecole elementaire.* Paris: INRP.

Groux, Dominique. 1993. *Propositions d'un curriculum d'ensemble (du jardin d'enfants à l'entrée à l'université) dans l'enseignement du français en Égypte.* Thèse de doctorat, Paris III.

———. 1994. Évaluation de l'impact pédagogique du curriculum de français des écoles de langue égyptienne. *Revue Française de Pédagogie* 108(3): 45–55.

———. 1996a. De l'Enseignement d'Initiation aux Langues Étrangères (EILE) à l'éducation bilingue. Actes du Colloque de l'ASDIFLE, 5, 6 et 7 septembre 1996, Université de Toulon et du Var. *Les Cahiers de l'ASDIFLE* 8: 261–270.

———. 1996b. *L'enseignement précoce des langues, Des enjeux à la pratique*. Lyon: Chronique Sociale.

———. 1998. Bekämpfung des Schulversagens durch frühzeitigen Spracherwerb. Die französisch-arabische Primarschule in der Rue de Tanger in Paris. *Bildung und Erziehung* 51(3): 271–278.

———. 1999a. Plaidoyer pour une politique linguistique cohérente en matière d'apprentissage précoce des langues. Dans : *Comparative Perspectives on Language and Literacy. Selected Papers from the Work of the Language and Literacy Commission of the 10th World Congress of Comparative Education Societies, Cape Town, 1998*, ed. by Leslie Limage, 265–280. Dakar: UNESCO Regional Office.

———. 1999b. Des conditions favorables pour un enseignement précoce des langues? L'apprentissage précoce des langues. *Résonances* 4(12): 3–4.

———. 2003a. Quel avenir pour l'enseignement bilingue euro-arabe? Dans: *L'éducation plurielle euro-arabe. De la réflexion à l'action*, 33–40. Paris: Jeunesse sans Frontières.

———. 2003b. Le meilleur âge pour apprendre. Pour un apprentissage précoce des langues. *Le Français dans le monde* 330(6): 23–25.

O'Neil, Charmian. 1993. *Les enfants et l'enseignement des langues étrangères*. Paris: Crédif-Hatier.

Porcher, Louis, et Dominique Groux 2003. *L'apprentissage précoce des langues*. Paris: PUF.

Pufahl, Ingrid, Nancy C. Rhodes, et Chrisian Donna 2000. *Foreign Language Teaching. What the United States Can Learn from Other Countries*. Washington, DC: Center for Applied Linguistics.

L'auteur

Dominique Groux est professeur des universités à l'IUFM de Versailles. Elle est actuellement détachée comme attachée de coopération universitaire à l'Ambassade de france en Allemagne et elle travaille à l'université de Potsdam (Allemagne). Ses champs de recherche sont l'éducation comparée, l'apprentissage précoce des langues, les échanges internationaux et l'éducation à l'altérité.

Addresse: 5, cité de Phalsbourg, 75011, Paris, France. E-mail: dgroux@noos.fr.

EDUCATIONAL DECENTRALIZATION, PUBLIC SPENDING, AND SOCIAL JUSTICE IN NIGERIA

MACLEANS A. GEO-JAJA

Abstract – This study situates the process of educational decentralization in the narrower context of social justice. Its main object, however, is to analyze the implications of decentralization for strategies of equity and social justice in Nigeria. It starts from the premise that the early optimism that supported decentralization as an efficient and effective educational reform tool has been disappointed. The author maintains that decentralization – on its own – cannot improve education service delivery, the capacities of subordinate governments, or the integration of social policy in broader development goals. If the desired goals are to be met, public spending must be increased, greater tax revenues must be secured, and macro-economic stabilization must be achieved without re-instituting the welfare state.

Zusammenfassung – DEZENTRALISIERUNG VON BILDUNG, ÖFFENTLICHE AUSGABEN UND SOZIALE GERECHTIGKEIT IN NIGERIA – Diese Untersuchung stellt den Prozess der Dezentralisierung von Bildung in den engeren Zusammenhang der sozialen Gerechtigkeit. Ihr Hauptthema ist jedoch, die Implikationen der Dezentralisierung für die Strategien zur Chancengleichheit und sozialen Gerechtigkeit in Nigeria zu analysieren. Sie geht von der Prämisse aus, dass der anfängliche Optimismus, der die Dezentralisierung als ein effizientes und effektives Werkzeug zur Bildungsreform unterstützt hat, enttäuscht wurde. Der Autor stellt die Behauptung auf, dass Dezentralisierung – für sich allein genommen – die Verfügbarkeit von Bildungsangeboten, die Kapazitäten der untergeordneten Regierungsebenen oder die Einbindung der Sozialpolitik in die weiteren Entwicklungsziele nicht verbessern kann. Wenn die erwünschten Ziele umgesetzt werden sollen, müssen die öffentlichen Ausgaben erhöht, größere Steuereinnahmen sichergestellt und makroökonomische Stabilisierung erreicht werden, und zwar ohne den Wohlfahrtsstaat wiedereinzuführen.

Résumé – DÉCENTRALISATION ÉDUCATIVE, DONS PUBLICS ET JUSTICE SOCIALE AU NIGÉRIA – Cette étude situe le processus de la décentralisation éducative dans le contexte plus proche de la justice sociale. Son objet principal, cependant, est d'analyser les implications de la décentralisation pour les stratégies de l'équité et de la justice sociale au Nigéria. Elle part de la prémisse que l'optimisme de départ qui soutenait la décentralisation comme étant un instrument de réforme efficient et effectif s'est révélé trompeur. L'auteur maintient que la décentralisation – seule – ne peut améliorer la distribution des services d'éducation, les capacités des gouvernements subalternes, ou l'intégration d'une politique sociale dans un élargissement des buts du développement. Si l'on veut atteindre les buts désirés, les dons publics doivent augmenter, des taxes sur les revenus plus élevées doivent être assurées, et une stabilisation macro-économique doit être réalisée sans une nouvelle remise en place de l'étatprovidence.

J. Zajda (ed.), Education and Social Justice, 115-138.

Resumen – DESCENTRALIZACIÓN DE LA EDUCACIÓN, GASTOS PÚBLICOS Y JUSTICIA SOCIAL EN NIGERIA – Este estudio sitúa el proceso de la descentralización de la educación en un contexto más restringido, el de la justicia social. Sin embargo, su principal objetivo no es el de analizar los efectos de la descentralización sobre la equidad y la justicia social en Nigeria. El trabajo parte de la premisa de que la expectativa optimista inicial, que había apoyado a la descentralización como herramienta de una reforma educativa eficiente y efectiva, ha quedado defraudada. El autor sostiene que la descentralización, por sí misma, no es capaz de mejorar los servicios de educación ni las capacidades de los gobiernos regionales ni la integración de una política social dentro de unos objetivos de desarrollo mayores. Si se quieren alcanzar los objetivos deseados, sin reimplantar el Estado de bienestar, habrá que incrementar el gasto público, asegurar una mayor recaudación fiscal y lograr la estabilidad macroeconómica.

Резюме – ОБРАЗОВАТЕЛЬНАЯ ДЕЦЕНТРАЛИЗАЦИЯ, ГОСУДАРСТВЕННЫЕ ЗАТРАТЫ И СОЦИАЛЬНАЯ СПРАВЕДЛИВОСТЬ В НИГЕРИИ – В данном исследовании рассматривается процесс децентрализации в более узком контексте социальной справедливости. Его главным предметом, тем не менее, является анализ влияния децентрализации на стратегии равенства и социальной справедливости в Нигерии. Она начинается с предпосылки о том, что ранний оптимизм, который поддерживал децентрализацию как действенный и эффективный инструмент образовательной реформы, развенчан. Автор статьи утверждает, что децентрализация сама по себе не может улучшить поставку образовательных услуг, возможности зависимых правительств или интеграцию социальной политики в более широкое развитие. Для достижения желаемых целей необходимо увеличить государственные затраты, обеспечить большие подоходные налоги и достичь макроэкономической стабилизации без переустройства государственного социального обеспечения.

Education and Policy Change

> "Ensuring the right of education is a matter of morality, justice and economic sense" (UNICEF 1999: 7).

Over the past two decades, Nigeria has experienced divergence, rather than convergence, in the provision of education. This is also the situation between local councils which are responsible for basic education. Inequalities have increased as the resource gaps between well-resourced and poorly resourced local governments and between rich and poor households in the country have widened. At the same time, educational disparities between regions, now called zones, in Nigeria and between people within the country have increased. Thus, many parts of the country and a significant proportion of its people have been largely excluded from education consumption and development (see Geo-JaJa 2005a). These distortions, possibly attributable to the logic of the "new right" ideology, make Nigeria an interesting case of decentralization. However, capturing the full effects of the unfolding changes is particularly difficult since recent political democratization processes have occurred under an unheralded election process yet to be determined by the courts.

The growing body of literature on decentralization shows that one of the most challenging and pressing issues facing education policy-makers at local and global levels is the problem of how to provide an equitable and affordable quality education for all. To achieve this objective requires extensive knowledge of the population: their number, characteristics, and economic conditions as well as the ways in which they will respond to education charges. This knowledge is key to deciding which mode of decentralization will appropriately address the issues of social justice and human security in education. This serves as the core point of the statement of UNICEF, which leads off this contribution. This understanding requires that human security and social justice issues be given top priority, while educational expansion and efficiency should come later.

In recent years, "decentralization" has emerged as a very popular term amongst "new right" education reformists and development practitioners. Yet there is no consensus on its exact meaning and theorization. Broadly, the term "decentralization", in reflecting changes in political, economic, and social values, is used to describe a gradual process of attaining efficiency and increasing participation under austerity. It has been a popular strategy for most central governments in developing countries to cushion financial burden or remedy economic crisis by debt servicing. This has implied a tighter fiscal and monetary policy, as well as the introduction of user fees for most social services.

By relieving central governments from providing social goods, the new right strategy has brought dramatic changes to the characteristics and functions of the state in developing countries around the world, particularly in Nigeria. This shift in opinion on appropriate educational finance polices has become a key determinant of government's role in meeting social demands for human rights – including education. However, studies show that its impact has not been uniform, with no consensus on whether it makes education pro-poor, improves education quality, or expands participation over centralization. Despite much dissent, it remained the dominant view, in part because it was propagated by the World Bank and by bilateral organizations which exercise enormous influence on economies in crisis. Irrespective of these inconclusive results, the measures for effective decentralization are based on the need to promote and support local institutional capacity, to attract and manage resources to provide transferred tasks, and to ensure and promote freedom in consuming social goods. Regarding education, all children must have the opportunity to consume satisfactory basic education, as states must fulfill their obligation to offer free and compulsory basic education. This means no school-aged child should be denied the opportunity to complete a satisfactory basic education (WEF 2000: 15). Attainment of these conditions rests on the political, financial, and cultural factors that are obtainable in a country.

The core objective of the present study is to evaluate policy options for education in Nigeria. We will attempt the following:

(1) To summarize the recent systemic decentralization of education in Nigeria.
(2) To determine the impact of decentralization on the commitment of the Nigerian state to education.
(3) To examine the financial challenges facing local governments in providing basic education.
(4) To explicate the impact of decentralization of public finance on adequacy, equity, and affordability of primary school education.

This study does not deal with all aspects of social policy; its main focus is primary education. In particular, it addresses the policy dilemma and does not undertake a real scientific description of the core, as data on Nigeria are difficult to obtain. Since there have been no previous recorded studies of this kind, this work will designate possible negative effects of educational decentralization on human rights and human dignity.

Education and Social Policy

Education is one of the key factors for social inclusion and human capital formation. In addition to its social and economic effects, education is perceived as a question of basic children's rights (see Universal Declaration of Human Rights 1948, Article 26). Studies such as Colclough (1982) or Lloyd and Blanc (1996) have identified the enormous benefits to families when all children receive primary education. According to Psacharopoulos (1992), education is widely regarded as the route to economic prosperity, the foundation of social equality, and the spearhead of cultural vitality. In the present contribution, education is considered a tool of social policy and social justice in two dimensions: (1) as a form of human-resource development; and (2) as a social policy for economic and social development affecting livelihood activities and citizenship needs. Thus, it can be said that "education is the single most vital factor for the realization of fundamental human rights, and promotes a civil society committed to transparency, good governance, and social inclusion" (UNICEF 1999: 13). Education in this new vision does not lose any of its transforming and human-rights potential.

Within this all-encompassing view, education is a key lever of sustained long-term productivity and social stability, as well as a key facilitator for breaking down barriers that exclude marginalized households from economic and political participation. Similarly, education is an indispensable instrument for nation-building and social justice affecting households' lifetime asset accumulation (Duflo 2002), hence the interest in the impact of fiscal decentralization on primary education. We refer to basic education as satisfying learning for life needs permitting citizens to live and work with dignity, fully empowered to participate in the development and improvement of society's quality of life. Such progress cannot be measured by economic figures but rather by improvements in basic social indicators such as literacy and social inclusion.

Background and Elements of Decentralization

Decentralization might put a country on a socially regressive path that could lead to the negation of all advances achieved under Principle 7 of the 1959 Declaration of the Rights of the Child. It declared: "The child is entitled to receive education which shall be free and compulsory, at least in the early stages." Similarly, Article 26 of the 1948 Universal Declaration of Human Rights affirmed: "Everyone has the right to education. Education shall be free, at least in the elementary and fundamental stages." The right to free primary education enshrined in the Convention of the Rights of the Child (1990, Article 28 and 29), ratified by almost all nations, asserted the responsibility of governments to provide free and compulsory primary education. Statements in these documents comprise the core argument for or against central governments' desire or responsibility to guarantee social justice for all citizens.

The gravity of a country's social conditions is reflected in decrease in the quality of public education, deterioration in education infrastructure, and low access of school-aged children. Interactive deterioration in the quality of education and health conditions is the most powerful social indicator of one country with two societies: integrated and the non-integrated citizens. This dualism is evident at both state and local government levels. These issues go to the crux of the question: What mode of decentralization should a nation implement or adopt? There is no easy answer. Other less glaring but dangerous factors are the effects of globalization and the granting and loan conditions imposed by international stakeholders in education (Geo-JaJa and Magnum 2003).

It is becoming increasingly clear that decentralization benefits a few at the expense of many. Multiple research studies document financial disparities in primary education under decentralization (Oxfam 2001, 2002; Bedi et al. 2004; Geo-JaJa 2004, 2005b) and widening disparities in per-student spending and student-teacher ratio in Nigeria (Hinchliffe 2002; Federal Ministry of Education 2003). Some argue that a positive effect on enrollment and social justice is unlikely, as central governments' authority for education decision-making is never totally delegated to subnational tiers of government, and as developing countries including Nigeria carry a substantial debt service burden. Other skeptical arguments are less convincing. These results may not be applicable to countries that are pro-poor or without debt overhang, given the incentive to invest and the skewed allocation of resources to long-term and short-term social activities.

One way to simplify this complex network of possible causes and effects is to return to a fundamentally simple idea: The decision to decentralize and decisions regarding primary education are closely linked to the social contract of central government and should not be regarded merely as market matters. Becoming aware of the dangers of educational decentralization is mobilizing many agents to seek alternative paths to social justice, considering people's dignity and values, such as social inclusion and open opportunity for all. Thus, social injustice is manifest in unaffordable and poor quality education as well as in denial of education that might lead to complete citizenship. Educational decentralization which accepts education charges is inconsistent with the general pronouncements of Principle 7 of the 1959 Declaration of the Rights of the Child; Article 26 of the Universal Declaration of Human Rights; and Article 13 of the 1966 International Convention on Economic, Social and Cultural Rights. Indeed, leaders of many sub-Saharan African nations are shocked as they find themselves sinking into education poverty, with millions of children victimized by child labor, homelessness, and illiteracy.

Decentralization: Efficiency or Equity?

Efficiency in resource mobilization minimizes distortions to the market from revenue generation or government intervention. In education this means maximizing the performance of the education system given a set of resources. Equity relates to fairness in resource utilization and allocation, allowing all children access to the quality of education that is practical for sustaining livelihood (pro-poor education). Compulsory schooling, or the opportunity to fulfill the right to basic education, can be a key to combating poverty and social injustice; it can also be a means of social integration and nation-building.

Decentralization can contribute to greater equity and efficiency in the distribution of expenditure for quality education. Attaining these aims is dependent on adequate resources for decentralized tasks and on good governance. As an essential component of sound decentralization policy, good governance requires role flexibility and stakeholder participation in program design and implementation, with necessary access to information for decision-making, as well as the ability to create an enabling environment for subnational governments to attain sustainable development through strengthened planning, increased management capabilities, and more flexible taxation bases. Thus, decentralization covers change in power relationships and transfer of responsibility and financial burden on public goods from central government to subnational governments. The major problem of decentralization is its inflexibility with economic rationalism. These prescribed methods are not adapted to local conditions and local education needs. Once again the resource-poor are asked to bear the brunt while the state spends national resources to build educational institutions that benefit the elite. These conditions raise doubts as to whether decentralization could indeed redistribute, share and extend power and enhance participation.

Decentralization: Process and Definition

Decentralization is complex in implementation and without a concise definition. Along with the potential for good educational results, it has the potential to redistribute social and political capital, which is rarely stated as a formal goal. The aims and outcomes of decentralization might be either consistent or inconsistent, depending on the circumstances under which they operate. This may be the core determinant of social justice under decentralization in any country. Social injustice may be defined as a way of life characterized by high illiteracy, inaccessibility to adequate education facilities, low quality of education, and inequity in the distribution of education's social and cultural capital. Simply put, social policy at a rhetorical level is not driven by concerns for social development and equity for all.

The fact that key social services such as education are concurrent responsibilities of central government and local government poses funding and organizational problems. Central government has determined policy over quality and quantity of education services to be delivered. In Nigeria, decentralization has not been able to translate into human development. The core desire is to ensure federal control over generated revenue, though appropriating it to lower tiers of government. The driving force is to get closer to citizens and communities by enforcing the principle of subsidiarity, vesting responsibility for services to citizens and providing financial resources commensurate to these tasks. Clearly this is adverse to subnational governments' capacity-building and autonomous decision-making in resource generation and distribution for social policy. If accepted as stated, decentralization becomes a method of implementing policies rather than an end to be achieved.

Decentralization: A Means to Checkmate the Welfare State

Until two decades ago, the Nigerian state financed and provided social services, and sought relations emphasizing face-to-face communication. The social welfare orientation was humane, and sensitive to the basic needs of citizens in their families and communities. At the center was the need for a strong state that could ensure children's right to quality basic education by mobilizing strong political commitment and allocating adequate funding. However, with the introduction of the new right ideology, governments are reluctant to invest adequately in primary education as a basic human right (Tomasevski 2003: 2; WEF 2000). It has been argued that this new approach to social provision, which extends structural adjustment programs and calls for deep social sector-wide transformation, negates education provision sensitive to human rights (Geo-JaJa 2004). Under this ideology, privatization and deconcentration have reduced the role of the sate, as well as shifted the means of intervention from de-commodifying bureaucrats.

The planned reduction of budget deficits and the servicing of debts have necessitated a fundamental rethinking of the role and responsibilities of the state and the public sector in consideration of the capacities of the Nigerian economy. Unfortunately this reduction necessitates both rationalization of services, responsibilities and social institutions formerly financed by the federal government and transfer of tasks currently performed by the state to lower tiers of government, to the private sector, and to individual households. Subsidiarity in this interpretation may be committed to dismantling the welfare responsibilities of the Nigerian state and delegating them to the various subnational governments. The practice of reducing welfare expenditure by devolving fiscal responsibilities to subnational levels of government has resulted in inequalities: denying some citizens equal access to quality education and significantly widening the gap between some well-resourced and poorly resourced local governments. Numerous studies have indicated that the decline in spending on social provisions has been accompanied with decline in the quality and access to basic education (UNICEF 1999; Stalling 2000; Colclough 2001; UNESCO 2003: 119; Bélanger and Liu 2004; Liu 2004).

Various studies have shown how, outside of the new right ideology, nationwide campaigns to boost educational spending and organization have increased enrollments (UNICEF 1999; Brazil 2000; Hall 2003), Since decentralization implies a tighter fiscal and monetary policy, the most important part of the decentralization process in Nigeria has been expenditure reduction which has virtually been unmatched in other countries in Africa. The central government has tried to satisfy debt obligations and balance the budget by balancing the social sector and by withholding Federation Accounts shares due to subnational governments. This irresponsible policy has culminated in comprehensive privatization and rationalization of social services (market-determined social-good provisions). This attempt initiated by the so-called "new right" group to reduce the role of the central government in providing social services, education in particular, can, however, also be interpreted within the theoretical framework of decentralization. This intertwined normative and perspective view of education reform is driven in part by neo-liberal ideology and in part by hope, but it is not borne out by experience.

It is understood that decentralization will be more circumspect under a relatively decentralized fiscal system. Clearly the trends towards privatization make the education sector highly externally efficient on economic grounds, but highly internally inefficient on equity and adequacy or social justice grounds. Those who are not able to invest in high-priced education might not receive commensurate economic or social returns as positive externalities are hedged. This section concludes that regardless of asserted efficiency, the effect of decentralization on social justice and equity in education in most developing countries is either limited or negative.

The Extent of State Resource Allocation to Subnational Governments

Today the Federation Account is the main instrument for financing decentralized education responsibilities to subnational governments. Central government undertakes substantive schemes of financial redistribution and grants to the education sector as stipulated in the constitution. But the functionality of each tier of government in providing assigned social service depends on two factors: (1) its carrying capacity; and (2) the unbiased sharing or granting of resources. The bulk of funding for primary education (i.e., teacher salaries) is provided through local governments' (20%) allocation from the Federation Account; according to Keith Hinchliffe (2002), this includes 87% of the funds for primary education. Available statistics are limited to 1999.

Without clear-cut criteria, the system appears locked in a battle between the federal government and executives of subnational government, as costs of teacher salaries for some local governments are higher than their total allocation from the Federation Account and Value Added Tax (VAT) collections. Very few local councils allocate recurrent funds to basic education. Evidence that some local governments have carrying-capacity problems after paying for teacher salaries casts doubt on the equity of the arrangements and the quality of education to be provided. Evaluation studies demonstrate that the formula for distributing funds has not led to equalizing education access or equity among local governments. Proper determination of a local government's fiscal carrying capacity would indicate whether they are able to finance decentralized services. In short, the model that best explains both decentralization and resource allocation to subnational governments for education provisions is the "political model".

The state has been more concerned with the manipulation of local governments as machinery for mobilizing political support than as facilitators for the delivery of social goods. This singular practice and the adoption of the political model have undermined the ability of local governments to reconcile shifted responsibilities and have set standards of quality with constraining financial demands. Thus, these vicious circles, the processes of circular and cumulative causation in which decentralization outcomes reinforce themselves, cannot ensure equitable distribution of satisfactory basic education in the long or short term.

To make local governments solvent will require determination of their fiscal carrying capacity and a radical change in the revenue allocation formula. Without this determination, chances of exacerbating inequality between local governments in the delivery of primary education (measured by the coefficient of variation in the expenditure on education) will be increased. Clearly, therefore, the mechanism of fiscal decentralization to reduce inequity and to guarantee children's rights to a satisfactory basic education will remain trapped in theoretical categories, political dichotomies, and conventional decentralization engineering, as it restrains rather than expands access, equity and social development. In part, the failure of decentralization to achieve desired education outcomes and social justice could be attributed to its inability to strengthen the financial capacity of subnational governments and to the accompanying privatization.

Universal Basic Education, Education Charges, and Social Justice

The consequences of decentralization in education are enormous for many households and for nation-building. Any kind of education charge is a tax on human security and human development, and most families cannot afford education charges. Education charges in any form – cost-sharing or cost-recovery – trap children in a cycle of illiteracy and human insecurity (Oxfam 2001). Further evidence will help to substantiate the argument that free access to quality education cannot be guaranteed under the deconcentration or privatization form of decentralization.

Within this remarkable constellation, Keith Hinchliffe (1999) shows that school failure – expressed in the form of high repetition and low completion rates, drop-out, over-aged illiteracy, and school crowding – is concentrated in poorly resourced local governments in Nigeria. Clearly this brings to light that with ongoing decentralization local governments are becoming more prominent among the causes of social inequality, further attestation to the polarization and bifurcation of the school system in terms of quality and affordability of private and public schools. To mitigate social and economic exclusion in designing decentralization policies the state must embrace wider social policies and ensure stable resources to subnational governments. There is the need to improve fiscal transparency at all levels of government, to develop a grant allocation formula, which requires fiscal carrying-capacity indicators, and, what is most essential, to adopt vertical and horizontal devolution of power. There is a scale of values to be taken into consideration. Nigeria can and should increase commitment to respond positively and in large measure to all requests for adequate funding to accomplish the tasks connected to education, particularly the promotion of primary education.

Education Charges and Household Education Demand

Bridging the widening gap in basic education can help reduce human insecurity and poverty. In this section, the root causes of the severe inequalities in education are considered. Furthermore, how worsening inequalities can contribute to increasing human insecurity and social exclusion are discussed. Parents in developing countries cite direct and indirect school fees as the major factor in deciding to keep children out of school. Ironically, as education charges are introduced and households and local governments are required to pay and maintain primary schools, respectively, the prospect of widespread social equilibrium and private returns from education diminish. Thus, gender bias is reinforced in most poor households.

In the author's on-going research in a small town called Opobo, Nigeria, parent interviews show that education charges play a significant role in households' education choices, tending towards discrimination against girls. Women indicated that girls are twice as likely to be taken out of school as boys when education charges are imposed. Women from poor households desired to give basic education to their school-aged children to enable them to grow up to live and work with dignity, something they themselves had not experienced. Contrary to claims often made by the new right, parents do not indicate reluctance to send daughters as well as sons to school, provided affordable good quality and effective schooling opportunities actually exist in their localities.

Education Cost and Derived and Lost Benefits

Unfortunately, the cost of education in Nigeria has been devastating; but most pronounced is its poor quality and the irrelevant manner with which Nigeria has attempted to meet social, cultural, and economic demands. The question now is how, in the face of decentralization, qualitative improvement can be made in things that drive knowledge and human development and thus promote social inclusion. Most, if not all of these educational issues could be addressed by combining knowledge and values of solidarity with a holistic approach to planning and managing the entirety of the education sector. But this has not occurred with decentralization, as its complexity explains the dismal education performance in Nigeria exhibited by lack of access to quality primary education.

In the old Western region, containing the states of Ogun, Oyo, Osun, Ondo, Kwara, and Lagos, eminent citizens recently gathered to celebrate the contribution of 50 years of welfaristic education policies during which the region invested heavily in education and made it affordable and free to all citizens, resulting in immense contribution to social mobility, societal transformation, and a distinctive competitive edge in all sectors of the society in an ethnically diverse country. Through such wider social policy, the region has been able to bridge social and economic gaps among citizens and facilitate individual self-actualization as well as engage many citizens in meaningful contributions to society. The Western region has been recognized for creating an innovative social program that has effectively combated poverty, raised its human resources, and achieved region-specific advantages within the Nigerian State. Furthermore, the strengthened political will of the region to boost education and, in particular, to invest more heavily in primary education where social returns are the highest assured the basic rights of almost 100% of school-aged children in the region.

Times have changed since the current political dispensation assigned low funding priority to education. Even if public education is productively inefficient, the social benefits associated with culture, civility, and knowledge lead to peace and nation-building; and some of the positive externalities of education accrue not only to individuals, but also to society at large. Indeed, Adam Smith, who provided the classic synthesis of the power and reach of the market mechanism two-and-a-quarter centuries ago, eloquently stated that it would be wrong to leave education to the market, as it is essential for peace and knowledge. He also asserted that education is very important for employability and political participation, and for deepening democratic values in society.

Now let us look at how nations have reacted to this important role of education and the matter of funding priority in some Western countries. In Japan, the first 9 years of schooling is free and compulsory; in the United States, education is free and mandatory for the first 12 years; similarly in England, despite challenging economic trials, the state fully funds public primary and secondary education up to the age of 16 years; and South Korea, Taiwan, Singapore, Hong Kong, China, and other East Asian countries have followed similar routes and firmly focused on basic education expansion. These illustrations depict that regardless of efficiency arguments posed by the new rights, the social policy of these developed and Newly Industrializing Economies (NIE) is consonant with the Convention on the Rights of the Child (1990, Articles 28 and 29) and the recommendations of the Salamanca Conference. Clearly, these examples illustrate the importance of a strong state in ensuring social justice, by guaranteeing children's rights to a satisfactory basic education. This will also guarantee their empowerment to participate as adults in the development and improvement of society's quality of life.

Quite apart from the assumption that decentralization increases efficiency and stakeholder participation, there is little evidence to support this causal relationship in most developing countries. In Nigeria, many intervening variables have hindered the ability of the government to facilitate and deepen social inclusion through education. Another way in which decentralization has had a negative impact on equity is that schools have become more selective – so much so that school-aged children from disadvantaged homes do not have equal access to a satisfactory free and compulsory primary education. Also noted is that the performance of students from areas with poorly resourced local governments or students from poorly resourced households has tended to decline, while that of students from well-resourced local governments has continued to rise. This observation raises serious questions about social equity and social justice. Decentralization itself does not ensure the closing of education gaps, nor has it increased school autonomy; it has merely caused a shift in power from central to local bureaucracies, fueling private educational inflation, distorting public education spending patterns, and leading to relative neglect of basic and primary schooling. In sum, decentralization has led to the general collapse of values that have contributed significantly to human security and social inclusion.

Given significant income inequalities, there are sharp differences in the effect of education charges on different households. Recent research findings show that education costs have led to differentiated demand and to the expansion of private (for-profit) schools, which are now attended by children of the rich (Geo-JaJa 2005b). Western nations have avoided education charges that are considered a tax on human development by finding a more acceptable balance of responsibility with households. Governments of these countries have recognized that primary education and literacy promotion are integral parts of social and economic integration of citizens into society. In contrast, Nigeria must do everything possible to prevent illiteracy from keeping millions of men, women and children from active citizenship in their country. The question is: Why has the problem of social injustice in primary education and the existence of millions of illiterates not challenged the state? It seems that the answer is sadly attested to by decentralization to balance efficiency over equity in Nigeria.

In the present contribution, the yardstick used to assess the effectiveness of decentralization is very consistent with the Universal Declaration of Human Rights (1948, Article 26) which states: "Everyone has the right to education. Education shall be free, at least in the elementary and fundamental stages" and, with Principle 7 of the 1959 Declaration of the Rights of the Child: "The child is entitled to receive education which shall be free and compulsory, at least in the early stages." The tenants of these principles and conventions to which Nigeria has agreed demonstrate a commitment to social justice through basic education.

Explaining the Trend in Education Charges

Mehrotra and Delamonica (1998) present studies of five countries (Burkina Fuso, Uganda, Bhutan, Myanmar and Vietnam) designed to illustrate the potential effects of education costs (uniforms, textbooks, building funds, and parent–teacher association contributions) in discouraging school attendance. A comparative analysis of the five countries suggests that the two with the lowest net-enrollment rates have the highest per-pupil recurrent cost (public plus private) relative to their per-capita income. A negative price elasticity of demand for children's education is documented by numerous studies of decision-making by households in developed and developing countries (Cheng 1994; Tsang 1994; Bray 1996; Zhang and Zou 1998; Birdsall and Orival 1999). For instance, in Ghana and Côte d'Ivoire (World Bank 1993) and Kenya (Bedi et al. 2004), increases in school fees and increases in the opportunity costs of attending school have negatively affected the right to quality education as well as the probability of enrollment. This culminates in the familiar problems of increasing differentiation in access to basic education along social class stratification. On the other hand, positive effects of a reduction in direct or indirect fees, or even the abolition of such charges, on equity and internal efficiency indicators were reported for Ghana, Kenya, and Malawi (Colclough 1996), Uganda and Tanzania (World Bank 1995; Oxfam 2002), and Botswana and Malawi (Colclough 1996).

A discernable pattern in these country studies is the decline in price elasticity as income rises, so that for rich households price increases have no impact on school-enrollment decisions if other factors are constant; but in poor households, the reduction in enrollment with increase in costs (direct or indirect) is significant. Within this context, financing schools through cost-recovery or cost-sharing mechanisms forces poor households to decide which child is to be excluded from attending school. Outcomes include low literacy rates, low levels of pupil enrollment, and high dropout rates – directly or indirectly affecting the child's human capital. Thus, the state must undertake the necessary reforms, allocate funding and be prepared to enter into partnership with elements of civil society and with stakeholders. Having outlined examples of the impact of education charges, attention will now be directed to the challenges that lie ahead in the Nigeria context.

Fiscal Decentralization in the Sphere of Education Equity: Reduction and Centralization

A large number of socially excluded and illiterate Nigerians live in both rural and urban areas (World Bank 1996). At this time in human history it is essential to provide citizens with the competencies, knowledge and values required for local and global livelihoods. The only real solution seems to be to introduce the system of earmarked capitation and to introduce adequate resources to support this priority sector (PAEG 1997). In the 1960s and 1970s, public spending on education increased more than in any other sector. During the 1990s and into the 2000s, the proportion of budgetary allocation to education averaged some 3% of recurrent expenditure. However, this figure, when compared with Botswana (21%), Ghana (26%), South Africa (24%), Uganda (26%), Swaziland (26%), Tanzania (14%), and Kenya (21%), is not impressive for a nation with more than 60% of school-aged children in school.

Table 1 presents the share of federal government expenditure on education. Overall, the shares as a proportion of government budget have varied between 24.7% in 1981 and 7.3% in 1990, and the trend has been largely downward. The 8.3% contribution by the federal government to the education sector in 2000 was lower than the 25% stipulated by UNESCO, and the 0.07% of GDP allocated to education in 2001 was the lowest in the world.

Table 1. Public expenditure on education as a percentage of total government expenditures (1980–2002)

Country/Year	Year allocation (%)																						
	80	81	82	83	84	85	86	87	88	89	90	91	92	93	94	95	96	97	98	99	00	01	02
Botswana	22.1	21.6	17.6	19.4	17.4	17.7	18.4	18.4	20.0	20.3	20.5	21.0	20.4	20.6	–	24.6	21.8	20.6	–	25.6	25.6	–	–
Cameroon	12.4	7.5	13.3	11.6	14.4	11.8	12.7	–	11.9	19.6	16.9	17.9	17.9	–	14.6	–	–	–	10.2	22.2	14.6	15.3	–
Ethiopia	12.7	9.8	10.3	8.9	10.5	9.8	10.8	11.5	10.5	9.9	9.9	10.6	14.3	15.4	13.7	14.0	13.7	14.0	13.8	11.3	13.8	–	–
Ghana	21.9	17.0	18.7	–	20.2	18.0	23.9	23.9	25.7	24.3	25.5	23.2	23.7	22.0	–	21.4	19.9	–	–	27.5	22.3	–	22.1
Kenya	19.6	20.6	19.9	20.6	19.8	19.6	22.6	21.3	22.1	19.8	19.9	20.1	21.9	18.9	21.4	–	16.7	21.4	22.5	22.3	–	–	–
Malawi	8.9	11.6	14.3	13.4	12.3	11.0	10.8	10.1	12.3	8.8	11.1	12.1	–	–	–	–	–	–	24.6	–	–	–	–
Mali	–	–	10.5	10.0	9.6	9.1	9.3	9.8	9.0	–	–	–	–	–	–	–	–	–	–	–	–	–	–
Mauritius	17.6	15.8	14.7	15.6	15.3	14.3	13.9	12.4	13.3	15.3	14.3	14.5	14.6	14.9	16.2	17.0	17.4	–	17.7	13.6	12.1	–	–
Nigeria	5.2	24.7	9.6	9.3	11.6	8.7	4.8	2.8	2.7	2.8	5.3	4.4	6.3	7.3	14.6	8.1	5.8	7.3	9.6	9.0	8.3	7.6	8.0
Tanzania	12.9	13.3	12.5	13.2	11.7	8.3	–	–	–	14.1	14.0	–	–	–	–	–	–	–	–	–	–	–	–
Swaziland	24.4	21.2	17.9	20.8	22.3	20.3	22.1	24.6	23.9	24.5	26.1	25.4	–	–	–	–	–	–	–	–	–	–	–
Uganda	16.9	12.6	12.4	10.9	11.7	12.7	15.0	–	–	–	11.5	15.0	–	–	–	–	–	–	–	–	–	–	–
Zambia	11.4	11.9	15.1	14.5	16.0	12.3	17.5	8.7	8.8	11.2	10.4	8.7	9.2	15.5	15.4	15.0	–	–	17.6	–	–	–	–

Source: UNESCO Statistical Year Book (various issues), IMF and World Bank Data Sources (WDI 2003 CD).

The concern with improved education quality and universalization of basic education is not congruent with provision of funding, as total education expenditure in real terms has continued to decline over the years. The reality is that decentralization has transferred responsibilities without granting comparable working resources to carry out assigned education provision tasks. Hinchliffe (2002: 24) draws particular attention to this situation: "Over time, the powers and responsibilities of the various levels of government in Nigeria have been changed as a result of both changes to the constitution and the perceived abilities of each government to undertake the financial and managerial responsibilities, which they have been assigned."

As responsibilities imposed on local governments do not reflect the financial resources available to them, schools are now subsidized through additional funds contributed by households and community-based organizations. It has become increasingly clear that if Nigeria is to secure the human capabilities required for development, it must ensure equity and access to pupils according to minimum standards based on user need; or if it is to promote social justice, the central government must determine local government fiscal carrying-capacity and revise the allocation of revenue accordingly.

Fiscal (De)centralization and Social Justice

The benefits anticipated from decentralization – efficiency, equity, adequacy, and economic and political participation – have not been realized in Nigeria, as decentralization has generally involved deconcentration and delegation. Under this narrow social-policy practice, the central government retains considerable powers at the local government level. Without exception, under this policy formulation the system allows the central government to determine the scope and substance of school curriculum, teacher compensation, and budget allocation, as well as who has access to basic education. In sum, it is argued that Nigeria provides a good example of how not to undertake decentralization in a federated system, corresponding with the author's opinion that decentralization in Nigeria aims more at shifting responsibilities than at promoting social justice.

The Current Extent of Decentralization: An Assessment

In making this assessment, the author adopts the accepted distinction between deconcentration (central government shifting responsibility to sub-national governments), delegation (central government delegating powers or transferring authority to subnational governments), and devolution (central government completely ceding powers and revenue-generating activities to subnational governments). The last is the only 'true' form of decentralization. Current practices appear to maintain and even increase decentralization while transforming the previous devolution into deconcentration/delegation. Evidence suggests that with decentralization the central government has receded and accepted the role of supporter and promoter of decentralization by aiding subnational governments in providing social services as well as allocating responsibility for their finances. It seems that decentralization in Nigeria aims more at shifting responsibilities than promoting social justice.

Figures from the Central Bank of Nigeria (CBN) and the Federal Ministry of Education seem to indicate that the above premise has been declining since the 1980s. For example, resources allocated to primary education represented only about 1.2% of the GDP in 1999 compared to 1.5% in 1990. Between 1996 and 2002 the primary education subsector received around 7.5–16.9% of the total government expenditures on education (Hinchliffe 2002: 8). From a ratio of 18.2% in 1980, the budgetary allocation to education as a percentage of total government expenditure declined to 8.7% in 1985, 5.8% in 1990, 7.6% in 2001, and just about 2% in 2003. Overall, as Table 1 shows, the shares of public funds allocated to education have varied over the years, ranging from a high of 24.7% to a low of 1.7%. Public expenditure per student has been cut by 32%. The obvious conclusion is that education expenditures in the 1990s were a smaller share of both GDP and total budgetary allocation than they were in the early 1980s, as both shares have fallen significantly. This funding gap has been compensated either by households or by local governments pulling money away from other areas (including health) into education. Unfortunately the failure of government to adequately fund primary education has been matched by disproportionately high levels of spending on defense. The fall in education's shares of the GDP and the movement of total government expenditure away from primary education suggest that attention needs to be given to the causes and implications of these trends.

Table 2 presents data on school enrollment from 1975 to 2002 along with supplemental enrollment by providing statistics on the number of primary schools, the total number of teachers, and the teacher/pupil ratio. Analysis of budgetary allocation shows what appears to be an anomaly between funding and enrollment, as primary enrollment jumped from 4,898,357 in 1975 to 12,117,483 in 1980, and in 1984 the number of primary schools had reached 38,211 with 359,701 teachers, enrolling 14,383,470 pupils. By 1990 the number of primary schools had declined to 35,433, enrolling 14,097,249 pupils, with 331,915 teachers. Thereafter, there followed a pattern of rise and decline in all categories. In 2002 there were about 50,518 primary schools housing 19,342,659 students, with 491,751 teachers. Obviously expansion of the system has not been parallel with expansion of the infrastructure and with teacher support needed to sustain it. According to recent statistics on primary education, 2015 primary schools are without a classroom or building of any type. Evidence from the World Bank (1998) supports this hypothesis. This is a remarkably low level of effort, in fact the worst effort level of all sub-Saharan African countries, considering the school-aged population

Table 2. Total enrollment, number of schools, and number of faculty by level of education (1970–2002)

Year	Enrollment	Number of schools	Teachers	Pupils completing primary six	Pupil/Teacher ratio
1970	3515827	14902	103152	–	–
1975	4889857	–	144351	–	–
1980	12117483	26723	343551	–	–
1981	13760030	36524	369636	–	–
1982	14311608	37614	386826	–	–
1983	14654798	37888	383989	–	–
1984	14383470	38211	359701	–	–
1985	13025287	33528	309032	–	–
1986	12914870	35433	308182	–	–
1987	11540178	34266	344221	–	–
1988	12690798	34911	331915	–	–
1989	12721087	34904	344221	–	–
1990	14097249	35433	331915	–	–
1991	13776054	35466	353600	1651204	37.0
1992	14805937	36610	384212	1922914	39.0
1993	15911888	38254	428097	2128157	37.0
1994	16831560	38649	435210	2190712	36.0
1995	17996209	39677	423059	2131035	36.0
1996	4073473	–	416745	1960084	34.0
1997	14695333	40425	407140	2042819	36.1
1998	16045567	40876	456672	2130691	38.3
1999	17907010	49326	432096	2391779	41.8
2000	19158439	49326	446405	2583670	43.9
2001	19385177	49306	487303	2385843	40.0
2002	19342659	50518	491751	2385178	45.0

Note: (1) Secondary school figures include secondary grammar/commercial, and technical/vocational.
(2) Tertiary school figures include universities/polytechnics/colleges of education.
(3) Federal Ministry of Education, Nigerian University Commission, and National Board for Technical Education.
*This indicator does not take into account the existence of second-shifts, multi-grade classes and practices that may affect precision.
Source: (1) UNESCO Statistical yearbook (various issues).

and the obvious overwhelming human needs. Also important to note is the large proportion of children who were not in school from 2000 to 2002 either because of late entry or re-entry or due to the politicization of Universal Primary Education by the government for selfish political gains in anticipation of the upcoming 2003 election.

Although the number of primary schools in Nigeria has increased, school enrolment continues to experience slow growth. Gross Enrollment Ratio (GER) for primary school children (6–11 years) in 1997 was 75%, and gross enrollment intake was 73%. Net primary figures, which are a better measure for reaching the goal of Universal Primary Education, remained at a low 52.9%. Surprisingly, these figures vary according to area (Abia, 96.2%; Jigawa, 17.2%). More perplexing is the difference in the literacy rate between the Northern and Southern states. In nine Southern states, the rates were higher than 75%. But within the same country, in nine states in the North the rates were less than 25%, with the lowest being Jagawa at 5%. There is a long way to go to eradicate illiteracy and attain 100% enrollment by the year 2010. The primary education system appears to impart poor quality education, with low internal efficiency, largely because the education system (not just the primary) is inadequately funded by the Nigerian state. Thus, the problems confronting primary education in Nigeria include inadequate funding, poor-quality infrastructure and facilities, and failure to ensure devolution, seen as a precursor to the current perpetuation of social injustice in Nigeria. According to the World Bank, sufficient resources, the Bank reiterated, are still not being made available to build and maintain the necessary infrastructure, to provide essential educational materials, or even to pay teachers a living wage (World Bank 1998). Yet 80% of Nigerians are engaged in the nonformal economy (World Bank 1995) and the number of individuals earning below US$ 0.40 a day is fast multiplying, For all the above practical reasons, some fairly strict conditions have to be satisfied and a safety net put in place if local councils financing education are not to offend equity and social justice or to impinge on the mandate of education as a human right.

Evaluation: Educational Decentralization for Whom?

In recent years, a number of countries have experimented with various types of charges in education funding. In theory such arrangements are expected to improve access and efficiency as a result of more choices and of competition with significant control. When the slogan is "to cut costs at any price", which is frequently the case under the new right strategy of decentralization, money is often reallocated away from the education sector. However, it is important to consider the effects of shifting away from a centralized social contract and budgetary allocation. The quality and access of basic education will inevitably be impaired. For society, investment in education reduces poverty and supports the expansion of knowledge which positively contributes to social benefits. The issue of investing in education has become even more problematic under fiscal decentralization as expenditures gravitate to general administration, internal security, and up-keep of local government politicians with clout. On the other hand, widening the coverage (which improves equal access to quality education), improving equity in resource allocation, and instituting needed indigenous reforms can contribute to minimizing human insecurity which has continued to ruin the lives of many Nigerians.

The shortfall in funding and the challenging role of the state within the social sector in Nigeria are inconsistent with rational notions of advancing equity, access and quality in Universal Primary Education. Furthermore, serious social conditions in the country are increasing through the rise of privatized education. To the detached observer, noting the contrast between the presumed benefits of decentralization and education as a human right in Nigeria, the education system displays a number of troubling trends. Most notable are the following:

- Inequality has grown alongside the expansion and deterioration in education
- The gap between rich and poor households is widening as the rich are increasingly sending their children to private primary schools (local and abroad) to ensure that they receive global education commensurate to that demanded by global universities and the global work place
- In a world of disturbing contrasts the gap between rich and poor local governments and between rich and poor households has continued to widen in educational provisions and consumption. It is increasingly apparent that this reality will not be changed through decentralization alone

These conditions are powerful social indicators which demonstrate the configuration of one country with two societies. There exist additional societies composed of local governments with low carrying capacity that are at the margin of affordable education. This results in a deeply divided society, along the dimensions of power, occupation, class, income, wealth, gender, and religion, in which illiteracy and exclusion from quality education are becoming serious realities. A social-justice approach helps to ameliorate such problems because it classifies institutional arrangements, assigns tasks and identifies subnational levels of government that are to receive and lose authority and responsibility. If the education gap is to be closed between the rich and the poor households and local governments, education decentralization needs a radical political and ideological shift toward a wider social policy initiative to achieve social justice in education. The approach that has been discussed emphasizes the importance of strict implementation of effective policy and the value of devolution of taxation powers (complete revenue collection and complete utilization) to subordinate levels of government.

In reaffirming basic education as a human right, the present study suggests what the Nigerian state must do to meet its commitment to the international instruments and conventions stating a child's rights to satisfactory basic education and to the recommendations of the World Education Forum (2000). The author is more convinced than ever that to achieve these goals, the state must do the following:

- Develop closer cooperation with subnational governments, communities and households in providing basic education
- Eliminate all charges for basic education and political determination of social policy within the next 5 years
- Work with local councils to identify the financing gaps for basic education and mobilize resources for restructuring and allocation to local governments with low carrying-capacity with a goal of strengthening capacity and basic education
- Ensure the engagement and participation of stakeholders and civil society in the formulation and implementation of education decentralization.

Although education is not a panacea for all of Nigeria's current problems, decentralization nevertheless constitutes a major challenge for a sustainable social-justice system and for human-capital formation. For various reasons, advances in education are now regrettably stagnating, causing social, economic, and political exclusion. But at a time when the state is finding it difficult to face up to its responsibilities on account of economic crisis, the solution it has sought is the political model of decentralization, which has exacerbated the process of social injustice. It is clear that the political model may exclude a significant proportion of people, particularly children from poor households, from the benefits of development unless governments remedy education funding inadequacies and evolve new social policies to make education policies household friendly. This implies a crucial role for the state.

To overcome this situation and to improve essential programs in education, decentralization of resources and responsibilities and an unshakeable concrete financial commitment by the state are essential. This study argues for the need to devise a new funding mechanism, as economic crises and the competing demands within families often make it very hard for them to send their children to school. The process of decentralization has not been an unconditional invitation to local governments to assume financial responsibility and for communities to retain authority over goals and didactic materials for education, but rather a well-calculated strategy on the part of the state to mobilize support and resources. Furthermore, this study indicates that the education system is no more egalitarian than the society of which it is a part, as net primary enrollment ratios of school-aged children have continued to decline, and disparities in funding and access to primary schooling have escalated to levels never experienced before. Other indicators illustrating low internal efficiency include high dropout, high illiteracy, and low school completion rates. Ultimately decentralization has not led to empowerment, nor has it led to strengthening human capabilities that may result in nationbuilding or to achieving greater efficiency and equity in education, as the discourse of social participation has been used to cloak the micro-institutional mandates. Finally, the social benefits from education and the entitlement of children to an education suggest that the state should play a strong role in financing and organizing basic education and health.

Conclusion

The present study has indicated that anything contrary to this funding formula is undesirable: Such attributes are regressive, and they exclude children from educational opportunities when compulsory attendance is not enforced. The author concludes that on its own decentralization cannot improve education service delivery, the capacity of subordinate governments, or the integration of social policy into broader development goals. If desired goals are to be met, public spending must be increased, tax revenue must be mobilized and broadened, and macroeconomic stabilization must be achieved without reinstitution of the welfare state. Therefore, the author reaffirms that the Nigerian state must not disappear with decentralization; instead it must accept a new role of supporter and promoter of equity and social justice, even as the scope of the market increases through liberalization in the wider context of globalization, by facilitating the revenue-generating ability and helping build the capacities of subnational levels of government for transferred responsibilities. Finally, the overemphasis on efficiency can eliminate equity and social justice altogether. In fact, it can negate social justice and human dignity, as the dominant ideology of the new right and neo-conservatism seek to create a socially stratified society in which the retreat of the state from education is matched only by the advance of market forces and globalization.

References

Bedi, Arjum et al. 2004. The Decline in Primary School Enrolment in Kenya. *Journal of African Economies* 13(1): 1–44.

Bélanger, Danièle, and Jianye Liu. 2004. Social Policy Reforms and Daughters' Schooling in Vietnam. *International Journal of Educational Development* 24(1): 23–38.

Birdsall, Nancy, and Francois Orivel. 1999. Demand for Primary Schooling in Rural Mali: Should User Fees be Increased? *Education Economics* 4(3): 279–296.

Bray, Mark. 1996. *Decentralization of Education: Community Financing*. Washington, DC: The World Bank.

Brazil. 2000. *EFA 2000, Education for All: Evaluation of the Year 2000*. Brasilia: National Institute for Educational Studies and Research.

Cheng, Kai. 1994. Issues in Decentralization: What the Reform in China Tells. *International Journal of Educational Research* 21(8): 794–808.

Colclough, Christopher. 1982. The Impact of Primary Schooling on Economic Development: A Review of the Evidence. *World Development* 10: 167–185.

———. 1996. Education and the Market: Which Part of the Neoliberal Solutions is Correct? *World Development* 24(4): 589–610.

Duflo, Esther. 2002. *The Medium Run Effects of Educational Expansion: Evidence from a Large School Construction Program in Indonesia.* Cambridge, MA: National Bureau of Economic Research. NBER Working Paper Series, 8710.

Geo-JaJa, Macleans A. 2004. Decentralization and Privatization of Education in Africa: Which Option for Nigeria? *International Review of Education* 50(2): 307–323.

———. 2005a. Globalisation, Education Reforms and Policy Change in Africa: The Case of Nigeria. In: *The International Handbook of Globalisation, Education and Policy Research*, ed. by Joseph Zajda, 517–536. Dordrecht: Springer.

———. 2005b. Sustainable Livelihood, Poverty Alleviation and Development: What Lesson From the IFAD/UNDP Credit-Input Strategy for NDDC? In: *Oil Democracy and the Promise of True Federalism in Nigeria*, ed. by Augustus Ikein, Steve Azaiki and Diepreye Alamieyeseigha. Lanham, MD: University Press of America.

———, and Garth Mangum. 2003. Economic Adjustment, Education and Human Resource Development in Africa: The Case of Nigeria. *International Review of Education* 49(3–4): 293–318.

Hall, Anthony. 2003. Education Reform in Brazil under Democracy. In: *Brazil Since 1983: Economy, Polity and Society*, ed. by Maria D'Alva Kinzo and James Dunkerley, 269–287. London: Institute of Latin American Studies, University of London.

Hinchliffe, Keith. 2002. Nigeria: *Public Expenditures on Education: Issues, Estimates, and Some Implications.* Washington, DC: The World Bank.

Liu, Fengshu. 2004. Basic Education in China's Rural Area: A Legal Obligation or an Individual Choice? *International Journal of Educational Development* 24(1): 2–21.

Lloyd, Cynthia, and Ann Blanc. 1996. Children: Schooling in Sub-Sahara Africa: The Role of Fathers, Mothers, and Others. *Population and Development Review* 22: 265–298.

Mehrotra, Santosh, and Enrique Delamonica. 1998. Household Costsand Public Expenditure on Primary Education in Five Low Income Countries: A Comparative Analysis. *International Journal of Educational Development* 18(1): 41–61.

Nigeria. Federal Ministry of Education. 2003. *A Handbook of Information on Basic Education in Nigeria.* Abuja, Nigeria: UNESCO and Ministry of Education.

Oxfam. 2001. *Education Changes: A Tax on Human Development.* Oxfam Briefing paper No. 3 Oxford: Oxfam.

———. 2002. *Every Child in School: A Challenge to Finance and Development Ministers*, Oxfam Briefing Paper No. 1705. Oxfam: Washington, DC.

PAEG (Poverty Alleviation and Elimination Group). 1997. Report of the Poverty Alleviation and Elimination Group of the Vision 2010 Committee, May. Abuja: PAEG.

Psacharopoulos, George et al. 1992. *Poverty and Income Distribution in Latin America: The Story of the 1980s.* Washington, DC: World Bank.

Stalling, Barbara, and Peres Wilson 2000. *The Impact of the Education Reforms in Latin America and the Caribbean.* Santiago, Chile: ECLAC and the Brookings Institutions.

Tomaskvski, Katarina. 2003. *Education Denied: Costs and Remedies.* London: Zed Books.

Tsang, Mun. 1994. Cost of Education in China: Issues of Resource, Mobility, Equality and Efficiency. *Education Economics* 2(3): 287–312.

UNESCO. 2003. *Education For All, Global Monitoring Report 2003/2004: Gender and Education for All – The Leap to Equality*. Paris: UNESCO.

UNICEF. 1999. *The State of the World's Children 1999: The Right to Education*. New York: Oxford University Press.

World Bank. 1993. *Investing in Health: World Development Report*. New York: Oxford University Press.

———. 1995. *Priorities and Strategies for Education: A World Bank Review*. Washington, DC: The World Bank.

———. 1996. *Poverty in the Midst of Plenty*. Washington DC: The World Bank.

———. 1998. *Hard Lessons: Primary Schools, Community and Social Capital in Nigeria*. Washington, DC: The World Bank.

WEF (World Education Forum). 2000. *The Dakar Framework for Action – Education For All: Meeting Our Collective Commitments*. Paris: UNESCO.

Zhang, Tao, and Hen-fu Zou. 1998. Fiscal Decentralization, Public Spending, and Economic Growth in China. *Journal of Public Economics* 67: 221–240.

The Author

Macleans A. Geo-JaJa is Professor of Economics of Education and holds the Chair of the Comparative and International Development Education Program at Brigham Young University. He previously taught at the University of Port Harcourt in Nigeria and at the University of Utah. He has a doctorate in Labor Economics. His main research areas are: education regeneration and nation-building, structural adjustment policies and globalisation, and social and economic aspects of education markets. He has been involved in numerous national and international projects, including the first ever Human Development Index of American Cities.

Contact address: David McKay School of Education, Brigham Young University, Provo, Utah 84602, USA. E-mail: geo-jaja@byu.edu.

SOCIAL JUSTICE IN CHINESE HIGHER EDUCATION: REGIONAL ISSUES OF EQUITY AND ACCESS

W. JAMES JACOB

Abstract – A topic of growing concern in Chinese higher education to policy-makers, scholars, and future student applicants is social justice. With the trend toward increasing enrollments in China's higher-education institutions, issues of equity and access have begun to surface, especially as they relate to China's minority population of over 100 million persons. The present contribution offers an overview of the regional boundaries of China, both geographic and historical. It then looks at the development of urbanicity in connection with higher education. Third, it describes the recent history of the gender gap in education both in general and in higher education in particular. Fourth, it examines the ethnic boundaries that exist in higher education. The final section analyzes related findings drawn from interviews and questionnaires administered to faculty members, administrators, and students at ten sample universities.

Zusammenfassung – SOZIALE GERECHTIGKEIT IN DER HÖHEREN BILDUNG IN CHINA: REGIONALE PROBLEME DER CHANCENGLEICHHEIT UND ZUGANGSMÖGLICHKEITEN – Ein Thema in der chinesischen Hochschullandschaft, das zunehmend mehr Interesse bei politischen Entscheidungsträgern, Gelehrten und zukünftigen Studienbewerbern findet, ist die soziale Gerechtigkeit. Während die Tendenz weiter in Richtung steigender Immatrikulationszahlen in Chinas höheren Bildungsinstitutionen ging, traten die Probleme der Chancengleichheit und des Zugangs an die Oberfläche, insbesondere, da sie in Verbindung mit Chinas Minderheitenbevölkerung von über 100 Millionen Menschen stehen. Der vorliegende Beitrag bietet einen Überblick über Chinas regionale Grenzen, sowohl die geographischen als auch die historischen. Er wirft dann einen Blick auf die Entwicklung von städtischen Strukturen in Verbindung mit der höheren Bildung. Drittens beschreibt er die jüngste Geschichte der Kluft zwischen den Geschlechtern in der Bildung allgemein und in der höheren Bildung im Besonderen. Viertens untersucht er die ethnischen Grenzen, die in der höheren Bildung bestehen. Der letzte Abschnitt analysiert relevante Ergebnisse aus Interviews und Fragebögen, die Fakultätsangehörigen, Führungspersonal und Studenten an zehn repräsentativen Universitäten vorgelegt wurden.

Résumé – LA JUSTICE SOCIALE DANS L'ÉDUCATION SUPÉRIEURE CHINOISE : QUESTIONS RÉGIONALES DE L'ÉQUITÉ ET DE L'ACCESSIBILITÉ – Un sujet de préoccupation grandissant dans l'éducation supérieure chinoise pour les politiciens, les écoliers et les futurs candidats aux études est la justice sociale. Avec la tendance croissante des immatriculations dans les institutions de l'éducation supérieure de la Chine, des problèmes d'équité et d'accessibilité ont commencé à apparaître, en particulier du fait qu'ils se rapportent à une minorité chinoise de la population de 100 millions de personnes. La présente contribution offre un passage en revue des frontières régionales chinoises, aussi bien géographiques qu'historiques. Puis elle se tourne vers le développement de l'urbanisation en connexion avec l'éducation supérieure. Troisièmement, elle décrit la récente histoire du fossé de la différence des sexes

J. Zajda (ed.), Education and Social Justice, 139-159.

dans l'éducation, aussi bien dans l'éducation générale que dans celle supérieure en particulier. Quatrièmement, elle examine les frontières ethniques qui existent dans l'éducation supérieure. L'ultime section analyse les conclusions connexes découlant d'interviews et de questionnaires remplis par des membres de facultés, des administrateurs et des étudiants dans dix universités prises comme modèles.

Resumen – JUSTICIA SOCIAL EN LA EDUCACIÓN SUPERIOR CHINA: ASPECTOS REGIONALES DE IGUALDAD Y ACCESIBILIDAD – La justicia social en la educación superior China es un tema de importancia creciente para los responsables de la política, los alumnos y los futuros candidatos a estudiantes. Ante el aumento permanente de matriculaciones en los institutos de enseñanza superior, en China han comenzado a aflorar problemas relacionados con igualdad y accesibilidad, ante todo cuando se relacionan con una minoría de unas 100 millones de personas. Esta contribución ofrece una sinopsis de los límites regionales de China, tanto geográficos como históricos, y pasa revista a la urbanización y su relación con la educación superior. En tercer lugar, describe la historia más reciente en cuanto a la desigualdad entre los géneros en general, y en la educación superior en particular. En cuarto lugar, examina los resultados, relacionados con lo que antecede, que se obtuvieron a partir de entrevistas y cuestionarios hechos a miembros de facultades, administradores y estudiantes en diez universidades elegidas para el muestreo.

Резюме – СОЦИАЛЬНАЯ СПРАВЕДЛИВОСТЬ В КИТАЙСКОМ ВЫСШЕМ ОБРАЗОВАНИИ: РЕГИОНАЛЬНЫЕ ВОПРОСЫ РАВЕНСТВА И ДОСТУПА – Все возрастающей заботой в китайском высшем образовании для политиков образования, ученых и будущих абитуриентов является вопрос о социальной справедливости. Наряду с тенденцией увеличения количества зачислений в китайские вузы начали возникать вопросы равентсва и доступа, в частности в отношении меньшинства населения в Китае - более 100 миллионов человек. В данной статье предлагается обзор региональных границ в Китае – как географических, так и исторических. Далее в статье рассматривается вопрос развития урбанизации в контексте высшего образования. В-третьих, в статье описывается недавняя история гендерного разрыва как в общем, так и в высшем образовании. В-четвертых, в статье рассматриваются этнические границы, которые существуют в высшем образовании. В заключение проводится анализ соответствующих данных из интервью и опросов, проведенных среди членов факультетов, администрации и студентов в десяти университетах, взятых в качестве примера.

Social justice in Chinese higher education is a topic of growing concern to policy-makers, scholars, and future student applicants. With the trend toward increasing enrollments in China's higher education institutions (HEIs), the issues of equity and access begin to surface, especially as they relate to China's 100 million plus minority population. Social justice in higher education bridges a number of disciplinary and academic areas. International educators have addressed social justice and education issues for a number of years. Paulo Freire (1970) viewed social justice as an inherent right of the people and often criticized education systems for feeding students with knowledge under a traditional "banking" model. Neo-Freirian scholars have identified schools and HEIs as ideal hubs for building critical pedagogical and thinking skills. Lee Anne Bell (1997) identifies three main goals that serve as necessary underpinnings in defining social justice education: social responsibility, empowerment, and equity. In addition to Bell's definition, Heather W. Hackman and Laura Rauscher (2004) argue that social-justice education must establish structures that examine issues of power and oppression that focus on critical thinking and practical skills development. Building on these definitions of social justice and education in this article, I discuss several boundaries in their relation to social justice in Chinese higher education.

Geographic and Historical Boundaries

In the restructuring of higher education in the 1950s, the government of China made a conscious attempt to ensure geographic distribution of HEIs, focusing on six geographic regions – North, Northeast, Northwest, Central South, Southwest, and East (see Figure 1). The initial goal of these reforms

Figure 1. Six geographic regions of China in the 1950s

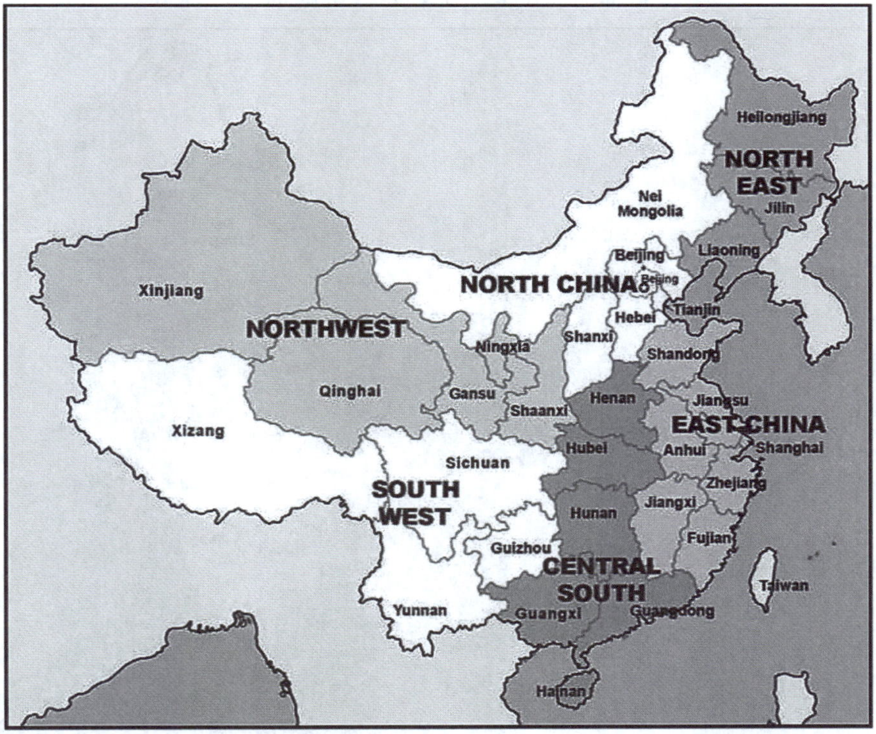

Sources: Adapted from Yang Rui (2000) and Ruth Hayhoe (1999)

was to establish one or two comprehensive universities, polytechnical universities or colleges, one major teachers college, one to three agricultural universities or colleges, and other specialized institutions in each specified region (Chen 2002). Then, from 1955 to 1957, to provide a more representative geographic distribution of HEIs nationally, the government initiated a small-scale restructuring by shifting five coastal universities to the hinterland and establishing twelve new institutions there. Since the 1980s, there has existed a recategorization of national regions based on the three primary economic regions of China – the Eastern Coastal Region, the Central Developing Region, and the Western Under-developed Region (Figure 2). In addition to the two geographical classifications provided in Figures 1 and the land may be geographically divided into seven primary regions: Northeast China, North China, East Central China, South China, Inner Mongolian Grassland, Northwest China, and the Tibetan Plateau.

Perhaps most relevant to Chinese higher education in this context is the correlation between economic, educational, and market-oriented reforms based on geographic region. Since the 1980s, the government has encouraged the coastal provinces to carry out many more reforms than were possible in

Figure 2. Economic regions of China established in the 1980s

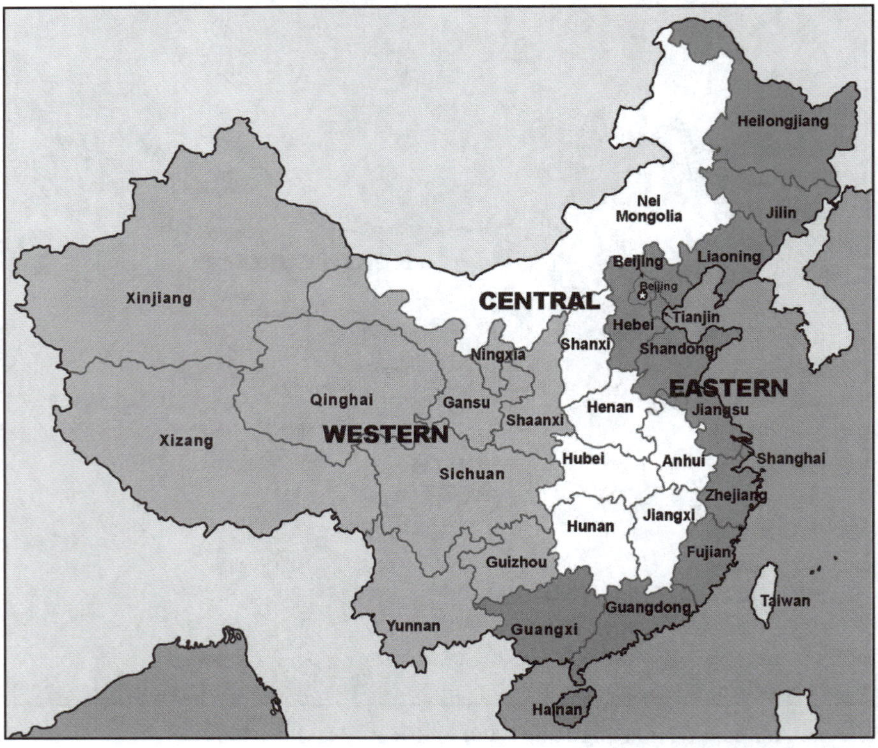

the more rural regions of the country. This geographic policy gave rise to the first four Special Economic Zones (Shantou, Shenzhen, Xiamen, and Zhuhai). Guangdong and Fujian provinces also benefited as recipients of several government financial contracts. Although these government policies clearly aided the development of the Chinese market economy, they also fostered inequalities based on geographic region. The eastern, coastal provinces benefited much more than the hinterland and remote regions.

Another geographic disparity has linked urbanicity with the various provinces of China. With a dramatic increase in economic output due to market demand for a large portion of the world's products primarily manufactured in the eastern regions, domestic migrant workers have sought employment from their native hinterland provinces to the easternmost provinces (see Table 1).

While urbanicity rates are increasing at the national level in China, these numbers do not seem to hold constant throughout every age group. In Table 2, figures show the percent of China's urban population distribution by age groups.

Since most HEIs are located in urban centers, it is clear, in view of the figures in Table 2, how higher education is becoming more readily available to the masses in urban locations than in rural regions. Urban populations also tend to be aging. For students in rural regions, however, access to higher education is generally more difficult than for students from urban locations. This is due to several factors, including socio-economic status, distance from familial support, and lack of sufficient financial resources. In terms of gender and urbanicity, the general Chinese population trend continues to be

Table 1. Urban population and urban population percentages, 1982–2000

Year	Urban population (in millions)	Urban population (%)
1982	206.31	20.55
1990	296.15	26.20
1995	353.40	28.58
1999	388.92	30.90
2000	455.94	36.09

Source: Adapted from William Lavely (2001)

Table 2. Urban population and urban population percentages, 1990–2000

Age	Aggregate		Rural		Urban	
	1990	2000	1990	2000	1990	2000
0–14	27.7	22.9	29.6	25.5	25.9	18.4
15–64	66.7	70.1	64.8	67.2	68.6	75.3
65+	5.6	7.0	5.6	7.3	5.5	6.3

Source: Adapted from Lavely (2001)

increasingly male. This is due largely to government family-planning policies, which give financial preference to families with only one child.

An estimated 100 million workers have migrated from rural to the manufacturing urban centers, leading to increased living congestion, transportation traffic, and crime rates (Whyte 1996; Solinger 1999; Fewsmith 2001; Eckholm 2003). While many critics cite the negative aspects of this migrant urbanization movement, others point out the positive dimensions. The urban–rural gap has been diminished insofar as several major manufacturing cities have granted permanent residency to migrants residing in cities and begun to give migrants' children equal access to education in urban schools (Chan 1995). Motives fueling the migrant-workers movement include the hope of these workers to send enough money back home to support their children, spouse, and even parents in realizing a better quality of life. Parents flock to the cities in pursuit of work for the purpose of financing greater educational opportunities for their children.

Gender Boundaries

China's enormous population has led the government to look with various lenses at how to curb population growth rates. The decision to limit birth rate to any degree ultimately addresses gender issues. For cultural reasons, many Chinese families desire to have at least one male child, as sons are traditionally responsible for caring for their elderly parents (Hansen 2004). Rather than being left without elderly care, if parents are limited to one child, many prefer to have a male child. William Lavely (2001) notes that the sex-at-birth ratio has "risen monotonically since 1980, a trend that has ominous implications for female welfare and for mating, and bleak ramifications for poor families whose life plans depend crucially on the recruitment of a daughter-in-law" (16). National census reports have shown a constant sex-at-birth ratio rise since 1982 (Table 3).

Thus, with a shear decrease in the number of female students, gender will become an increasingly pertinent issue in the future of higher education. While women in China have realized more educational opportunities than in many

Table 3. Sex ratio of births and sex ratio of the population age 0–4, 1953–1999

Year of census or survey	Sex ratio of births	Sex ratio of the population age 0–4
1953	–	107.0
1964	–	105.7
1982	108.5	107.1
1990	111.4	110.2
1995	115.6	118.4
1999	117.0	119.5

Source: Adapted from Lavely (2001)

developing countries (Epstein 1991; Wen and Cai 1994; Hayhoe 1999), the sex-at-birth ratio may be one factor that threatens to hinder this achievement.

In addition to the Chinese sex-at-birth-ratio phenomenon, other gender barriers disadvantage female students, some of them cultural. Others are even global in nature. For instance, in 1990 illiteracy rates for women (32%) were more than twice the national average for men (13%). In his national study on minority education in China, Jacques Lamontagne (1999) found a strong correlation ($r = 0.842$) between the level of female illiteracy and the magnitude of the illiteracy gender gap (150–51). Other than in the Xizang (Tibet) Region, Lamontagne noted that the gender gap is steadily decreasing on a national level. In his analysis, Lamontagne provided a comparison between major ethnic groups that have either small or large gender illiteracy gaps. According to Lamontagne's study, in educationally less-advantaged provinces, women remain in a slower phase of transition toward literacy than in other provinces of the country. Xizang is the only province in which the educational gender gap has not yet peaked.

Ethnic Boundaries

China's population consists of many different nationalities and ethnic groups, although over 90% of the total population are ethnic Han. The name "Han" derives from the people of the Han dynasty (206 B.C.–A.D. 220), a period recognized for its great unity among the people in China. During the Han dynasty the people of virtually all geographic regions in China came to view themselves as part of the same ethnic group. This is because of several unique characteristics, including similar values derived from the ideas of Confucius and other classical writers, a common written language, and an agricultural system based on producing grains such as wheat, rice, and millet.

Since the formation of the People's Republic in 1949, China has identified 55 ethnic nationalities; these range in size from several thousand to several million members. The largest ethnic groups include the Zhuang, Hui, Uygur, Mongols, and Tibetans, yet there are many other ethnic groups that speak a unique language and maintain a unique culture. Language has remained a barrier to minority students in higher education. In China, minority students learn and speak their native tongue or dialect at home and in their social circles, while simultaneously having to learn Mandarin in school and for business. According to John N. Hawkins (1983), most Chinese minority languages are significantly different from the Han dialect. Although minority students receive preferential treatment on the national higher-education entrance exams, it is often not enough to compensate for the lack of language fluency required at the higher education level. Another disparity that tends to de-link minorities from higher-education opportunities is the fact that the majority of China's minority members live in predominantly rural and hinterland regions. Geographically disadvantaged regions, coupled with minority obstacles, only compound higher education opportunities for these students (Hawkins 1988; Jiang 2002; Andreas 2004; Kynge 2004).

China's ethnic minority populations accounted for approximately 8% of the country's total in 1990 and 8.4% in 2000. Based on the two most recent censuses, ethnic Chinese minorities totaled 90.6 million in 1990 and 104.5 million in 2000 (National Bureau of Statistics 2002). Between 1982 and 1990 the minority population grew at an annual average rate of 3.83%. (During this time period, over 14 million people who had previously been classified as ethnic Han were reclassified as minority group members – see Postiglione 1999.) This rapid annual rate was largely due to a relatively high natural increase, as well as the government's reclassification of ethnic groups from the Han majority to newly recognized minority ethnic groups (Poston and Jing 1987; Poston 1993). In the 1990s, however, minorities grew at less than half this rate, at 1.51% per year. This trend probably stems from the successful implementation of family-planning policies in the minority regions. Due to government family-planning restrictions, the minority ethnic groups generally have higher birth and growth rates. The Chinese government has supported minority groups with benefits such as better medicine and nutrition, improved economic development, and policies of preferential admissions to higher education.

The government has established five autonomous regions that specifically relate to ethnic minority populations in China, namely Inner Mongolia (established in 1947), Xinjiang Uygur (est. 1955), Guangxi Zhuang (est. 1958), Ningxia Hui (est. 1958), and Xizang (est. 1965). Additionally, China has 30 autonomous prefectures and 120 autonomous counties. Though autonomous in many ways, these regions remain part of the People's Republic. Originally the autonomous regions were granted autonomy to use their respective minority languages in public meetings, the press, and in education. Minority policy changed, however, at the onset of the Cultural Revolution. Minority group members thence needed to learn to speak and write Han in addition to their own respective languages (Hawkins 1983: 189).

Minority students have maintained an enrollment rate between 1.0% and 6.0% of total higher-education enrollments since 1949 (see Table 4). The average percentage of minority enrollees in Chinese universities from 1949 to 2000 was 4.5% of the total number of higher education students.

Note how less than 1.0% of the national body of higher-education students were of minority status in 1949. Not long after the creation of the People's Republic, minority enrollments rose to over 3.0% and maintained this percentage until the beginning of the Cultural Revolution, when all HEIs were closed during the first years of the movement. Preferential admissions were again extended to minority students at the end of the Cultural Revolution, with minority students making up roughly 6.5% of the national subsector student body. This percentage vacillated throughout much of the

Table 4. Minority students at Chinese universities, 1949–2001

Year	Number of students	Percentage
1949–1950	1,255	0.93
1959–1960	28,163	3.47
1979–1980	42,944	3.75
1989–1990	137,948	6.60
1999–2000	247,700	6.06

Sources: Updated from Sautman (1999: 180); *Educational Statistics Yearbook* 1989 (1989); *Educational Statistics Yearbook of China* 1995–2002 (2003)

late 1970s and the 1980s. Barry Sautman (1999) notes that the most likely reason for the slight decline of minority-enrollment percentage is the rapid expansion of higher-education enrollments that began in the mid- to late-1990s and gained momentum at the turn of the 21st century.

In 1951, the government ambitiously sought to educate and train teachers from ethnic backgrounds throughout China. This effort established over 100 normal HEIs specifically to meet the various needs of the respective ethnic groups throughout the country. Simultaneously, the government set up departments for ethnic teachers' training in various comprehensive universities and nationality colleges. After more than 50 years of governmental support, approximately 900,000 teachers of ethnic origins have been trained throughout the country, a feat some 35 times the original ethnic minority teacher status at the beginning of this reform effort (CERNET 2000a).

More recently, the government has established a number of research institutions at various national and local HEIs (CERNET 2000b). Several regional research institutions have also been established, including one at Xinjiang Normal University, one of the sample universities in this study. These research centers focus and publish on various ethnic education issues and trends.

Although significant strides have been made to meet the needs of minority students in China, some scholars argue that there is still room for improvement. Ethnic minority students lack the linguistic, cultural, and political identity foundations to compete with the ethnic Han majority in the Chinese higher education arena. Preferential treatment of minority students may ease higher education institutional admissions, but it has also led to corruption among some students who pose as ethnic minorities just to obtain improved examination scores and increase their overall advantages toward admissions (Johnson and Chhetri 2000). With the amount of emphasis the government has placed on increased higher-education enrollments in the past decade, the same level of emphasis is needed to ensure that minority students are likewise granted equal educational opportunities. The rapid increase in higher-education enrollments worldwide does not necessarily lead to greater diversity in HEIs or equality of opportunity for minority students (Lewis and Dundar 2002). Coupled with geographic and urbanicity variables, it is often difficult to meet the growing higher educational needs of the Chinese ethnic minority groups.

Methodology

The cross-sectional analysis presented here of ten case-study universities was conducted in the 2003. The following types of data were collected for the investigation and analysis portion of this study:

a. Qualitative interviews with university administrators ($n=10$), faculty ($n=21$), and students ($n=20$).
b. Questionnaires administered to selected administrators ($n=48$), faculty ($n=147$), and students ($n=989$) from the participating universities in this study.
c. Archival data, including information from academic journals, government archives, internet sites, books, dissertations, and academic conference presentations.

School Selection

In order to measure the impact of the market economy on higher education in each of the major regions in China, the sample of universities was stratified from both the original geographic distribution outlined in Figure 1 and also according to the identified economic regions as portrayed in Figure 2. A further stratification of universities was made according to top-ranked universities from the literature review of higher-education ranking systems in China. In this manner, the top-ranked universities were selected from each of the six geographic regions in Figure 1 and from the three economic regions in Figure 2. Thus, the following numbers of universities were included from the respective geographic regions: one university from the Western Economic Region; two universities from the Central (one from Guangdong, which spans both the Central South and Eastern Economic Regions); and seven universities from the Eastern (two universities span the Eastern and Central Economic Regions – Peking and Tsinghua Universities). No universities were selected from the Southwest Region in Figure 1 because the advisory committee felt that findings from Xinjiang Normal University from the Northwest Region could be generalized to the Southwestern Region as well.

Instruments

The questionnaires used in this study are based on those of UCLA's Higher Education Research Institute (HERI). This was the first time these surveys were administered at higher-education institutions in China. Established in 1966, HERI's surveys include the United States' largest and oldest empirical study of higher education, involving data on some 1,800 institutions and over 11 million students in the United States. The survey addressed such issues as trends, admissions, governance, finance, curriculum, student life, scholarship opportunities, and international exchanges. This article does not advocate a cookie-cutter instrument for all international contexts; HERI surveys have demonstrated, however, a long history of monitoring higher education trends in the United States. Using the HERI surveys also provides an opportunity for comparisons between higher education trends in the United States and China. Whereas this study was conducted in 2003, it could be strengthened substantially with longitudinal follow-up studies. Qualitative interview instruments were designed by the author in order to triangulate quantitative findings from the HERI surveys.

Regional Empirical Findings

This section concludes the present study by introducing and analyzing some of the quantitative and qualitative findings from the ten sample universities. The first set of findings draws largely from questionnaire data administered to students, faculty, and administrators. Juxtaposition of the findings shows differences between participant groups regarding ethnic background, religious affiliation, gender, socio-economic status, and native geographic region (see Table 5). Next, this section examines faculty and administrator salaries (see Tables 6 and 7). The final portion of this analysis shares some of the findings from the qualitative, in-depth interviews relating to equity of access in higher education.

Just over 5.0% of the student participants were of an ethnic minority background other than Han. This variance increased to 10.2% among faculty members and 8.3% among administrators. Where roughly two-thirds of administrators and about half of the faculty spoke Mandarin Chinese as their native dialect; only 28.6% of the graduate students and 35.3% of the undergraduate students spoke Mandarin as their native tongue. The overwhelming majority of minority dialects identified among the study's participants (the only group with a Mandarin majority was among administrators) highlights the ethnolinguistic diversity that exists in Chinese higher education.

While religion was not sampled from study faculty and administrator participants, only 10.5% of the students professed to believe in a religion (2.8% did not respond). The percentage breakdown for students who professed to belong to a religion was as follows: 7.2% professed Buddhism, 1.3% Muslim, 0.8% Christian, 0.4% Hindu, and another 1.3% another form of religion. Table 5 juxtaposes undergraduate and graduate student distance from their respective universities to their home location, SES, and parental education level. Over half of the undergraduate and approximately two-thirds of

Table 5. Home location, SES, and parents' education of student participants

	Undergraduate students ($n = 797$)		Graduate students ($n = 192$)	
	Frequency	Percentage	Frequency	Percentage
Distance (km) between University and Students' Home				
5 or less km	53	6.6	9	4.7
6–10 km	31	3.9	6	3.1
11–50 km	73	9.2	15	7.8
51–100 km	71	8.9	8	4.2
101–500 km	156	19.6	25	13.0
Over 500 km	401	50.3	129	67.2
Did not respond	12	1.5	0	0.0
Concerns about financing education				
None (confident that they will have sufficient funds)	394	49.4	81	42.2
Some (but probably will have enough money)	329	41.3	86	44.8
Major (not sure if they will have enough funds to complete higher education)	71	8.9	24	12.5
Did not respond	3	0.4	1	0.5
Highest level of father's formal education				
No formal schooling	11	1.4	17	8.9
Some primary school	46	5.8	15	7.8
Primary school graduate	71	8.9	21	10.9
High school graduate	182	22.8	49	25.5
Some university	240	30.1	42	21.9
University graduate	99	12.4	19	9.9
Some graduate school	126	15.8	27	14.1
Graduate degree	8	1.0	0	0.0
Did not respond	14	1.8	2	1.0

Table 5. Continued.

	Undergraduate students ($n = 797$)		Graduate students ($n = 192$)	
	Frequency	Percentage	Frequency	Percentage
Highest level of mother's formal education				
No formal schooling	46	5.8	24	12.5
Some primary school	87	10.9	37	19.3
Primary school graduate	68	8.5	32	16.7
High school graduate	207	26.0	39	20.3
Some university	232	29.1	31	16.1
University graduate	70	8.8	16	8.3
Some graduate school	79	9.9	11	5.7
Graduate degree	0	0.0	1	0.5
Did not respond	8	1.0	1	0.5
Parents' annual income				
Less than RMB 10,000	231	29.0	78	40.6
RMB 10,000–14,999	133	16.7	33	17.2
RMB 15,000–19,999	73	9.2	16	8.3
RMB 20,000–24,999	77	9.7	6	3.1
RMB 25,000–29,999	39	4.9	4	2.1
RMB 30,000–39,999	60	7.5	8	4.2
RMB 40,000–49,999	37	4.6	7	3.6
RMB 50,000–59,999	54	6.8	18	9.4
RMB 60,000–74,999	30	3.8	5	2.6
RMB 75,000–99,999	17	2.1	6	3.1
RMB 100,000–149,999	14	1.8	3	1.6
RMB 150,000–199,999	7	0.9	3	1.6
RMB 200,000–249,999	4	0.5	2	1.0
RMB 250,000 or more	6	0.8	1	0.5
Did not respond	15	1.9	0	0.0

Table 6. Faculty and administrator annual salaries

	Faculty ($n=147$)		Administrators ($n=48$)	
	Frequency	Percentage	Frequency	Percentage
Amounts				
Less than RMB 20,000	26	17.7	14	29.2
RMB 20,000–29,999	37	25.2	11	22.9
RMB 30,000–39,999	22	15.0	8	16.7
RMB 40,000 or more	48	32.7	9	18.8
Did not respond	14	9.5	6	12.5

the graduate students were from homes over 500 km from the sample universities.

Only a small percentage of students expressed major concerns about financing their higher education (8.9% of undergraduates and 12.5% of graduate students). It is interesting to note that 82.1% of the undergraduate students' fathers graduated from high school, while just about three-fourths (73.8%) of their mothers were high-school graduates. This gender discrepancy held constant at the graduate-student level as well; only 50.9% of the mothers compared with 71.4% of the fathers had graduated from high school. There was a great deal of variance between the two student groups in terms of parental annual income. Whereas 40.6% of graduate students' parents made less than RMB 10,000 per year, only 29.0% of undergraduate parents made an equivalent annual amount. Based on Table 5, the overall socio-economic status of the undergraduate-student group is higher than that of the graduate-student group. This held true for parental education level as well. Recognizing that 82.1% of the undergraduate participants' fathers and 73.8% of their mothers held at least a high-school degree; this is well beyond the national educational level average.

Regarding faculty and administrator salaries, findings provide the overall annual income (Table 6), as well as those stratified by geographic region of the participant schools (Table 7). The average income for administrators came to RMB 31,167 and RMB 29,204 for faculty members.

These amounts show a great deal of variance; the lowest-paid faculty member received only RMB 1,000 per year, compared to the highest-paid who made RMB 100,000 per year. Administrators made anywhere from RMB 3,000 to RMB 250,000 per year. (Note that one member of this study's advisory committee felt that these figures may be potentially misleading as some faculty members might actually make less than RMB 1,000–3,000 per year.) Even more striking than just the amounts of faculty and administrators is the geographic distribution of these salaries, as portrayed in Table 7. Faculty salaries ranged from an average of RMB 33,630 in the

Table 7. Faculty and administrator annual salaries, by region

	Faculty ($n = 147$)			Administrators ($n = 48$)		
	N	Mean salary	X^2	*N*	Mean salary	X^2
Mean salary by geog. region of university						
East	45	30,200	275.85**	15	46,867	110.22*
Central South	45	32,956		16	33,750	
North	27	33,630		6	15,000	
Northeast	15	30,933		5	21,400	
Northwest	15	5,267		6	9,333	
Southwest	0	0		0	0	

*$p < 0.1$; **$p < 0.001$

North to RMB 5,267 in the Northwest ($X^2 = 275.85$, $p < 0.001$). This discrepancy emphasizes the huge gap that separates higher education institutions in the eastern and coastal regions compared with the predominantly rural and remote regions in China's hinterland. Administrator salaries ranged from RMB 46,867 in the East to RMB 9,333 in the Northwest ($X^2 = 110.22$, $p < 0.1$).

Again, the Northwest region bemoans the small salaries associated with China's hinterland regions. Also striking among the administrator group is the difference in pay between its faculty and administrators (which claimed the highest faculty salary average among the geographic regions) and only RMB 15,000 per year for its administrators, ranking fourth-highest behind the East (RMB 46,867), Central South (RMB 33,750), and Northeast (RMB 21,400).

When asked how Chinese universities can become more equitable in terms of access, interviewees responded by suggesting that the National College Entrance Examination needed significant reforms, assistance should be mandatory for students in rural regions, and low socio-economic status students needed financial support to make their higher-education experience a reality. Other suggestions that interviewees commented on include increasing enrollments to all qualified students; helping minority students who are hindered by linguistic, cultural, and rural barriers; and equalizing opportunities for both gender groups. Regarding the unique nature of Chinese higher education admissions, one faculty member said:

> Because of various deficiencies in the current higher education system, Chinese institutions cannot reach an equivalent level of access equality currently experienced by several Western nations. If we adopted a purely American model, only the best performing students with the most opportunities would be permitted into HEIs, thus widening the gap between the rural and urban students.

Yet the examination system has several weaknesses, identified by interviewees as well. Perhaps the most common critique of an admissions system that relies solely on examination scores is that the exam system does not necessarily account for students' talents, gifts, and ethics. It fails to address issues of socio-economic background and language fluency. One administrator said: "I think the national college entrance exam system must be ameliorated to make the score embody the actual knowledge level of the individual student. Furthermore, we should focus on closing the widening gap that exists between the various geographic regions based on selection criteria." Another faculty member added:

> The exam system is not entirely equitable. Since there is only one exam, some students whose grades are normally outstanding, endure problems while taking the test and blunder on their exam scores. Some minor problems that are likely to occur while taking the exam, such as problems in filling out the selection of disciplines, could jeopardize the students' chances from attending good HEIs.

Thus, while most interviewees felt the examination-based selection system had some merit, it also had room for refinement. In order to meet the entirely equitable selection criteria, interviewees felt that items such as language, socio-economic status, talents, and character must be included.

The second most-common suggestion for making Chinese universities more equitable in terms of access concerns the need to assist applicants from rural regions. Commenting on the struggles associated with geography, one faculty member said: "No matter what geographic region students may be in, there will always be inequalities in terms of college access. Yet, rest assured that inequalities are especially large for ethnic minorities and those living in rural regions of the country." An administrator added:

> More fundamentally speaking, access opportunities are inequitable because of the diverse quality and development of fundamental education levels in different geographic regions. Because of the diverse economic development situations of applicants, students have received a huge variance in the quality of instruction at their respective primary and secondary schools. While some geographic regions attempt to offset these inequitable discrepancies through bonus scores on higher education entrance exams, other deprived regions do not. In many remote regions, high school students will migrate just to score better on exams in hopes of bettering their chances to be admitted to a better HEI.

So rather than just looking at college entrance examinations, many interviewees felt that this issue must be addressed by looking beforehand at the quality and level of education students receive in the vast Chinese state. It is impossible to generalize findings from one region to another. Furthermore, regional inequities are compounded by issues such as minority groups, language of instruction, and socio-economic status.

A third most-common suggestion for making higher education more equitable concerns higher-education financing. In the past, higher education was funded entirely by the government. With the influx of millions of students into the subsector, it is impossible for the government to continue this practice. Furthermore, higher education costs continue to grow at an increasingly rapid rate. Many Chinese universities have made strides in providing avenues for students who struggle financially to further their higher-education ambitions. One administrator interviewee said that her university had established a slogan: "We will not permit a student to leave our school based on financial difficulty." In order to accommodate this slogan, the university has established a series of scholarships, loan schemes, and work experiences for needy students to pay for their studies. Yet these scholarships are still linked to excellent performance on the college entrance examination. Therefore, many qualified students who do not perform well on the college entrance exam find themselves restricted because of financial limitations.

When asked whether students in rural and ethnic minority regions are discriminated against in terms of higher-education opportunities, the majority of interviewees responded affirmatively. The majority felt as if the greatest discrimination in higher-education opportunities faces those of ethnic minority backgrounds. Interviewees identified several factors as stumbling blocks for minority groups obtaining a higher education in China. These include linguistic cultural barriers and living in predominantly rural region. The majority of respondents did not feel that granting bonus points on the national college entrance examination remedied the inequality gap in accessing higher education. Preferential treatment can also be viewed as a stumbling block. One graduate student recognized the difficulty minority students face once enrolled in a HEI:

> Take my school as an example. After arriving at my school, I noticed that minority students have a distinct language barrier, so there are many additional problems they face in terms of studying, examinations, and finding a job after graduation. There are generally two distinct groups at my university – those from the rural regions and those from the cities. It is very hard for the two groups to mix together. Students from rural regions and minority ethnic groups will continue to feel inferior while students from urban centers will continue to maintain a sense of superiority.

Faculty members have also noted difficulties minority students face. Commenting on a minority cultural barriers, one faculty interviewee said:

> Minority student success in school largely depends on whether or not their parents' ideology and hope for their children to attend university is considered a priority. If students reside in urban centers, their chances for attending higher education increase. The level of parental education background is also a significant predictor of higher education entrance.

Even though preferential treatment is extended to many minority students, the majority of interviewees in this study agree that the barriers far outweigh the bonuses.

Another common discrimination against students in rural regions is the quality of their schools, teaching, and limited resources for facilities and technology. Thus, while the urban centers of China continue to mesh with the global economy and higher education landscape, the rural regions tend to be left behind. This is always a game of catch-up, according to one interviewee, who viewed the plight of the poor and rural students as a vicious cycle of mediocrity and poverty. In order to overcome these deficiencies in the rural regions, one administrator suggested: "Teacher education must be improved. Many teachers aim to help the poor ... One of the results in the restriction of the teachers' level of education is the low quality of teaching; therefore, students in these areas are always at a disadvantage when applying for HEIs." Other interviewees felt that increased incentives should be made available by the government to keep quality teachers and administrators in rural primary and secondary schools. This is not an easy task; increased wages and salaries are three times or more in urban centers what they are in the rural regions of the country.

Conclusion

The market economy has contributed to the need for individuals to obtain higher degrees, especially in a primarily knowledge-oriented economy. This contribution has discussed several social-justice boundaries facing the Chinese higher-education subsector, particularly in relation to the issues of equity and access. Drawing largely from the literature, it has examined geographic, ethnic, gender, and urbanicity barriers associated with higher education. Each of these factors is influenced by the market economy in China and HEI graduates need to develop social justice education skills such as critical thinking, independent problem-solving, and community involvement. Market trends point away from a purely insular and planned economy towards one that encompasses greater differentiation, decentralisation, and privatisation. Where traditional Chinese higher education focused internally on creating jobs sponsored primarily by the state, job placement opportunities of the future are much broader. This period of unprecedented economic growth emphasizes the need of developing a global scholar in Chinese higher education.

Geographic and urban disparities continue to pervade the higher-education subsector, though governmental efforts are being made to curb this disparity. Ethnic minority groups numbering over 100 million people in China have also received much needed attention regarding access and equity policies. Yet given the majority of the ethnic minority groups residing in hinterland locations, these two social-justice issues will need additional governmental attention in the future. The market has emphasized the importance of national and global languages in education. But will additional emphasis on English and Chinese further ostracize already marginalized groups? And since culture is so closely linked and intertwined with language, how can HEIs help maintain strong cultural identities while simultaneously equipping students with the necessary skills to compete in a market-oriented economy?

While the overall birth ratio of females is decreasing throughout the country, in many regions females continue to be more disadvantaged as compared with males. Yet the increase in male birth ratios also makes it more competitive for male students to compete for higher education enrollment opportunities. Based on a study of ten sample universities, the present contribution also examined salary differences between elite urban HEIs and leading universities in more rural or hinterland regions. Possessing the world's largest education system and potentially largest national higher-education subsector, China merits the attention of global scholars, policy-makers, educators, and investors. Equally important to meeting the growing market demands for higher-education expansion, social-justice issues of equity and access must be resolved.

References

Andreas, Joel. 2004. Leveling the Little Pagoda: The Impact of College Examinations, and their Elimination, on Rural Education in China. *Comparative Education Review* 48(1): 1–48.

Bell, Lee Anne. 1997. Theoretical Foundations for Social Justice Education. In *Teaching for Diversity and Social Justice: A Sourcebook*, ed. by Marianne Adams, Lee Anne Bell, and Pat Griffin, 3–15.

CERNET. 2000a. *Education for Ethnic Minorities in China: Making a Great Effort to Train Teaching Staff of Ethnic Origins*. Beijing: China Education and Research Network.

CERNET. 2000b. *Education for Ethnic Minorities in China: The Support to and Cooperation with the Ethnic Regional Education*. Beijing: China Education and Research Network.

Chan, Merry Jean. 1995. Floating Populations. *Harvard International Review* 17(4): 62–65.

Chen, David Y. (2002). The Amalgamation of Chinese Higher Education Institutions. *Education Policy Analysis Archives*, 10 (20).

Eckholm, Erik. 2003. Tide of China's Migrants: Flowing to Boom, or Bust? *New York Times* 29: A1.

Educational Statistics Yearbook of China. 1989. Beijing: People's Education Press.

Educational Statistics Yearbook of China, 1995–2002. 2003. Beijing: People's Education Press.

Epstein, Irving, (ed.). 1991. *Chinese Education: Problems, Policies, and Prospects*. Vol. 20. New York: Garland Publishing, Inc.

Fewsmith, Joseph. 2001. *China since Tiananmen: The Politics of Transition*. Cambridge: Cambridge University Press.

Freire, Paulo. 1970. *Pedagogy of the Oppressed*. New York: Herder and Herder.

Hackman, Heather, W., and Laura Rauscher. 2004. A Pathway to Access for All: Exploring the Connections between Universal Instructional Design and Social Justice Education. *Equity & Excellence in Education* 37(2): 114–123.

Hansen, Mette Halskov. 2004. Ethnic Minority Girls on Chinese School Benches: Gender Perspectives on Minority Education. In: *Education Culture and Identity in Twentieth-Century China*, ed. by Glen Peterson, Ruth Hayhoe and Yongling Lu, 403–429. Ann Arbor: The University of Michigan Press.

Hawkins, John N. 1983. Educational Policy and National Minorities in the People's Republic of China: The Politics of Intergroup Relations. In: *Education and Social Change in the People's Republic of China*, ed. by John N. Hawkins, 176–202. New York: Praeger.

———. 1988. The Transformation of Education for Rural Development in China. *Comparative Education Review* 32(3): 266–281.

Hayhoe, Ruth. 1999. *China's Universities 1895–1995: A Century of Cultural Conflict*, 2nd ed. Hong Kong: Comparative Education Research Centre, The University of Hong Kong.

Jiang, Xueqin. 2002. China Struggles with How Best to Educate Minority Students. *The Chronicle of Higher Education* 48: A46.

Johnson, Bonnie, and Nalini Chhetri. 2000. Exclusionary Policies and Practices in Chinese Minority Education: The Case of Tibetan Education. *Current Issues in Comparative Education* 2(2): 1–11.

Lamontagne, Jacques. 1999. National Minority Education in China: A Nationwide Survey Across Counties. In: *China's National Minority Education: Culture, Schooling, and Development*, ed. by Gerard A. Postiglione, 133–171. Vol. 42. New York: Falmer Press.

Lavely, William. 2001. *First Impressions of the 2000 Census of China*. Seattle: Sociology Department and Center for Studies in Demography and Ecology, University of Washington.

Lewis, Darrell R., and Halil Dundar. 2002. Equity Effects of Higher Education in Developing Countries. In: *Higher Education in the Developing World: Changing Contexts and Institutional Responses*, ed. by David W. Chapman and Ann E. Austin. 169–193. Westport, CN: Greenwood Press.

National Bureau of Statistics. 2002. *Statistical Yearbook of China 2002*. Beijing: China Statistical Publishing House.

Postiglione, Gerard A. 1999. Introduction: State Schooling and Ethnicity in China. In: *China's National Minority Education: Culture, Schooling, and Development*, ed. by Gerard A. Postiglione, 3–19. Vol. 42. New York: Falmer Press.

Poston, Dudley L. 1993. The National Minorities of China. Paper presented at the International Population Conference/Congress International de la Population, Montreal.

Shu Jing. 1987. The Demographic and Socioeconomic Composition of China's Ethnic Minorities. *Population and Development Review* 13(4): 703–722.

Sautman, Barry. 1999. Expanding Access to Higher Education for China's National Minorities: Policies of Preferential Admissions. In: *China's National Minority Education: Culture, Schooling, and Development*, ed. by Gerard A. Postiglione, 173–210. Vol. 42. New York: Falmer Press.

Solinger, Dorothy. 1999. *Contesting Citizenship in Urban China: Peasant Migrants, the State, and the Logic of the Market*. Berkeley: University of California Press.

Wen, Peizhi, and Hong Cai. 1994. Women Students in Higher Education in China: A Personal Insight. *Women's Studies International Forum* 17(5): 533–537.

Whyte, Martin King. 1996. The Social Roots of China's Economic Development. In: *China's Transitional Economy*, ed. by Andrew G. Walder, 37–57. Oxford: Oxford University Press.

Yang, Rui. 2000. Tensions between the Global and the Local: A Comparative Illustration of the Reorganisation of China's Higher Education in the 1950s and 1990s. *Higher Education* 39(3): 319–337.

The Author

W. James Jacob is Assistant Director at the Center for International and Development Education at the University of California, Los Angeles, where he also received his Ph.D. in Comparative and International Education. His current research focuses on program evaluation, social change and development, and higher education organizational analysis in developing countries with geographic emphases in China and East Africa. He worked as a policy analyst and evaluator of HIV/AIDS education programs in Uganda from 2001 to 2005, where he was simultaneously the principal investigator of a Sub-Saharan African HIV/AIDS literacy-education research program. He is currently co-directing a Global Higher Education Trends Analysis study on the influences of the market economy on higher education.

Contact address: Graduate School of Education and Information Studies, Center for International and Development Education, Box 951521, Moore Hall, Los Angeles, CA, 90095-1521, USA E-mail: wjacob@gseis.ucla.edu.

THE UNIVERSITY FOR OLDER ADULTS: ON CUBA'S UNIVERSALIZATION OF THE UNIVERSITY

CLARA LIG LONG RANGEL AND ANTONIA ZENAIDA SANCHEZ PROENZA

Abstract – In this study we focus on a new program in Cuba, university studies for older adults or seniors. Specifically, we look at the Special Municipality of the Isla de la Juventud (Isle of Youth) in the context of the larger policy of "universalization of higher education." We provide information about Cuban perspectives on adult education, discuss the "workshop" as an important mode of educational work, and present information on both the preparation of those who teach older adults and the training of "facilitators" in the workshop mode. This contribution also presents student evaluations, as well as a critique of the program.

Zusammenfassung – KUBAS SENIORENUNIVERSITÄT: EIN BLICK AUF DIE UNIVERSALISIERUNG DER UNIVERSITÄT – In diesem Beitrag legen wir das Augenmerk auf ein neues Programm in Kuba, nämlich Universitätsstudien für ältere Erwachsene oder Senioren. Insbesondere werfen wir einen Blick auf die Gemeinde der Isla de la Juventud im Kontext der weiteren Politik der „Universalisierung der höheren Bildung". Wir liefern Informationen über die kubanischen Blickwinkel auf die Erwachsenenbildung, diskutieren den ‚Workshop' als eine wichtige Methode der Bildungsarbeit und präsentieren Informationen sowohl über die Vorbereitung derjenigen, welche Senioren unterrichten, als auch über die Ausbildung der Facilitatoren in der Workshop-Methode. Dieser Beitrag enthält auch Evaluationen von Studierenden sowie eine Kritik des Programms.

Résumé – L'UNIVERSITÉ DE CUBA POUR LES PERSONNES DU TROISIÈME ÂGE : UN REGARD SUR L'UNIVERSALISATION DE L'UNIVERSITÉ – Dans cet article, nous nous concentrons sur un nouveau programme à Cuba, les études universitaires pour les adultes plus âgés ou les personnes du troisième âge. Plus spécifiquement, nous nous tournons vers la Municipalité Spéciale de la Isla de la Juventud (l'Île de la jeunesse) dans le contexte d'une politique plus large de « l'universalisation de l'éducation supérieure ». Nous fournissons des informations à propos des perspectives cubaines sur l'éducation des adultes, discutons de « l'atelier de travail » comme d'un mode important de travail éducatif et présentons une information aussi bien sur la préparation de ceux qui enseignent aux personnes du troisième âge que sur la formation des facilitateurs sur le mode de l'atelier de travail. Cette contribution présente également des évaluations étudiantes aussi bien qu'une critique du programme.

Resumen – LA UNIVERSIDAD DEL ADULTO MAYOR EN CUBA: UN VISTAZO A LA UNIVERSALIZACIÓN DE LA UNIVERSIDAD – Dedicamos este trabajo a un nuevo programa educativo de Cuba que ofrece estudios universitarios para adultos mayores. Específicamente, echaremos un vistazo a la Municipalidad de la Isla de la Juventud, en el contexto de una política amplia de 'universalización de la educación'. Ofrecemos información sobre las perspectivas cubanas en educación de personas

J. Zajda (ed.), Education and Social Justice, 161-173.

adultas, describimos el 'taller' como modo importante dentro del trabajo educativo y presentamos información sobre la preparación de aquellos que imparten la enseñanza a los adultos mayores y la capacitación de los 'facilitadores' que trabajan en los talleres. Esta contribución también presenta las evaluaciones hechas por los estudiantes y críticas del programa.

Резюме – КУБИНСКИЙ УНИВЕРСИТЕТ ДЛЯ ПОЖИЛЫХ ЛЮДЕЙ: ВЗГЛЯД НА УНИВЕРСАЛИЗАЦИЮ УНИВЕРСИТЕТА – В данной статье акцент ставится на новой программе в Кубе – университетской программе обучения для взрослых старшего возраста или пожилых людей. В частности, рассматривается Специальный муниципалитет Исла де ла Хувентуд (остров Молодежи) в контексте большой политики «универсализации высшего образования». Авторы предоставляют информацию о перспективах в образовании взрослых на Кубе, обсуждают «рабочую группу» как важный вид образовательной работы и предлагают информацию о подготовке тех, кто обучает пожилых людей, и подготовке «помощников» для обучения в режиме рабочей группы. Данная статья также дает оценку самих студентов, а также критику программы.

Introduction

Growing old with sufficient quality of life is both a process and the result of learning, though it is often erroneously thought to start only after one has reached mature adulthood. The University of Cuba's new view of universalization has broken with the traditional setting of the university campus so as to bring the academy to the student in his or her own community and to promote the idea that older adults also can access university classrooms in order to share their knowledge and experiences and to learn and unlearn with others about this new stage of life under the guidance of specialists and renowned academicians. The present contribution compiles information about the significance that the University of the Older Adult (*Universidad del Adulto Mayor*, or UAM) has for older adults and their families, as well as for the teachers who worked on this research project under the auspices of the Cuban Workers' Confederation (*Central de Trabajadores de Cuba*, or CTC), the Association of Cuban Educators (*Asociación de Pedagogos de Cuba*, or APC), and the Ministry of Higher Education (*Ministerio de Educación Superior*, or MES). In what follows, we describe the teacher–student relationship in the workshop as the preferred way of organizing the pedagogical process; then we propose a plan to help teachers and tutors to improve, since they are key figures in this process. Our objective here is to present the experience of the UAM in the Special Municipality of the Isla de la Juventud (Isle of Youth) in light of aspects that are essential to the process of universalization.

Presentation

> Today university teaching is progressively extending throughout this country's municipalities as an unavoidable need for a powerful revolution in education. ... In view of the new realities and circumstances, it will be necessary to see how the program is constructed, and what type of innovations will have to be applied in it; and it will be necessary to alter the way in which we move from one concept to another (Castro Ruz 2003).

In an increasingly globalized world, the changes that have been introduced in Cuban educational policy as part of the "battle for education and culture" have encouraged numerous "programs of the revolution", particularly and more recently the universalization of higher education. This program has brought about the adoption of new methods and teaching styles and a reflection on something much farther-reaching than the essential theoretical elements on which those changes are based (Lig Long Rangel 2001; Sanchez Proenza 2004).

Universalization, as the Minister of Higher Education C. Fernando Vecino Alegret (2003) has said, "is the explosion of higher studies; the university campus is not dispersed or atomized, but expanded, with a constant flow of information and education", which encourages specialists in and students of pedagogy to explore in scientific work topics such as lifelong learning in, with, and for older adults as alternative means of reflecting on and understanding the main trends in educational practice. This is how the concepts of the micro-university, the local university, and the local teacher have emerged, and how the concept of the tutor has changed with respect to the way in which he or she figures in the educational process. In this context, universalization is defined as

> all the transformations that have taken place in higher education in order to reach all sectors of society, not only enabling its central facilities to give ever greater possibilities of access but also through its presence in all the municipalities throughout the country, allowing higher levels of equity and social justice and thereby contributing to the development of a higher general culture, one that is essential to all citizens (CTC 2003: 2).

At the same time, other demographic changes have occurred in the world. The world's population has been growing increasingly older since 1980, and the Cuban population is no exception. In Latin America, Cuba is one of the countries with the oldest populations. Its socio-political structure places it in a position to help to ensure the active participation of communities, families, and older adults as the main actors in the effort to understand a culture of growing old.

Development

Since the dawn of the 21st century, the most revolutionary sectors of humanity have been reflecting more intensely on the future – conditioned by the advance of knowledge, particularly in science and technology – in the interest of paving the way to a future of progress for all human beings.

However, the situation in Cuba is quite different. A great deal of work has been done to achieve quality in education throughout the learner's life, an objective of UNESCO's Education for All project for 2015. Thus, the satisfaction of the adult population's current and future needs is of concern to the CTC, the APC, and the MES, among other organizations and institutions. These organizations have close ties in this regard.

The Cuban Workers' Confederation (CTC) is a national guild whose role is to make certain that national and municipal guidelines and directives are followed regarding the care for and security and welfare of active and retired workers. This body is in charge of coordinating with the *Organismos y Empresas de la Administración Central del Estado* (Systems and Enterprises of the Central State Administration), as well as with mobilizing qualified personnel to support the UAM program in accordance with the directives of workers' centers.

The Association of Cuban Educators (APC) is a non-governmental organization in charge of implementing the educational policy established by the MINED and MES, and, in cooperation with the CES, of tailoring the policy to the particular conditions of each territory, using an integral approach. It works to improve the staff connected with the UAM, particularly its tutors and teachers, as well as its administrative structures, and it supervises and inspects the UAM.

The Ministry of Higher Education (MES) develops strategies for the management of the process of universalization based on assessments of what is necessary for the creation of study plans and educational and instructional activities for the preparation of practicing professionals and students of education. It directs the activities of the UAM in keeping with the plan for instruction and education.

The Centers for Higher Education (CES) are centers for advanced studies that have as part of their mission the education and improvement of professionals in every field and to guarantee the qualifications of those professionals who either belong to the CES or are adjunct teachers at the UAM, and who are responsible for the proper functioning of the UAM (as determined by a Dean's or Rectorial Resolution). In the case of the Isla de la Juventud, the centers include the University Center "Jesus Montane Oropesa," the University of Pedagogy "Carlos Manual de Cespedes," and the Medical University of the Isla de la Juventud.

The Local Facilities of the UAM (Las Sedes Zonales de las Universidades del Adulto Mayor, or *SeZUAM)* are located in each residential area on the Isla de la Juventud: Gerona, La Fe, and La Demajagua. It is there that the educational process takes place with and for the UAM students, and also where the teachers at the CES act as facilitators, steering that process of human enrichment in accordance with the study plan and in close connection with the assessment of local needs. Such local facilities contribute to the sustained existence of the microuniversities in each area.

Microuniversities, designate the spaces in which the essential part of the educational process takes place for older students; this process is possible thanks to the presence of teachers and tutors there. The CES and the microuniversity are two elements that are closely interconnected without either of them losing its identity. They are functionally integrated; in both, personal components of this educational process are present.

It is obvious that the education of the older adult requires knowledge of this stage of life, appropriate types of classes, the role of the teacher, and objectives of and potential for learning. As Fidel Castro Ruz (2003) has said, "It will be necessary to deepen our knowledge in view of the new realities and circumstances." The present study can be seen as a contribution to the development of andragogy as the science of adult education.

General Characteristics of the Relationship Between Older Adults

Development theorists have not paid much attention to mature adulthood, which is often characterized as a regression since it is marked by losses or problems affecting the sensory and motor systems. Often the older adult is seen as a geriatric patient (University of Havana 2003), and this view has occasionally impacted on relations with older adults. To a certain degree, the reason for this is that the relation between human beings is based on cultural experiences that are passed from generation to generation and on the distinctive characteristics of the time in which the individual lives (characteristics reflected in the beliefs, prejudices, and attitudes shared by different social groups), as well as the individual's expectations, that is, what he or she expects from others and from him- or herself.

Currently a new perspective on mature adulthood is taking shape. Mature adulthood is a stage in life in which one continues to develop one's personality and one's ability to learn. The older adult is a subject undergoing development, a person involved in a process of change and in whom new psychological traits emerge. According to Orosa Fraiz (2000), it is a challenge for specialists to understand psycho-pedagogical development in the aging process, to identify what the social situation is for development among the aged, and to deepen their knowledge of the systems of activity and communication, among other aspects that contribute to the full development of their personality.

It is important to assess how the relation with and among older adults is influenced by the self-transcendence, that is to say, the need that they have to be among others, a need that does not appear in the same way in other stages of life. That is why "others" are required to heighten personal development, and not to constrain it, since especially for the older adult "the other" is often more important than the older adult him- or herself.

In daily interactions with the older adult, we should not be overprotective, nor should we marginalize him or her or emphasize the losses brought on by old age, since this has a negative impact on the image that society, the family, and the older adult have of old age. We cannot allow the deterioration of the image of the older adult, or leave him or her alone with his or her thoughts and anxieties, since he or she could get depressed and become ill. In this sense, specialists on aging contend that images of and negative attitudes towards old age constitute factors of high socio-psychological risk, similar to hypertension in a pregnant woman or the biological effects of low weight on a newborn infant.

It is important to recall, as Jose Ysem de Arce (1999: 4) expresses it in his article on emotional intelligence in the older adult, that "one of the first needs of every human being is to be accepted, loved, embraced, and to belong to something and somebody – all feelings on which self-esteem is based. Self-esteem consists of feeling able, helpful, and dignified. Thus, one cannot talk about self-esteem if the person realizes that others consider him replaceable."

Typically one ignores the fact that communication is the main source of social support required by older adults and that it is a basic component also at this stage of life for their psychological development, for the achievement of their potential. The UAM presents itself as a sphere in which shared educational activity becomes another important factor in development; other students of the same age, the teacher, and the tutor constitute different levels of assistance in the process of learning and unlearning.

The essential objective of the educational process at the UAM is to transform oneself into "another". It broadens the culture of growing old expressed in a higher quality of life and increases the individual's potential for general and integral development. In Cuban pedagogy, one says that teaching guides development – and educational activity is necessarily conductive to development. This saying also applies to adult education, or andragogy, which is why it is still worth:

- Distinguishing between pedagogical and andragogical models. Older adults are people who are passing through a stage of life and who begin their studies at this time; the requirements of their studies must consider their characteristics.
- Starting with what it is necessary to learn at that age and what one wants to learn, both of which are influenced by the personal histories of the older adult students, their experiences and pains, and how they want to learn after unlearning.
- Considering horizontal interpersonal relations, from adult to adult rather than from teacher to students, since they both have knowledge.

- Seeing the teacher as co-facilitator and the older adult student as co-responsible in his or her learning, which is understood as an individual product.
- Developing the educational process as one of orientation/learning, not as teaching/learning.
- Guaranteeing the interaction of participants in a natural alternation of roles.
- Approaching the educational process as a continuum and as self-evaluation and co-evaluation.
- Maintaining the quality of all activities that are engaged in with older adult students.

In view of the foregoing general characteristics of the interaction with older adults, as well as the most common ways of organizing the teaching-educational process in higher education, three years of work with older adult students have led us to identify the *workshop* as the preferred way of organizing the educational process at the UAM.

The Workshop as a Form of Organization of the Educational Process

The workshop is a mode of collective work, one that is not exclusive to the educational process. With some concrete objectives and employing careful methodology, it increases a group's capacity to perform a common task. The workshop is a mode of work that values the knowledge accumulated by each person through his or her own activities; at the same time, it is a place in which to produce knowledge on the basis of the practical and theoretical knowledge that the members of the group have internalized.

Working in workshops presupposes a task taken up by a group of people who assume common objectives; thus, their main feature is their cooperative character. To improve educational practice, cooperation is the main instrument cooperation means addressing a shared task, participating with other people, each of whom assumes part of the collective responsibility.

Our workshops took place not only and not so much with the intention of understanding a particular problematic but to promote the elaboration of separate projects in alternation with increasing success in daily tasks. These workshops were also distinguished by the fact that the techniques and procedures used in them were dynamic and flexible both methodologically and operationally (Lig Long Rangel 2001).

Evaluation of and in the Workshops

From the very beginning, evaluation was understood not as a fragmented process but as a continuum, as a process of dialogue, understanding, and improvement not only of the results but also of the rationality and fairness of the educational activities engaged in. In the course of the workshops, two complementary dimensions were conceived: the systematic or formative evaluation and the final or summary evaluation.

Formative or Systematic Evaluation
In the course of each workshop, opinions and feelings were collected so as to evaluate along the way the content, methodology employed, the participation in, and the quality of the debates. This allowed us to adjust the activities engaged in, with older adult students in the implementation of UAM and to make our initial proposal more flexible.

Final Evaluation
Participatory techniques were used to reflect aloud on the following questions:

- What should be said about the workshops?
- What learning technique should be used?
- What new feelings have surfaced?
- What plans and projects are to be undertaken?
- What points of dissatisfaction, error, or deficiency were found?

The most common responses can be summarized as follows:

What Should be Said about the Workshops:
- Here we could express what we think and feel.
- The workshops were very useful to us and were of high quality.
- It was good, nice, and new to learn together.
- We congratulate the educators that worked with us.
- We want the educators to repeat the workshops.
- Thank you for the solidarity.

What Should be Learned:
- How to face this stage of life with optimism.
- The possibility of achieving harmony in family life without imposing criteria (ways of thinking).
- Respect for the other as a rule for communication and happy coexistence.
- We have much to give to and receive from others, even if they are younger.
- To retire is not to retire from life; it is the beginning of another phase of life.
- How to assert our rights with respect and love.

What New Feelings Have Surfaced:
- Happiness, hope.
- Satisfaction from listening to one another.
- The wish that the workshops would not end.
- Satisfaction with oneself, and pride in what was experienced.
- The realization that we can still learn.

What plans and projects are to be undertaken:
- Register for the available courses next year.
- Do daily exercises.
- Make time for ourselves; go for walks and visit old acquaintances.
- Take care of our health and visit the family doctor.
- Participate in the dance club.

Dissatisfactions, errors, or deficiencies:
- Being absent sometimes.
- Thinking that one has already learned everything over the years.
- The room did not have a blackboard and other means of interaction.
- We could not take things home with us to read.
- At the beginning, we were ashamed to talk and communicate our worries.
- We did not always have our snack.

Despite the quality of each workshop and its acceptance by the older adult students, we noted a limitation in its application, one that should not be underestimated: Not all the instructors (teachers and tutors) were prepared for it; not all were familiar with the characteristics of this stage of life; and in practice some demonstrated incomprehension of their role as facilitators. Rapid preparation was necessary to redress these limitations.

Plan for the Preparation and Improvement of Facilitating Teachers and Tutors

From the beginning our objective was to prepare professionals and academicians to be able to direct and evaluate the integral development of older adults (Sanchez Proenza 2004). At first and due to the fact that the teachers were mainly health-care professionals engaged in medical teaching and some were from other areas, different aspects were stressed in each of the groups of teachers: either pedagogical or socio-medical aspects. Specific objectives focused on the acquisition of information on health, socialization, legal, housing, and other problems that most often concern older adults. This helped to better prepare the teachers for activities focused on development, safety, and health care, as well as those aimed at motivating older adults' capacities for learning and self-management. Such preparation supplied the teachers with information about the policies and services that are directed to meet the demands and needs of older adults.

At this point, the preparation plan corresponded to the program designed for older adult students. Teachers knew the topic beforehand. We knew where to find the information and share it among ourselves. Moreover, each of us went to the workshops as if he or she was one more member of the group. Along the way, we noticed some inconsistencies regarding the roles of teachers and tutors, as well as some shortcomings in the preparation plan. We then worked to reorient our efforts.

Functions of Facilitators (Teachers and Tutors)

Here the facilitators act as role models in the educational process; they instill confidence in the older adult students and act as their guides and supporters, and for that reason the facilitators represent a key element in the process of universalizing the UAM. In this capacity they:

- Participate in the integral characterization and evaluation of older adult students.
- Orient and steer the realization of teaching activities for the actualization and integration of the course content for the geriatric education of older adults, as well as their families and communities.
- Help to ascertain fundamental socio-familial problems in the students' macro- and micro-spheres in keeping with their individual needs and in view of the prospect for their solution by means of the investigation.
- Coordinate the activities required for the welfare of the older adult students with the team of local facilitators and the municipal body that regulates the schools and universities for older adults.
- Assess and control the investigative and extracurricular activities for older adult students in the university program and stimulate exchange of experiences and the presentation of work at meetings.
- Participate in activities designed to prepare teachers and help them to succeed.
- Participate or complete investigations on topics related to the education of older adult students and the aging population.

From the foregoing it should be clear that developing activities that help the local tutors and teachers to improve is necessary so as to assure their preparation to achieve their crucial tasks in this process of pedagogical universalization (Sanchez Proenza 2004).

Interdisciplinary Program for the Preparation of Facilitators

It is assumed that all teachers who have had a higher level education, regardless of their area of specialization, have been sufficiently prepared to perform well, given their knowledge of their field of work and the considerable professional experience they have accumulated therein. However, in their previous training they did not necessarily gain knowledge of how to work with older adult students. It is necessary, therefore, to find ways to supplement their knowledge base in view of both their new task in the context of the universalization of the university and their role as teachers or tutors in their respective facilities.

Introduction

It is well known that older adults can experience various problems – economic or health-related problems, social isolation, inactivity, etc. – that impinge upon their perception of their usefulness and reduce their self-esteem. To resolve these problems, it is necessary that health care institutions and workers, older adults, and the community in general face them in a pro-active way, viewing the problems not merely as difficulties but as opportunities to act.

To do so it is necessary to prepare human resources, particularly the professionals and academics who act as facilitators in the UAM. This is the main objective of the interdisciplinary program, the content of which has been broken up into modules.

Objective of the Program

To prepare the facilitators of the UAM to accomplish their tasks optimally.

Contents

Module 1: The teacher and the tutor, their role as facilitators at the UAM

1. *Foundations of the UAM.* Guiding documents of the study program. Interacting with older adults. Organizational forms of the teaching process. The workshop and techniques of participation. System of evaluation as a process of dialog, understanding, and improvement.
2. *The Teacher and Tutor as Facilitators.* Their functions. Their role in the process of universalization. Joint action with the families' communities, medical doctors, and nurses.
3. *Scientific Activity.* Characteristics of scientific activity on the part of older adults. Final paper. Characteristics and requirements. Supervision of the writing of the paper. Presentation of scientific papers. Communication and/or publication of the results. Educational research. Research projects to be designed and carried out by the teachers and/or tutors.

Module 2: Introduction to gerontology

1. *Introduction to the General Aspects of Social Gerontology.* Socio-cultural aspects of aging. The role of the older adult in different societies. Image and self-image of the aged. Older adults' change of roles; adjustments and readjustments. Older adults and their families. Mistreatment of older adults. Preparation for aging and retirement, gender differences. Importance of social networks and principal support organizations for older adults. Legislation.
2. *Education and Human Development.*The prolongation of life expectancy and its social consequences. Changes in the individual and the needs they generate. Learning throughout life. Human groups and their role as spaces for social learning. Techniques for working in groups and for participation: research as a means to evaluate and improve work with older adults.

3. *Healthy Aging*. Importance of healthy habits in life. Gastrointestinal care; most frequent dental problems. Nutrition. Functionality and autonomy; prevention of accidents and the risks of overmedication. Older adults and sexuality. Biological aging, cognitive deterioration and stimulation, physical activity, and retirement.

Module 3: New computer and telecommunication technologies

1. *Computer Technology*. Its use. The new computer and telecommunication technologies as teaching and work tools. Use of the CD. Use of software in the development of capacities. Networks. Electronic mail. Web pages.
2. *Audiovisual Media*. The screen. The projector. Educational television and video.

Conclusions

In the current situation of the accelerated aging of the Cuban population, it is imperative that a gerontological culture be developed in order to help to increase the general quality of life. The UAM constitutes an educational undertaking that helps to generate attitudes, plans, and programs that offer alternatives to develop such a culture as part of the general culture. The process of universalizing the UAM emphasizes the interrelation between the Centers for Higher Education, the Cuban Workers' Confederation, and the Association of Cuban Educators, as well as between them and the local facilities, which is essential in order to make the facilitators' work viable and to assure that older adults receive good care. In this sense, the preparation and improvement of the facilitators aims at insuring the universalization of the UAM.

Note

This study was translated from the Spanish by Marcus Brainard.

References

Castro Ruz, Fidel. 2001. Discurso pronunciado en el acto de graduación del primer curso emergente de formación de maestros primaries [Speech given on the Occasion of the First Graduation of Primary Teachers]. *Tabloide especial* 4, March: 3.

———. 2003. Discurso pronunciado [Speech]. *Periódico Granma, September 8: 7.*

Central de Trabajadores Cuba (CTC). 2003. Estructura y funcionamiento interno de las Cátedras Universitarias de Adultos Mayore [The Structure and Internal Functioning of Professorships for Universities of Older Adults]. Havana: Ministry of Education.

Lig Long Rangel, Clara. 2001. Talleres de Capacitación Pedagógica [Pedagogical Workshops on Enabling Students]. *Revista Electrónica de Medicina Isla de la Juventud* 2(4).

Orosa Fraiz, Teresa. 2000. La Tercera Edad y la Familia. Una mirada desde el adulto mayor [Senior Citizens and the Family: On the Older Adult]. Havana: Editorial Félix Varela.

Sánchez Proenza, Zenaida. 2004. Formación y superación del personal docente en el proceso de universalización pedagógica: una práctica diferente [The Education and Improvement of Teachers in the Process of Pedagogical Universalization: A Different Approach]. Isla de la Juventud, Cuba: Ministry of Education.

University of Havana. 2003. Encuentro Nacional de Cátedras y Filiales Universitarias de Adultos Mayores [National Conference of Universities of Older Adults and Affiliates]. Havana: Ministry of Education.

Vecino Alegret, Fernando. 2003. Entrevista [Interview]. *Periódico Granma*, December 16: 8.

Ysem de Arce, José. 1999. *Inteligencia emocional en el adulto mayor* [Emotional Intelligence in the Older Adult]. University of Bio-Bio. Paper presented at the International Conference on Senior Citizens in November in Talos, Chile.

The Authors

Clara Lig Long Rangel has a Masters of Education from the Pedagogical University of Enrique José Varona in Cuba. She holds a chair in adult education at the Medical University of the Isla de la Juventud. She is the president of the Isla de la Juventud branch of the Association of Cuban Educators (APC), a non-profit NGO. She has addressed guidance and links between education and work, didactics and pedagogy in her work.

Contact address: Universidad Pedagógica y Facultad de Ciencias Méldica, Isla de la Juventud, República de Cuba. E-mail: clara@ahao.ijv.sld.cu.

Antonia Zenaida Sánchez Proenza holds a Masters of Education from the Pedagogical University of Enrique José Varona in Cuba. She is Adjunct Professor and Deputy Director of Research and Postgraduate Studies at the Pedagogical University of Carlos Manuel de Céspedes, Isla de la Juventud. Her research interests cover the nexus between education and work, didactics and biology. She is currently working on teacher education and higher education.

Contact address: Universidad Pedagógica y Facultad de Ciencias Méldica, Isla de la Juventud, República de Cuba. E-mail: fcmij@infomed.sld.cu.

QUALITY AND EQUITY IN EARLY CHILDHOOD CARE IN PERU

REGINA MOROMIZATO IZU

Abstract – The present study examines educational policy documents and programs on early childhood development and education in Peru. The author provides an evaluation of early childhood learning programs and their outcomes in different education centers in Peru. Health, nutrition, development, and participation are identified as key areas of concern. The study concludes with a reference to the importance of monitoring quality and equity in early childhood care.

Zusammenfassung – QUALITÄT UND CHANCENGLEICHHEIT IN DER FRÜHKINDLICHEN PFLEGE IN PERU – Die vorliegende Studie untersucht Dokumente zur Bildungspolitik sowie Programme zur frühkindlichen Entwicklung und Erziehung in Peru. Die Autorin bietet eine Auswertung von Programmen zum frühkindlichen Lernen sowie deren Ergebnisse in verschiedenen Bildungszentren in Peru. Gesundheit, Ernährung, Entwicklung und Teilhabe werden als Schlüsselthemen identifiziert. Die Studie schließt mit einem Verweis auf die wichtige Bedeutung der Überprüfung von Qualität und Chancengleichheit in der frühkindlichen Pflege.

Résumé – QUALITÉ ET ÉQUITÉ DANS L'ASSISTANCE À LA PRIME ENFANCE AU PÉROU – La présente étude examine les documents et les programmes de la politique éducative pour l'éducation et le développement de la prime enfance au Pérou : L'auteur fournit une évaluation des programmes d'apprentissage de la prime enfance et de leurs résultats dans différents centres d'éducation au Pérou. Santé, nutrition, développement et participation sont identifiés comme des domaines clefs de préoccupation. L'étude conclut sur une référence à l'importance de la qualité et de l'équité de l'encadrement dans l'assistance à la prime enfance.

Resumen – CALIDAD E IGUALDAD DE OPORTUNIDADES EN LA ATENCIÓN DE LA PRIMERA INFANCIA EN PERÚ – Este trabajo examina documentos y programas educativos sobre el desarrollo y la educación de la primera infancia en Perú. La autora proporciona una evaluación de los programas de aprendizaje para la primera infancia y de sus resultados en diferentes centros de enseñanza de Perú. La salud, la nutrición, el desarrollo y la participación se han identificado como áreas de importancia central. El estudio termina indicando cuán importante es controlar la calidad y la igualdad de oportunidades en la atención de la primera infancia.

Резюме – ПРОБЛЕМА КАЧЕСТВА И РАВЕНСТВА В ВОСПИТАНИИ ДЕТЕЙ В РАННЕМ ВОЗРАСТЕ В ПЕРУ – В данном исследовании изучаются документы об образовательной политике и программы по раннему развитию ребенка и его воспитанию в Перу. Автор статьи предлагает оценку программ по раннему обучению детей и их результаты в разных образовательных центрах Перу. Здоровье, питание, развитие и участие определяются как ключевые проблемные области. Исследование завершается ссылкой на важность мониторинга качества и равенства в раннем детском воспитании.

J. Zajda (ed.), Education and Social Justice, 175-189.

There have been non-conventional childhood care programs in Peru since the 1970s. They have evolved over the years, having adjusted to the different realities and requirements of each region in the country. After more than 30 years of activity on this front, it is instructive to reflect on where the programs have succeeded, as well as where they have fallen short, in order to generate new proposals concerning childhood care as a foundation for social development, proposals based on the premise that it is necessary to invest in quality programs focused on early childhood, especially for those young children who are living in adverse circumstances.

In the present study, I begin by providing a brief overview of the focus on development, the programs geared to young children, and the relation of these programs to social changes – especially in the family – that have occurred in Peru in the last decades and that have led to the creation of viable non-conventional programs in early childhood care which have the potential to grow and which cost less than their conventional counterparts, while not necessarily being of lesser quality. Then I shall sketch the Strategy of Integral and Integrated Childhood Care, which has been implemented in the National Program to Assist Children – Wawa Wasi; it is a strategy that has grown out of lessons learned and the identification of successful approaches. The guiding assumption in what follows is that all this is important for the implementation of new approaches to early childhood care.

The Focus on Early Childhood Care

The focus on development evolved over the course of the last century and into the present. During the first half of the 20th century, and especially after the global crisis of the 1930s, the main concern was to encourage growth in the industrial sector by replacing imports. The assumption was that economic development would result in the development of countries.

However, in the 1970s it became clear that the achievement of high growth rates did not necessarily lead to an increase in people's quality of life. As a result, new indicators for measuring the level of quality of life – such as mortality, child mortality, and years of schooling – began to receive more attention.

These indicators have made it possible to gain real insight into the situation in which our children find themselves, despite the fact that in many countries data is scarce on children below 5 years of age. Due to the new indicators, quantitative issues have been given more weight, and qualitative aspects intimately connected with the conditions bearing on children's survival, especially those children who live in sectors with the highest poverty, have been set aside.

Nonetheless, the focus on human and social development has given rise to profound reflection on our concept of the child. In the 1960s, children were seen as a human resource in which it was necessary to invest in order to secure efficient, productive agents for the country's continued growth. Together with such concepts of development, the reflection on the child has evolved so as to accommodate positions that express concern for the whole, integral, and harmonious development of children – that is, concern for the child him- or herself, the child seen as a subject with rights and not only as an "economic" investment in the future. Reflection on the evolution of these concepts is important since they are determinants and benchmarks in the design of childhood care programs.

But how have such programs evolved? In Latin America, many have gone through a phase of "state assistance", which began after the economic crisis in the 1930s, when a great deal of attention was paid to the health and nutrition of the children of working mothers. After the 1950s, due to the focus on economic growth and the emphasis on education, the expression "educational" *(educativa)* gained currency; many preschools were founded that aimed at helping children aged 3–6 years to prepare for primary school. (In Peru the expression "preschool" [*preescolar*] has since been rejected; instead, "primary school" [*inicial*] is used, because it is meant to be preparation for life and not just for getting into school.) However, due to the cost of running those preschools, it was not possible to meet the demand for childhood care, nor was it a model that could be replicated in areas with limited resources.

In view of the guidelines for the equity and democratization of education, some non-conventional educational programs were expanded which were designed as effective and less costly alternatives for people in greater need. This resulted in many alternatives being offered in the region which ranged from programs that gave help of some kind (say, regarding nutrition or health) to programs that involved more integral services. There were also programs that involved the whole community, as well as programs that have not succeeded in working with the community. This state of affairs is worrisome, for, because only the mother or her proxy is involved, and not the nuclear family, the effort remains partial.

The National Action Plan for Children was elaborated after the 1990 World Summit for Children in New York and established the goal of a 10% increase in programs for children between 6 months and 3 years of age. Likewise, due to the current policy – sponsored by UNESCO in light of the 1980 World Conference on Education for All in Jomtien – of extending childhood care to the age of 5 years, some classes have been created for 5-year-olds at many schools, thereby increasing participation to 75% of children in this age group. There has not been such growth in the provision of services for children under 3 years of age.

In this connection, the Peruvian Ministry for Women and Social Development (MIMDES-Peru) has implemented the National Program to Assist Children – Wawa Wasi, which is currently helping some 40,000 children between the ages of 6 months and 4 years who are living in precarious situations and/or in poverty. To this end, a strategy of integral and integrated childhood care has been introduced which draws on the reflections and learning experiences from over 30 years of conducting alternative or non-conventional early childhood care programs.

Integral and Integrated Childhood Care in the Wawa Wasi Program

Through the implementation of multiple strategies, and thanks to the organizational capacity of the management committee, as well as to the extremely valuable help of caregiving mothers with some technical assistance from local teams seeking to deliver quality care, the Wawa Wasi program seeks to foster the human and social development of children. With this focus, the Wawa Wasi program's strategy of integral childhood care follows the guiding principles set out in the National Action Plan for Children 2002–2010:

Equal Opportunity for All

The strategies that have been developed to provide children with integral and integrated childhood care have as their main objective the achievement of the full development of the children's capacities, while trying to minimize the effects of poverty. For this reason, articulating the action points in health, nutrition, childhood education, and child-rearing are fundamental in order to provide the opportunities and conditions that children require to grow and develop into healthy and happy individuals.

Give Priority to Children as Subjects with Rights and Sustainers of Development

Talking about human and social development in early childhood programs implies a different way of understanding children. That is why the strategies that have been promoted for integral childhood care are rooted in the firm conviction that children have the right to receive quality care in health, nutrition, and education, as well as to have a family and a community that provides them with protection and love, and that the strategies are appropriate for their age and socio-cultural context.

Increased Interest in the Child and its Right to Participate

The strategies that have been developed place special emphasis on caring for the welfare of children who participate in the program. Wawa Wasi (children's homes) are not physical spaces in which children are "kept." On the contrary, they are physical, emotional, and social spaces in which children find satisfaction for their basic needs: rest, food, play, love, care, and protection. And they are also spaces in which children have the opportunity to interact with a loving adult, other children, and different materials that allow them the free exploration that optimizes the learning process.

The Family as the Fundamental Institution for the Development of the Human Being

To include child-rearing in the strategy of integral childhood care implies the acknowledgment of the role family members, and especially parents, play as primary agents responsible for the child's welfare. Thus, it is necessary to engage in coordinated work along the lines of a Wawa Wasi – a home that contributes to the achievement of positive results in child development.

Integral and Integrated Childhood Care from an Ecological View of Human Development

> Adequate childhood care must begin in the family, the community, and institutions. Thus, integral childhood care during the early years proves to be an essential strategy for the fight against poverty, because it helps children to overcome the vicious cycle that reproduces, diversifies, and makes poverty more complex. From this perspective, early integral childhood care is not only a strategy for increasing the degree of child development; it is much more than that it: is a strategy for achieving the human and social development of a country, a strategy that promotes the construction of new relationships, organizational forms, values, and norms (Adapted from Myers 1995).

From the perspective of child development focused on human and social development, it is important to understand the multiple variables that are interrelated and that affect child development positively or negatively.

When we talk about human and social development, we are referring to the full development of the human being, his or her possibility of transcendence, the humanization and recognition of the human being as a social being by nature that needs others in order to survive and develop. In this framework, childhood care does not take place in an isolated physical, emotional, and social space; rather, the child is part of a family, a community, and a cultural system that he or she will come to know and whose values, habits, beliefs, etc., he or she will progressively internalize.

We believe that the ecological perspective on human development, whose main representative is Urie Bronfenbrenner, provides a better understanding of the dynamics of systems and the relationships among them. It grants an important role in child development to the environment, which comprises four systems or "nested structures." In the following figure, the ecological perspective is applied to the Wawa Wasi program so as to illustrate the systems involved therein (Figure 1).

We regard the child as a social being who develops in contact and direct interaction with his primary environment: his or her home and family. The relationship between the primary caregiver and the child forms the *microsystem*, but this is influenced by the presence and participation of other relatives,

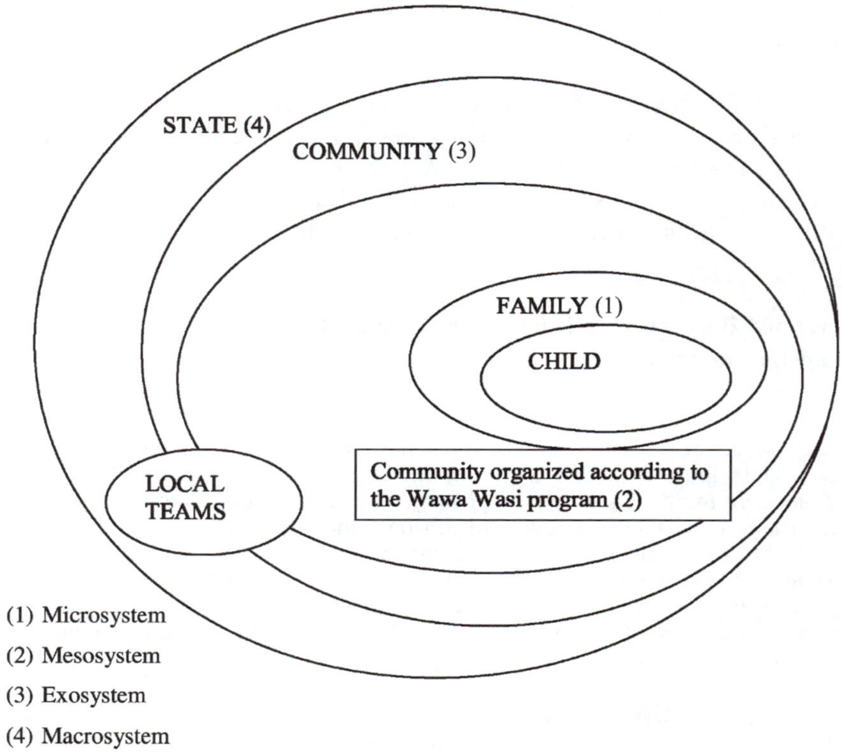

Figure 1. The Wawa Wasi from an ecological perspective

friends, and neighbors, who make up an informal social support network, the *mesosystem*, in which bilateral relationships are established.

It is at this level that the relationship of mothers as caregivers and other members of the immediate community to the child are located. We know that children involved in the Wawa Wasi program spend a considerable part of their day there building up the confidence and security they need to develop adequately in different areas of their lives.

But the work that is done in the Wawa Wasi is not sufficient on its own; parents and family in general also must participate in the rearing and education of their children since, as was noted above, the family is the primary environment that influences human development.

Within the *exosystem* we find factors that affect and interact with the first two levels – for instance, the economic and working conditions of the members of the community in which the children live, social services in the community, mass media, and other legally established structures.

Finally, the *macrosystem* is formed by a culture's models, beliefs, and ideologies, which permit the continuity of values that sustain social organization.

From this perspective, we can say that the intervention carried out in the program is not only *integral* but also *integrated.* This obliges us to have an interdisciplinary view of the problematic of the child in Peru.

In talking about *integral childhood care*, we have in mind care that aims at achieving the *integral development* of the child from a holistic and comprehensive perspective. In this respect, it is necessary to point out that child development is conceived of as the progressive building-up of the properly human functions (language, reasoning, memory, care, esteem). It is the process in which the capacities of human beings are initiated, the process in which there is a series of qualitative jumps that lead from lesser capacity (more dependence, fewer possibilities of response) to greater capacity (more autonomy, more possibilities to solve problems, to be creative, etc.) (Bassedas et al. 1998).

This definition has the following components:

Acknowledgment of All Dimensions of Child Development in Our Intervention

We regard the child as a complete being who evolves in an integrated manner. However, for methodological reasons and to explain concepts, we can grasp the development as a system with different subsystems that constitute different dimensions of the development, such as motor, cognitive, affective, communicative, and social dimensions. At each stage, all the capacities of the human being come into play, and there are synergies between them. Thus, we maintain that a person's capacities act as a whole: if something affects one capacity, the effect will also be observed in the others.

Understand the Complexity of Child Development

We start by recognizing the double meaning of development: as process and as system (Ghersi 2003). In talking about process, we are referring to the move towards higher and more complex levels of organization presented in a sequential manner. In talking about system, we are referring to the necessary interactions between different subsystems and processes, their interdependence and reciprocal effects in childhood development, which establish a close relationship between maturation, learning, and development.

Identification of Factors that Aid in the Healthy Development of Children

We agree with the interactionist position, which affirms that psychological processes are enabled by the genes that differentiate us as members of the human species, being framed by a calendar of maturation that establishes that some acquisitions are possible at certain points in time if and only if the relationships and interactions of the person with his or her environment allow it. This leads us to talk of the existence of specific and strategic moments for acquiring certain abilities, especially during the first years of life. It is absolutely necessary to ensure that this calendar of maturation is not altered and that the children are healthy and have good nutrition, since these are basic conditions for the development of capacities and the acquisition of new abilities.

Understanding child development in its complexity in relation to the factors that condition it is the first step that allows us to talk of *integrated childhood care*, that is to say, the integration of different strategies that have been developed in the areas of health, nutrition, and education in coordination with families and communities and with the aim of generating synergies to achieve the human and social development of the children participating in the Wawa Wasi program.

Identifying the factors and implementing strategies that favor child development in Peru requires an interdisciplinary and intercultural perspective. Keeping in mind the factors that influence development in general terms, we nevertheless do not lose sight of the particularities of each region in Peru, especially when implementing the strategies of care for our children. These factors are related to biology, physiology, and psychology, as well as to the environment. They do not act in isolation; they "mix" with and influence one another. Nowadays they are called epigenetic variables because in them factors of both a biological and an environmental character flow together.

Biological, physiological, and psychological factors are directly associated with the growth and maturation of the various structures and systems of our organism that enable us to survive and adapt to our environment. In the case of the Wawa Wasi program, we stress the fundamental role that the subcomponents of health since they nutrition play, since they contribute to children's good health and thereby generate the biophysiological conditions that will allow them to acquire different abilities. It is necessary to continually monitor nutrition, diseases, and health since they affect child development. In the case of early childhood education, the strategies employed respect the child's process of maturation and try not to violate or overburden his or her capacities, taking care not to alter his or her nervous system and normal neurological functioning. In the case of child-rearing, it is vital to work with the families to improve approaches to child-rearing that are directly related to the child's physical and mental health.

Regarding *environmental factors*, we refer to the context in which the child lives, the interrelations established between him or her and other people, objects, and different situations and experiences to which the child is exposed. Environmental factors exert a strong influence on the development of abilities and the acquisition of knowledge. That is why the subcomponents of early childhood education and child-rearing involve strategies that are strongly linked to the conditions of the environment, socialization, and relationships that children have to develop optimally. Both subcomponents are strengthened by the subcomponents of health and nutrition in relation to the promotion and prevention of diseases, the generation of healthy spaces, and the diffusion of good practices of child-rearing.

Although each of these aspects emphasizes some subcomponent or other, that does not mean that the strategies and actions implemented are partial. It is precisely the understanding of the complexity of child development that enables us to observe that biological, physiological, psychological, and environmental aspects are not independent but interrelated. Thus, childhood care has to be *integral* and *integrated.*

The Office for Integral Childhood Care

The most significant problems that the children in question here face are: (1) bad conditions of basic hygiene, (2) high rates of disease, (3) a higher rate than the national average of acute malnutrition, (4) deficits in their relationship to objects, fine motor skills, and communication, (5) inadequate practices of child-rearing, and (6) low parent participation in childhood care in the Wawa Wasi.

The Office for Integral Childhood Care (*Unidad de Atención integral*) stresses the need to work jointly and has designed an integrated approach that allows multidisciplinary teams to find points of convergence for the different strategies that have been implemented in each of the subcomponents of health, nutrition, early childhood learning, and child-rearing, with the aim of generating synergies that optimize time, effort, and resources and thereby guarantee quality and improvement in child development.

The logic of generating an integrated intervention is based on the factors that influence child development; for instance, if children have health problems, it will be difficult for them to improve their state of nutrition, which will affect in turn their success in learning. A vicious circle will arise that will affect the extent to which they are able to develop their capabilities. For that reason, four challenges are presented below that in practice work in parallel and point towards the same aim of human and social development (Table 1).

In Figure 2, it can be observed that each challenge builds on the preceding one, where efforts are directed towards the human and social development of the children participating in the Wawa Wasi program.

The adequate implementation of strategies aligned with each of these challenges requires that one rely on an organized community (component of community management), the existence of processes for the development of

Table 1. Four Challenges

Challenge 1:	Improve the conditions of basic hygiene and generate adequate health practices.
Challenge 2:	Improve child nutrition.
Challenge 3:	Increase development levels and generate adequate conditions for learning.
Challenge 4:	Encourage the active and committed participation of parents.

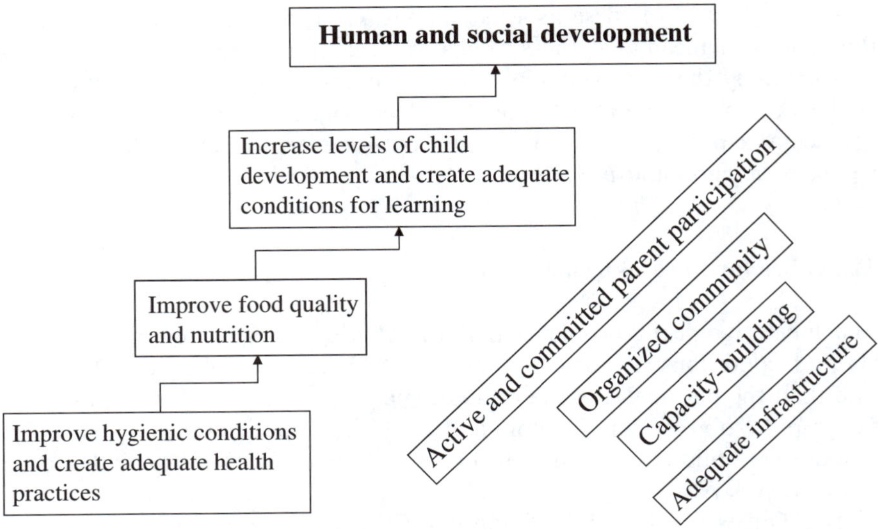

Figure 2. Logic of integrated intervention

capacities for those involved in the implementation of strategies (component of enabling capacities), and an infrastructure that guarantees the minimal conditions for the operation of the Wawa Wasi and related nutritional services (component of infrastructure). From this general scheme, different strategies are articulated for each of the challenges, as Figures 3–6 indicate.

Challenge 1: Improve the Conditions of Basic Hygiene and Adequate Health Practices.

In this figure, at issue is the healthy focus on aspects linked to the environment in which children develop. With this view of people's health and the subcomponent of child-rearing, different strategies of promotion and prevention regarding the implementation of healthy spaces for and practices of child-rearing were implemented (Figure 3).

Another aspect linked to this healthy focus bears on food safety; it involves availability, access, and care in the preparation and consumption of food. These basic aspects guarantee adequate nutritional care.

Challenge 2: Improve Child Nutrition

Aspects to be emphasized in the formulation of Challenge 2 include the implementation of appropriate methodologies for different age groups. This

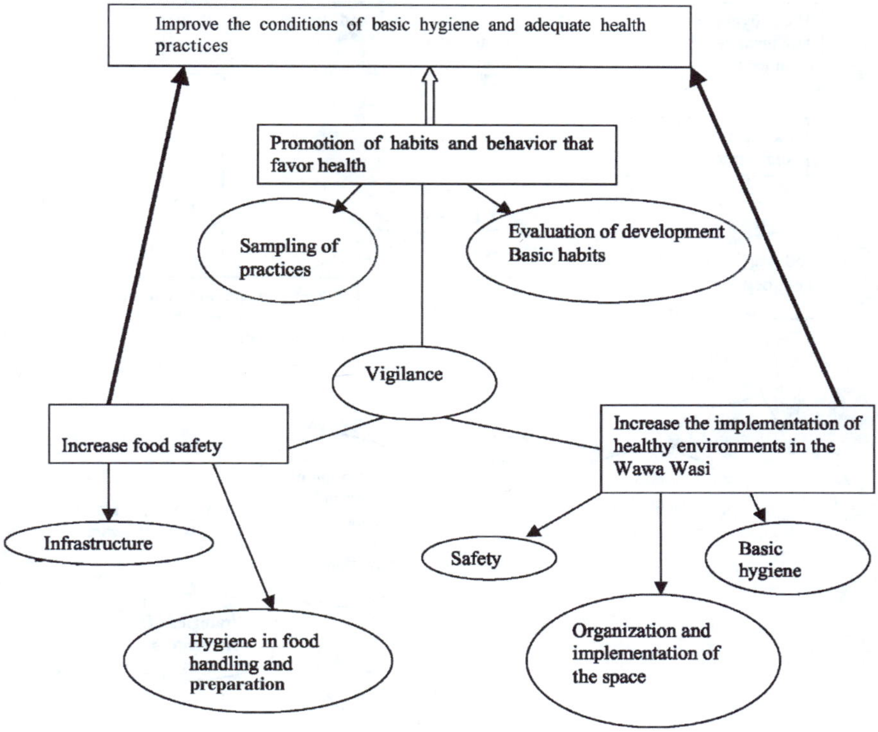

Figure 3. Improve the conditions of basic hygiene and adequate health practices

involves not only meeting children's nutritional needs but also giving children the appropriate amount of food, as well as using food typical of each region (Figure 4).

Among the intervention strategies for children with problems of malnutrition in the program are: active nutrition to guarantee that they eat their food, the introduction of more calories into their diet, the promotion of healthy eating habits, and the coordination with the Ministry of Health for the treatment of childhood diseases.

Challenge 3: Increase Development Levels and Create Adequate Conditions for Learning

With respect to Challenge 3, the strategy of early childhood education that has been implemented since 2003 is interesting. Here a system of evalution has been developed that measures the success in learning and the effects of the educational strategy (Figure 5).

One of the advances made with this strategy is the use of interactive panels as a simplified instrument of evaluation that enables caregiving mothers

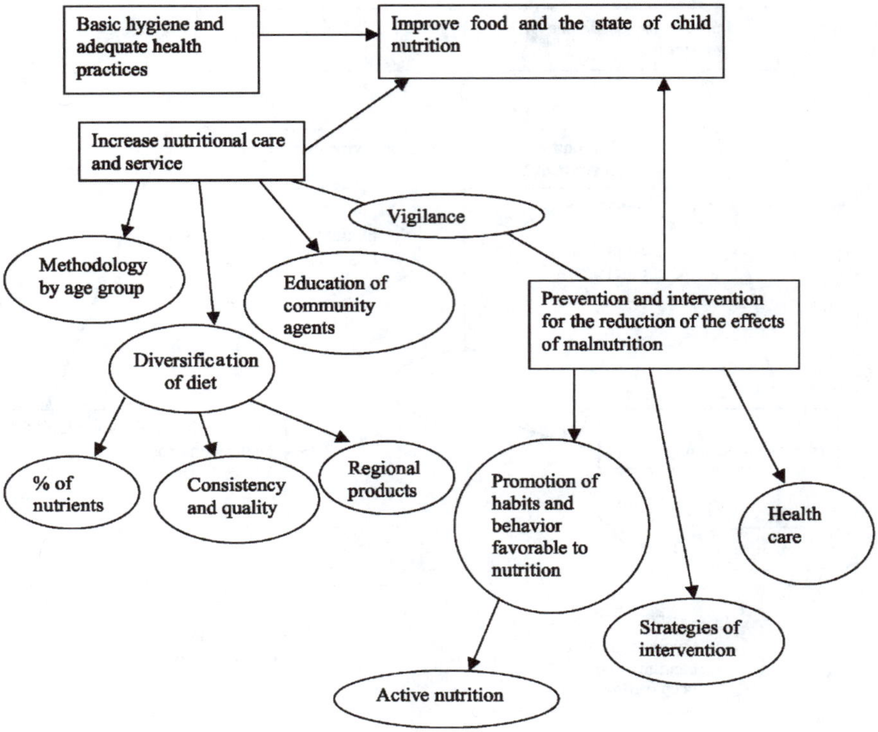

Figure 4. Improve child nutrition

the opportunity to participate in the monitoring of childhood development. Another aspect to be highlighted is the concept of an educational strategy that recovers the active role of the child, strengthening the value of play as a means of socialization and learning.

The matrix of articulation allows local teams to plan strategies to be employed in the Wawa Wasi, which implies strategies that strengthen basic habits of nutrition and hygiene and form rotating modules that encourage children to explore different materials freely.

Challenge 4: Encourage the Active and Committed Participation of Parents

Challenge 4 is vital to the achievement of the objectives proposed in the program and is closely linked to the work with the families using the program. Through this challenge, strategies for promotion and prevention are developed using non-formal means of communication, such as community theaters and counseling done by the caregiving mothers (Figure 6).

The sampling and collection of child-rearing practices at the national level will allow us to learn more about the ideas, beliefs, and myths that different

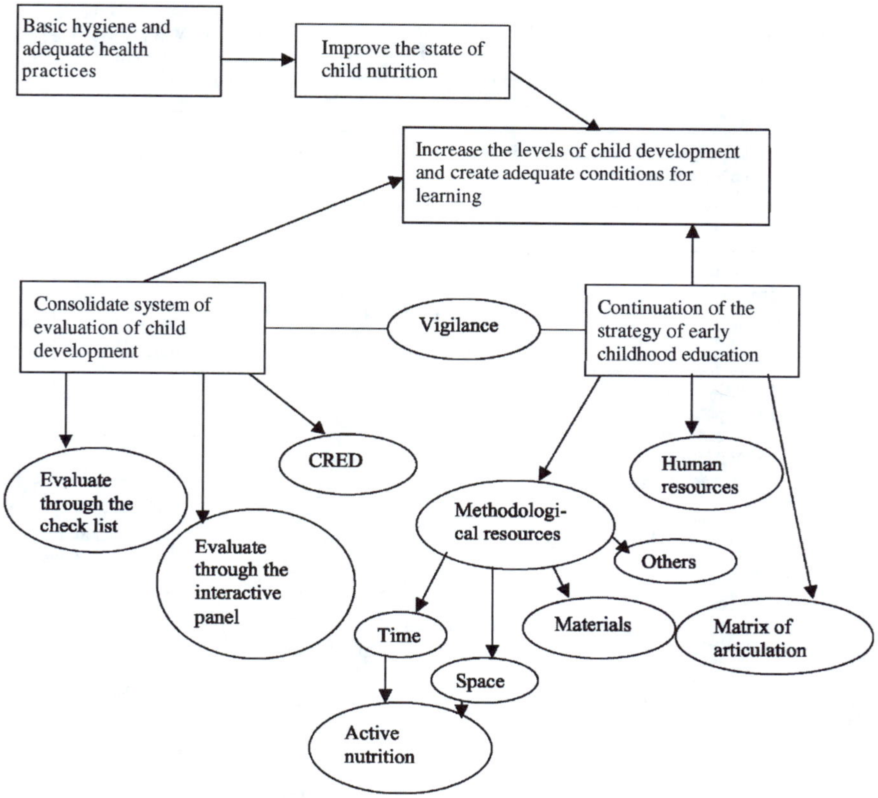

Figure 5. Increase development levels and create adequate conditions for learning

communities have with respect to childhood education. This will provide a frame of reference for identifying benchmarks and generating a constructive response aimed at promotion and prevention.

Another important aspect is the formation of family networks with the aim of supporting the strategies developed in the Wawa Wasi.

Towards Quality Care ... for Life

Talk about quality with regard to social programs, such as the Wawa Wasi program, remains ambiguous, confusing, and imprecise, since it is not sufficient simply to import this from quantitative logic, but above all requires a qualitative perspective.

In quantitative terms, quality refers to aspects linked to the accomplishment of objectives from a cost-benefit perspective. This is valid and important in order to control the investment in resources employed on behalf of

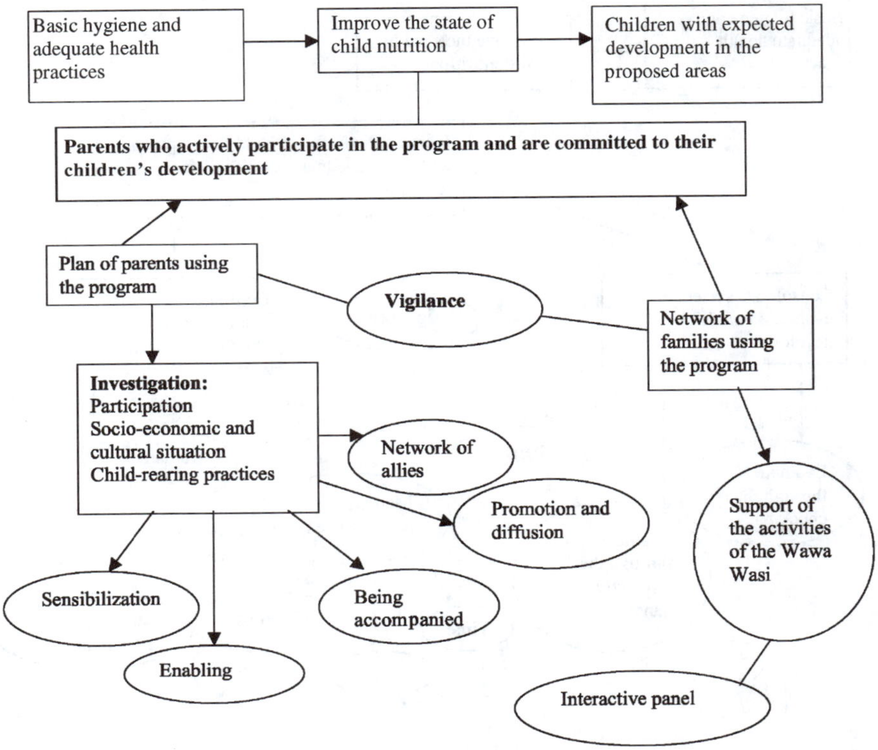

Figure 6. Encourage the active and committed participation of parents

the communities. But quality in purely qualitative terms is even more complex, though indispensable when working with human beings, since it provides us with important data about the population for which we are caring. It is necessary to know not only the percentage of children that have some type of malnutrition, but also who they are, how they live, and the conditions in which they have to survive, how they build up relationships, which ideas or beliefs their parents have about how to rear and educate them, etc.

Taking quantitative together with qualitative data will allow us to create, adjust, and strengthen the strategies we have been promoting. That is why regional centers inform central headquarters each quarter about the progress in each regarding the four challenges mentioned above. (Each challenge has a series of indicators on which the regional centers report quarterly. These are processed and analyzed in a way that allows the optimization of resources for monitoring the centers.) These reports make it possible to complement the monitoring system and allow the Office for Integral Childhood Care – Technical Office for Operations, together with the local centers, to search for and develop better alternative solutions to those unsolved difficulties. Although the data reflected in each quarterly report are quantitative, they enable the search for qualitative aspects. It is then possible to establish a relationship between multiple variables that allow us in turn to understand the progress in and the limits to achieving the objectives.

Finally, in monitoring quality we especially have to emphasize *vigilance*, a term that appears in all the schemes presented in the foregoing. This remains the responsibility of all parties – community agents (Vigilance Board, Management Committee), caregiving mothers, and families, the local teams with respect to how the Wawa Wasi are working, nutritional and general management services, the Office for Coordination, and society in general – involved in the program for childhood development, since the care for and welfare of our children is a responsibility we all share.

Notes

This study was translated from the Spanish by Marcus Brainard.

References

Bassedas, Eulalia, Teresa Huguet, and Isabel Solé. 1998. *Aprender y enseñar en educación infantil* [*Learning and Teaching in Child Education*]. Barcelona: Grao.

Ghersi, Ethel. 2003. Desarrollo Infantil [Child Development]. Working paper for the class "Estimulación Temprana 1" [Early Childhood Stimulation I] at the Pontificia Universidad Católica del Perú (PUCP).

Myers, Robert. 1995. *The Twelve Who Survive: Strengthening Programmes of Early Childhood Development in the Third World*, 2nd ed. Ypsilanti, MI: High Scope Press.

The Author

Regina Moromizato Izu holds a Masters in Social Management from the Pontificia Universidad Católica of Peru and is pursuing doctoral studies in childhood, youth, and social sciences at the Universidad Manizales – CINDE (Colombia). She is currently teaching in alternative early childhood programs at the Pontificia Universidad Católica of Peru. She has conducted various research projects and consulting work for government agencies concerning programs bearing on early childhood, the family, and the community.

Contact address: Facultad de Educación, Pontificia Universidad Católica de Peru, Lima, Peru. E-mail: rmoromi@pucp.edu.pe

CULTURAL COMPLEXITY, POST-COLONIALISM AND EDUCATIONAL CHANGE: CHALLENGES FOR COMPARATIVE EDUCATORS

ANNE HICKLING-HUDSON

Abstract – This study explores various elements in the struggle for a post-colonial refashioning of cultural identity through education. Drawing on experiences in Australia and the Caribbean, the author illustrates how educational systems undergoing decolonisation reflect socio-cultural tensions of race and power. The author discusses the complexities for comparative educators in engaging with suppressed knowledge, recognising the yearnings of the marginalised, challenging the conditions that lead to poverty, and refashioning education for social justice in an era when the achievement of justice seems increasingly difficult. She argues that comparative educators can benefit from using post-colonial thinking to understand cultural complexity and promote life-affirming practices in educational change.

Zusammenfassung – KULTURELLE KOMPLEXITÄT, POSTKOLONIALISMUS UND PÄDAGOGISCHE VERÄNDERUNG: HERAUSFORDERUNGEN FÜR VERGLEICHENDE PÄDAGOGEN – Diese Studie erforscht verschiedene Bestandteile im Kampf um eine postkoloniale Neugestaltung von kultureller Identität durch Bildung. Unter Bezugnahme auf Erfahrungen in Australien und dem karibischen Raum illustriert die Autorin, wie Bildungssysteme unter dem Einfluss der Entkolonialisierung soziokulturelle Probleme wie Rassenspannungen und Machtstrukturen widerspiegeln. Die Autorin diskutiert die Schwierigkeiten für vergleichende Pädagogen darin, mit unterdrücktem Wissen umzugehen; darin, die Bedürfnisse derer, die gesellschaftlich am Rand stehen, wahrzunehmen; darin, den Bedingungen, die zur Armut führen, entgegenzutreten; und darin, die Bildung für soziale Gerechtigkeit in einem Zeitalter neu zu gestalten, in dem die Durchsetzung von Gerechtigkeit zunehmend schwierig erscheint. Sie legt dar, dass vergleichende Pädagogen aus der Nutzung von postkolonialen Denkweisen profitieren können, um kulturelle Komplexität zu verstehen und lebensbejahende Praktiken in der Veränderung des Bildungswesens voranzutreiben.

Résumé – COMPLEXITÉ CULTURELLE, POSTCOLONIALISME ET CHANGEMENT ÉDUCATIF : LES DÉFIS POUR LES ÉDUCATEURS COMPARÉS – Cette étude explore les éléments divers de la bataille pour un remodellement postcolonial de l'identité culturelle à travers l'éducation. Se basant sur des expériences en Australie et aux Antilles, l'auteur illustre comment les systèmes éducatifs sous-tendant la décolonisation reflètent les tensions socio-culturelles de races et de pouvoir. L'auteur discute des difficultés pour les éducateurs comparés à s'engager pour des savoirs étouffés, à reconnaître les désirs ardents des marginaux, à défier les conditions qui mènent à la pauvreté, à remodeler l'éducation en faveur de la justice sociale dans une époque où l'obtention de la justice semble extraordinairement difficile. Elle soutient que les

J. Zajda (ed.), Education and Social Justice, 191-208.

éducateurs comparés peuvent tirer profit d'un usage de la pensée post-coloniale afin de comprendre la complexité culturelle et de promouvoir des pratiques soutenant la vie au sein d'un changement éducatif.

Résumen – COMPLEJIDAD CULTURAL, POST-COLONIALISMO Y CAMBIO EDUCATIVO: RETOS PARA EDUCADORES COMPARATIVOS – El presente estudio explora diversos elementos de la lucha por una recomposición postcolonial de la identidad cultural a través de la educación. Haciendo referencia a experiencias hechas en Australia y el Caribe, la autora ilustra cómo los sistemas educativos que están pasando por la descolonisación reflejan las tensiones socioculturales de raza y poder. La autora expone las complejidades que tienen que encarar los educadores comparativos al enfrentarse con conocimientos reprimidos, reconocer las demandas de los marginados, desafiar las condiciones que causan pobreza y recomponer la educación para lograr la justicia social en una era donde conseguir justicia parece ser cada vez más difícil. La autora sostiene que a los educadores comparativos les podría resultar beneficioso utilizar un pensamiento postcolonial para comprender la complejidad cultural y para promover prácticas que mejoren la calidad de vida en el cambio educativo.

Резюме – КУЛЬТУРНАЯ МНОГОГРАННОСТЬ, ПОСТ-КОЛОНИАЛИЗМ И ОБРАЗОВАТЕЛЬНЫЕ ПЕРЕМЕНЫ: ВЫЗОВЫ КОМПАРАТИВНЫМ ИССЛЕДОВАТЕЛЯМ В СФЕРЕ ОБРАЗОВАНИЯ – В данном исследовании изучаются раличные способы пост-колониального изменения культурной идентичности с помощью образования. Основываясь на опыте Австралии и Карибского региона, автор статьи иллюстрирует, как образовательные системы, претерпевающие деколонизацию, отражают социо-культурные трения, возникающие между той или иной расой и властью. Автор статьи обсуждает трудности, стоящие перед компаративными исследователями, которые заключаются в неполной информации о знаниях, определении и признании маргинальных групп, изменении условий, ведущих к бедности, и изменении образования для социальной справедливости в эпоху, когда достижение справедливости кажется все более трудным. Автор статьи утверждает, что компаративные исследователи могут использовать пост-колониальное мышление, чтобы лучше понимать культурную многогранность и поддерживать жизнеутверждающий опыт в образовательных переменах.

Imagine images of the British Queen, a mahogany sculpture of an African head, and the Jamaican singer Bob Marley with his flowing dreadlocks. What could the three possibly have in common? In the present contribution, I explore the tensions and complexities of the struggle for a post-colonial refashioning of identity that are suggested by these images. They are pictures on three Jamaican postage stamps. The Queen, the dreadlocked Bob Marley, and the mahogany head sculpted by Edna Manley symbolise Caribbean tensions and contestations over identities and directions. Some Jamaicans still idolise the British monarchy and the perceived stability of colonial rule. Others contest the racism and oppression of that history by means of art that celebrates the African characteristics that used to be despised, and through songs articulating suffering, resistance, hope and liberation. The art and the music are two of many strands in the movement to reclaim pride in black culture and to struggle against imperialism, racism and injustice (Nettleford 1978). Such contestations spill over into the educational systems of postcolonial societies, be they mainly 'White', 'Black', 'Asian' or multi-racial. The pictures on the stamps remind us of the legacies of 'whiteness' and its 'others' with all the overlapping connotations of authoritarianism and complicity, desire and repulsion, safety and danger, apathy and resistance, dogmatism and ambivalence. In these debates, born of the hybridity of post-colonial culture, the protagonists are multiracial. The sculptress Edna Manley and the singer Bob Marley are both of Jamaican-English parentage. Caribbean and other post-colonial societies are thoroughly 'Creole' – culturally and racially mixed over centuries of interaction.

My argument is that using a post-colonial framework to analyse this cultural complexity is a key to helping students and researchers explore education in a way that recognises and escapes colonised frames of thinking. I explore how disadvantaging structures continue to perpetuate inequities through schooling, and I discuss change approaches from incremental to revolutionary. The context is that of considering how the fresh currents of thinking in comparative education can help us to recognise, explore and disrupt entrenched preconceptions that may be limiting our possibilities for changing in the directions that would create more equitable societies in a globalising world culture.

Some researchers who explore post-colonial theory in comparative education studies are scholars whose lives have been shaped by post-colonialism, either in the sense of having lived in a former colony and through its decolonisation process, or of having lived in a metropolitan centre in the morally problematic situation of being beneficiaries of the gains of empire. They foreground the struggles of decolonisation in education, and the views and voices traditionally seen as belonging to the 'other'. They call for analytical attention to culture and the texts and discourses of teaching and learning, and engage with views of education that contest the modernist paradigm. My outlook stems from my being a product of the global currents of colonialism, decolonisation and post-colonialism. My homeland, Jamaica, became independent in 1962, and so I had much of my schooling under British colonialism. In the era of decolonisation, I took degrees (in History and Education) in three Commonwealth universities, in the Caribbean, Hong Kong and Australia, and worked and studied as an educator in the United Kingdom, Jamaica, Grenada, the United States and, finally, Australia. I have 'lived' comparative education, as a student, a teacher and a researcher in various post-colonial and multiethnic settings. In this paper, I apply some insights from my own experience of the post-colonial condition to thinking about comparative education and how we teach it.

Race, Power and Cultural Complexity

The concepts of race, power and cultural complexity are the ones that I will emphasise. My experience of teaching in many post-colonial countries increasingly confirms my view that students of education need to understand post-colonial perspectives to make sense of their studies. These perspectives, deconstructing the manifestations and implications of Eurocentrism and racism in the post-colonial world, should frame the study of education and its specialised components. How racism has distorted knowledge, socio-cultural relationships and economic patterns is clearly visible in the curricula and structuring of educational institutions worldwide, and there is a moral imperative for teachers, students and other citizens to challenge them. As educators, we can learn from comparing how the curriculum of 'whiteness' (read 'White supremacy') is implemented in different countries (Churchill 1995; Hage 1998; Kincheloe et al. 1998; McKay 1999; Hickling-Hudson and Ahlquist 2003) – and even more importantly, how it is being challenged and overcome. These are the two faces of power, viewed as both a negative and positive force, working dialectically on and through people, its operations both enabling and constraining (Aronowitz and Giroux 1985: 216). This complex study would be well placed in comparative education, a field which combines historical and sociological macro-views of education as a global system as well as finely textured analyses of education at its micro-levels (Bray and Thomas 1995).

My years of university teaching in Queensland, Australia, where intercultural perspectives are not well developed, have made me aware of the fact that talking about race is often highly unwelcome to people of European descent. Sarah White (2002) points out that "talking about race in development is like breaking a taboo". Development assumes colour-blindness. There is no analysis of development policies by race, as there is by gender, and there are few programmes of anti-racism training. The silence about race, White points out, is a silence full of implications. It both masks its centrality to the development project, and emphasises this centrality. Although 'race' has no biological validity, it is a socio-historical construct which is an important aspect of identity, as well as being a principle influencing particular types of social structures, transforming physical space, the human body, consciousness, institutions, and contributing to the concept and techniques of modernist development. The central facts in development are international capital, regional power blocs and the position of nation states, but its metanarratives and its assumptions of superiority have racial undertones. Development, colonial power, and racist explanations depict 'otherness' in a manner which eschews and escapes the task of making sense of other worlds (Omi and Winant 1986; Mundimbe 1988; White 2002).

Edward Said (1994: xxix) points out that "Partly because of empire, all cultures are involved in one another; none is single and pure, all are hybrid, heterogenous, extraordinarily differentiated, and unmonolithic."

Much Western thought and practice ignores global hybridity. This omission contrasts with intercultural ideas which reflect the diversity, complexity and sophistication of cultures. Many people genuinely ally themselves in the struggle against the evils of racism. But despite improvements, anti-racist legislation and practice have failed to put an end to the web of disadvantages visited upon many people because of their skin colour. Furthermore, White-dominated societies are experiencing a racist backlash against multiculturalism and anti-racism (Mikaere 2001). The situation calls for teachers to face the complexities of challenging the manifestations of continuing racism – discrimination, exclusion, cultural suppression and other forms of injustice.

Post-colonial theory explores this complex patterning of racism and the range of responses it engenders. 'Post-colonial' in the sense used here does not, of course, mean to suggest that we have finished with the colonial. It refers to the thinking that deconstructs the operations of Eurocentrism in colonial and neo-colonial polities, and that develops alternative analyses and propositions based on different ways of knowing (Masemann 1990; Hall 1996; Willinsky 1998; Tikly 2001; Hickling-Hudson et al. 2004; Ninnes and Burnett 2004). The themes of the present remarks draw implications from the knowledges of indigenous and colonised peoples suppressed and hidden by the hegemony of Eurocentric education. They stimulate comparison of the neo-colonial education systems which were part of the European empires. They emphasise flesh-and-blood issues of how education affects people, and provide thoughts about the elements of cultural complexity that Western educators need to take on board in order to collaborate in developing the human face of comparative education.

Uncovering Hidden Knowledge

Aboriginal Australian ways of knowing have opened my eyes, and those of at least some of my students, to the richness, complexity and importance of a world-view which is strikingly different from the modernist Western one. An illustration of this comes from the Australian Aboriginal painting entitled 'To Hold Our Earth Firmly', and the ideas of Australian Aboriginal people of the Pintupi nation which produced this painting. It is in the style of dense dots and symbols arranged in swirling patterns and earth-colours characteristic of the art styles of Aboriginal peoples of Australia's central desert region. The story of the painting is publicised in the book by Kevin Keeffe *From the Centre to the City* (1992). Keeffe explains that the artists, who were also schoolteachers, collectively produced the painting and in 1989 brought it thousands of miles from their Central Australian homeland to the capital, Canberra. Attending a conference on education there, they presented the painting as their 'paper'. In that action, they disrupted the norms of presenting a written paper, and challenged the White, Anglo-Australian audience to engage with the message of the painting in a manner different from anything they had experienced before.

I have used this painting and this story as a method of getting my Australian students to encounter, most of them for the first time, the philosophically and artistically sophisticated knowledge and skills of Australian indigenous peoples. I start the class by presenting to them a photo of the painting from Keeffe's book, explaining how the artists used it at the education conference. Then I give them the key which explains how to decode the highly complex symbol system of the dots and lines and their juxtaposition in the canvas. In small discussion groups, the students work out the message of the painting. When the students have exchanged their interpretation of the painting, I present to them the interpretation of it given by the Pintupi artists themselves, as told by Keeffe. The painting tells a story of the disruption of the integrated traditional philosophy and culture of the Pintupi people after they were forced by White Australians to live in sedentary settlements where British education was imposed in the 1950s. White newcomers ruled the schools and the elders were stripped of their traditional role of teaching the young. By the 1970s some adults and children had learnt the negative lessons of alcoholism and petrol-sniffing. In the 1980s there was improvement in that some Pintupi teacher aides were allowed to help the White teachers in the school, and gradually took on more responsibilities, but the elders with their community and traditional knowledge were still excluded.

The painting puts forward the vision and hope that in the future, the school would become "an integral part of the community in a balance determined by the older men and women: those who 'hold the earth firmly'", while the artists will be the teachers who carry out their "professional and kinship responsibilities of holding and looking after the students in the school" (Keeffe 1992: 28).

Students are both fascinated and shocked, because the Pintupi explanation of the painting is so much deeper, so much more complex and complete than the thin and superficial interpretation that they, the students, tend to produce in their discussion groups. Over the decade in which I have taught this lesson, I have found it by far the most effective method of stimulating White Australian students to respect indigenous Australians as their cultural equals, rather than as victims of history to be pitied, defended or despised. For the first time, students are faced with a knowledge system that is different from the Anglocentric system in which they have been socialised. This disrupts their preconceptions. In discussion, they acknowledge not only that the painting is aesthetically beautiful, but also that the Pintupi knowledge system represented by the artwork is highly sophisticated, succinct and 'literate' in the use of symbols to convey thought-provoking messages.

The students are also impressed by the creative and passionate challenge posed by the artists to the conventional organisation of education, and of the Anglo-Australian conference. They are intrigued by the idea of Aboriginal schoolteachers challenging high-status White delegates to 'read' and engage with the social critique of the painting. For White Australian student teachers to articulate these insights is a step forward, since their socialisation and education has not disposed them to think in these positive ways about the indigenous peoples from over 400 language groups who inhabited their country for an estimated 40,000 years before the arrival of Europeans.

I ask my students to consider indigenous intellectual achievements not only in Australia but also in the Americas (see Weatherford 1988; Churchill 1995) as a way of advancing the idea of post-colonial engagement with unfamiliar knowledge that can challenge and disrupt scholarly conventions of Eurocentrism. This uncovers many layers of cultural dilemmas including the conventions of access to knowledge and the ongoing problem of its appropriation and commodification by Western interests (Morgan 2003). If social class and development economics are the central 'tropes' of comparative education, a post-colonial perspective that recognises and engages appropriately with hidden knowledges adds important insights to any socio-economic analysis of education.

Racism as Violence, Dispossession, Desire ... and Resistance

Mies and Shiva (1993) depict modernist development as a process of violence, dispossession and desire. We can depict racism in education in the same way. It is a process of cultural, intellectual and physical violence which strips its targets of their dignity and dispossesses them of their culture and resources. The dispossession that peoples of non-European ethnicities suffered under colonialism still shows in the patterns of poverty and cultural suppression throughout the world. But as well as shaping identities, subjectivities, and structures, racism also engenders challenge, desire, ambivalence, complicity and a range of other responses. Such issues of race, neo-colonial development and cultural identity are being grappled with all over the post-colonial world. The way in which I understand them stems from my double location in Australia and the Caribbean.

My teaching and research have involved me dialectically in the struggle for recognition of the vital global role of the knowledges and work of formerly colonised peoples, and in the racialised education structures that continue as a legacy of colonialism. School students are often subjected to a callously ethnocentric version of knowledge, as I have observed with colleagues when visiting schools in both Australia and the United States (Hickling-Hudson and Ahlquist 2003: 69). In my attempt to prepare student teachers to counter this, I provide them with the opportunity to study how systemic institutional racism continues to locate disproportionate numbers of 'Blacks' at the bottom of multiracial societies, the racialised discourses which characterise different kinds of curriculum texts, and which perpetuate personal insults such as those drawing on 19th-century imagery to call dark-skinned people 'gorilla', 'nigger', 'boong' or 'blackie'. I and my family have been the target of these insults, a reminder of the emotional violence that indigenous Australians have to live with daily. In the 1990s, the people of a rural town in Australia wanted to name a new football stadium the 'Nigger Brown' stadium in honour of a long-dead local sporting hero (blond and blue-eyed) whose surname 'Brown' had led his friends to nickname him 'Nigger'. The outrage this stadium name provoked among indigenous and other Australians led to acrimonious debate, but eventually to the withdrawal of the name.

Student teachers debate with each other as to whether there is anything wrong with such a name for a public place. Some think there is not, because after all, it was the man's nickname! Some are indignant, while others do not see as objectionable the conflation of the term 'Black' as a designation for people and an epithet of negativity, as in a 'black' mood, day, film, deed, thought, Friday, market or economy. After all, they say, words have multiple meanings, and this usage of 'black' is traditional in English. This attitude is demonstrated with depressing regularity in everyday talk and in newspapers. Even a prestigious national daily paper can unselfconsciously, on the same page, juxtapose an editorial column headed "Don't Close the Lid on Black History" and a letter headed "A Black Day for Yorta Yorta People" (*The Australian* 2002). Yet racism is not the only component in culture, and there is also much to celebrate in the unique intercultural creations and relationships of Australia's post-colonialism. As in any culture, students learn as much from uncovering these complexities as they do from thinking about the continuing negativities that have to be challenged. Essential to the macro-understanding of globalisation is recognising that "the 'I' is being challenged in crucial ways. Before we recognise the 'Other', we have to know ourselves well" (Stromquist 2002: 2; see also Fox 2003).

As a young graduate, I chose what seemed like a contradiction for a highly qualified person in my society – to go and teach in very poor areas. Searing social disparities marked the contrasts between the elegantly well-resourced Jamaican elite schools that were the only schools I knew throughout my youth, and the impoverished schools in which as a young adult I taught (in the United Kingdom and Jamaica) and which, as a teacher–educator, I later encountered in my supervision of the practicum of student teachers. The dissonance between being caught up in some of the struggles of daily life for the impoverished and oppressed, and my elite education as a middle-class and Anglicised child of the British Empire, had a powerful effect on me. Recently, I rediscovered the diary which I kept during my years teaching at a Jamaican comprehensive high school to which the children of the poor were relegated. The following paragraphs draw from it, highlighting the interrelation of race, class, dispossession and challenge in countries emerging from colonialism.

Poverty was at the basis of many of the problems at the school. There were different degrees of poverty, but for many students it meant being hungry throughout the day, and being unable to buy sufficient numbers of the schoolbooks and materials that were required. The government introduced a programme of free school lunches to help children whose families could prove that they needed this help. In my homeroom class of 40 students, 10 were signed up for school lunch. The rest were able to bring 40 cents a day to buy snacks at the school canteen. The teachers raised money to provide a breakfast programme, but funds were scarce and irregular, so breakfast was minimal, providing only a few of the neediest students with a milky drink and some bread to start the day.

Some family situations were dire. Rosalie, one of my 16-year-old students in the top stream, missed school for several weeks during the year of her school-leaving exams. When she returned, we learnt that her absence stemmed from the necessity for her, as the eldest sibling, to look after her younger brothers and sisters while her mother had been committed to the mental hospital for medical treatment. Her father was absent, contributing little or nothing to the household. She had to go to various relatives and friends in turn begging them for a minimum of daily food for the family. She had no money to pay the expensive entry fees for her school-leaving exam (the British General Certificate of Education, 'O' Level). Her despair and tears cut to the heart. Even though some teachers clubbed together and paid exam entry fees for her and a few others, this did not solve her pressing problems. She did not know when her mother would fall ill again, making it necessary for her once again to drop out of school. She could not afford textbooks, and had already missed so much tuition that it was unlikely that she would be able to pass the exams. She had no guarantee of eating regularly, since her mother, due to her illness, had lost the job she once held. There was no state welfare system to assist families in this sort of crisis. The charitable payment of exam fees is a drop in the ocean, for how many youngsters can teachers help, and how to make decisions to help one rather than another? Most of the students needed financial help. Many could not afford the exam entry fees. Another student in my school-leaving exam class, a 16-year-old whose parents had long abandoned him, survived in the same precarious way as Rosalie had done, by asking for food from a different friend or relative each day. He was able to pay his exam fees by 'hustling' on the streets, earning small amounts of money by working in odd jobs. This option was not open to girls. Cases abounded of students living on the edge of daily hunger and precariousness.

Impoverishment meant not only hunger and the inability to meet educational costs, but sometimes lack of basic health care. Several of the students I taught were reading so close to the page that they obviously needed glasses, but with no state programme of eye care, there was no possibility of getting them. I contacted some of my friends in Jamaica and in the United States and asked them to raise money to contribute towards a programme for funding optometrist tests and glasses for the children. They were generous, but their contributions could only provide a handful of students with the glasses they needed. It was then that I was struck by the full realisation of the obscenity of situations that make charity necessary. Forcing people to depend for their basic human rights of food, health care and education on the irregular goodwill of the relatively wealthy is simply cruel, inhuman and unacceptable. The targets of this abuse have every right to fight to better their condition, and perhaps it is only they who can effectively lead this fight. It was a watershed moment in my political understanding and development.

Accompanying poverty was the inadequate quality of the primary school background of most of the children who came into this school at age 12 or 13. Though most had been taught the basic 'three Rs', others had been so poorly taught, in conditions of such overcrowding, that they entered secondary school functionally illiterate and innumerate. Some never caught up. But some had been taught well, were placed in the top stream, passed their external exams, and against the odds of their background, went on to professional and other careers. I still meet some of my students today, adults with their own families and careers, who stop me in the street, on the beach, or on the campus of the University of the West Indies with 'Miss, don't you remember me? I was in your history class!'

In the programmes of educational restructuring, the colonial social class divisions of the society remained deep. The majority of students continued to be allocated to the neglected All Age government-funded schools, but some got the chance to go to the upgraded 'New Secondaries' which provided a vocational schooling to age 16. At the elite grammar schools catering for a small minority of the secondary school-aged population, curriculum programmes were geared towards the new external regional exams of much higher status set by the Caribbean Examinations Council (CXC). The status difference was symbolised in the school texts – printed locally on cheap newsprint for the New Secondaries, and glossily illustrated and printed by international publishers for the prestige schools. It was not until the 1990s, 30 years after independence, that the government in Jamaica started to lay the foundation for equalizing the curriculum throughout the high-school sector.

Neo-colonial schools contribute to emotional anguish and low self-esteem by battering students with assaults on their self-image and identity. When a Caribbean History curriculum was first introduced in the region, in the 1960s, the textbooks and examination questions reflected a colonial interpretation which continued through the 1970s and beyond. They were prepared by a combination of scholars from the United Kingdom and Caribbean thoroughly socialised in imperial history. Some questions required students to imagine that they were slave traders, and write essays setting out how they would organise the African slave trade, or from the viewpoint of sugar plantation owners explain how slaves would be used. None asked students to take the viewpoint of the African majority. It was the negative self-image of many of the youngsters that I taught that made me fully understand the damage being done by this kind of racialised neo-colonial discourse.

An important experience for me was learning how to recognise and name neo-colonial interpretations and how to contest them in the public arena. I collaborated with other teachers to write a series of newspaper articles entitled *Whose History?* which critiqued the new CXC examination syllabus in Caribbean History for perpetuating the forms and paradigms of the old British one. Challenges such as these led to changes, and the CXC curriculum for all subjects gradually became more epistemologically sensitive and reflective of the complexity of Caribbean history, culture, science and society. These Caribbean examinations are intellectually demanding and internationally recognised, and this has encouraged significant advances in curriculum design and textbook writing. But we need to reflect on the extent to which this new examination system contributes to stalling social progress with the ambivalence of desire for the old ways in which we have been socialised. It remains an elitist exam, and we should ask how far it clings to aspects of past colonialism in that it excludes ways of knowing other than those based on academic literacies, does not engage with the oralities and folk forms of our region, and acts as a gate-barring entry to all but those who can afford an expensive, middle-class high-school education and (still) costly exam fees. Curriculum, textbook and examination ideology should constantly be under scrutiny (King and Morrissey 1990), and this is an aspect of schooling that comparative educators can make visible.

Unsettling Neo-Colonial Education: Revolution, Reversal and Lagoon Flows

I have drawn on my experiences to illustrate the power dynamics in neo-colonial intersections of class and race, and to make the point that such situations still exist in some countries just as I encountered them many years ago. How difficult it is to shift these problems is indicated by several recent Caribbean research studies, including those of Evans (2001), Samms-Vaughan (2002) and Jules (2002). One of the problems of neo-liberal globalisation is that the type of economic growth engendered does not reduce poverty. According to UNICEF, one in four children in the Caribbean live in poverty. The following percentages of people were living below the poverty line between 1994 and 1997: Antigua 12%, Grenada 30%, St Lucia 25%, Jamaica 32%, Dominica 33%, Guyana 43%. This has a direct impact on reducing the capability of families to ensure that children can reach their potential (Ramsaran 2002). Many home and family factors stemming from poverty in Jamaica still prevent efficient utilisation of educational resources. Children may be financially unable to attend school, they may assist the family in earning an income rather than attending school, they may attend school but lack school materials to support learning, they may be too undernourished to learn, and their families may disintegrate under economic stress (Samms-Vaughan 2002). Other social problems, including the repressive and often violent nature of the conventional school, combine with poverty to render schooling problematic (Jules 2002; Evans 2001).

The problems of an under-resourced and inequitable education system abound. Yet, due to the efforts of Caribbean governments to achieve change with few resources, many aspects of education have been improved, though there are limitations to the improvements (Hickling-Hudson 2004a). The political, economic and educational systems in which we are enmeshed continue to bear the stamp of European colonialism even when we reform them. It will take more radical efforts than any we have yet seen to reshape systems and identities in ways that counter the racist, sexist and classist denigration of our colonial and neo-colonial histories (Willinsky 1998), and instead nurture social health.

The Grenada Revolution of 1979 to 1983 was a significant event in the history of educational change in the decolonising world. The movement had poisonous strands evidenced by the fratricidal fighting after a few years that led to the collapse of the revolution. But in spite of this and its crushing in 1983 by the United States, the sociopolitical and educational approaches forged by the people of Grenada and their supporters during those years are still important today. Educational change in Grenada illustrates many layers of the theme of cultural complexity and the difficulties of change. One aspect of the theme relates to the new insights in pedagogy that some educators developed by being introduced for the first time to the teaching of Paulo Freire. I was invited to be part of a teaching team assembled by Grenadian education leaders and Freire, who had agreed to work for a few weeks in the new revolutionary process. I have described the 2-week workshop of teachers led by Freire and its educational and political implications (Hickling-Hudson 1988). Mention of this great Brazilian educator reminds me of how unusual it is for educators from the English-speaking Caribbean, like myself, to work with Latin Americans, our separateness a legacy of the linguistic and cultural divide built into the region by its five former colonisers, Spain, Portugal, Britain, France and the Netherlands. The cultural and political richness of the experience of working with Freire and his colleagues from Mexico, Argentina and Columbia became a watershed in my development as an educator. The dialogic education method that he taught remains of major significance in giving both students and teachers voice and showing them ways of relating their education to the socio-political context.

As a teacher-educator and educational planner in Grenada, I gradually absorbed several other types of insights. I participated in and witnessed the efforts to reshape society and education along lines of social justice. Complexity characterised the model of education that the revolution was promoting. There was ambivalence in the strategies that creatively challenged racism and elitism, and yet continued to perpetuate the dogmatism of class-based assumptions. After the invasion by the United States, a series of elected Grenadian governments backed by aid and tutelage from the United States set about erasing programmes of the revolution. These regimes dismantled the Centre for Popular Education, which had organised adult literacy and continuing education. The university scholarships to Cuba and other socialist countries were discontinued. They stopped the curriculum-development process which had produced new readers for Grenadian children, developing their literacy in both Creole and English. They dismantled the National In Service Teacher Education Programme (NISTEP), which had started to provide education and professional training for the backlog of untrained teachers, 70% of the teaching body. The huge popular participation in political processes with their grassroots educational component was also eradicated (Hickling-Hudson 1989, 1995; Hickling-Hudson and Ahlquist 2003).

Yet the memories of these significant experiments remain in written and spoken accounts, and also in some programmes which were gradually restored in Grenada, for example, elements of in-service teacher education, and a resumption of the university scholarships to Cuba (Hickling-Hudson 2000b). The short-lived revolution of four-and-a-half years had delineated the goal of a qualitatively new type of education, and had taken initial steps towards it. Chris Searle's books have recorded the outpouring of the peoples' Creole voice in public poetry and discussion. The poetry in *Words Unchained* (Searle 1984) ranged over themes that explored many aspects of the revolution, including recognition of folk roots, articulation of the effort needed to push changes forward, assertion of women's equal contribution to national development, and a new sense of cultural pride and dignity. Comparative educators have been in the forefront of researching how post-colonial social movements such as those in China, Cuba, Nicaragua and Grenada grappled with the unsuitability of Eurocentric education, and their achievements as well as shortcomings in how they sought to reframe it (Carnoy and Samoff 1990; Arnove 1994).

There is much to add to the repertoire of educational change by returning to the ideas of some indigenous groups in Australia. Educational knowledge is unsettled and stretched by indigenous ways of thinking which challenge not only the curriculum, but the very shape and nature of the school. This is vividly shown by the dissonance in the experiences of a White educator, Michael Christie (2000), working in an indigenous community where schooling is now controlled by Aboriginal educators and community members. Christie, gradually absorbing some understanding of indigenous philosophies, came to see not only how powerful they were for learning, but also how they revealed the arrogance of the White Australian imposition of a narrow type of schooling. As he explains it, the Yolgnu philosophy of education, based on the concepts of '*Ganma*', '*Garma*' and '*Galtha*', departs fundamentally from the modernist Western school. *Ganma* symbolises an intercultural (Aboriginal and Western) learning situation, which is to the elders akin to what they see happening in a '*Ganma*', a lagoon within the mangroves where salt water coming in from the sea meets streams of fresh water coming down from the land. Each body of water has its own flows, and the lagoon is highly productive as a food source, just as each body of learning has its own logic and their meeting is highly creative and different from the originals.

The school should be like *Garma*, a public area for open ceremonies which everyone can participate in and enjoy. "Educationally Garma means the open forum where people can talk and share their ideas, differences can be talked through, and everyone can work to reach agreement" (p. 13). *Galtha* is a place where people from different territories assemble to make important negotiations, agreements and plans, and is also a process of meeting and negotiating. So in education, *Galtha* is "the nexus between plan and action, theory and practice" (p. 14).

The insights of this approach have much to teach us about the complex interplay of paradigms and cultures in the reshaping of education. Yolgnu philosophy resonates with, yet goes beyond the observations of McCarthy et al. (2003: 460, 461), that

> postcolonial cultural workers point to the limitations of monological and homogenizing approaches. They argue that culture and identity are the products of human encounters and the inventories of cross-cultural appropriation and hybridity ... [C]urricular knowledge should be an interdisciplinary product of heterogeneous sources, and pedagogy should be organised around the thesis of the constructed nature of all knowledge.

The exploitative practices of colonialism are manifest in the poor resourcing of education systems, the asymmetries and exclusions based on social class, race and gender, and the hegemony of mono-cultural curricula. The work of building alternatives is incipient and uneven. Drawing on concepts of 'race', power dynamics and cultural complexity in contexts of diversity and hybridity helps us to investigate the diverse and interacting systems of meaning in our decolonising world.

We hear much about development issues and how they affect education as a system, but not enough about post-colonial issues and how they affect the lives and learning of the students and teachers involved. Fruitful lines of research would explore the yearnings of the marginalised and their experience within traditional education, investigate the extent to which educational reform constitutes charity – a flimsy and temporary bandage over deep wounds, and show that changing education involves striving for curricular justice as much as for institutional and structural justice. Such research will lead us to the dialectical insight that the only way the marginalised will receive education justice is to fight for it, but that their fight is hindered by the exclusions they have suffered. The struggle for justice can best be carried on by alliances. I have learned how important it is to work collaboratively with educators, whatever their ethnicity, who are developing effective work to combat racism, sexism and other patterns of oppression (Hickling-Hudson 2004b).

Conclusion

Comparative education could carry out more research than at present (Broadfoot 1999; Crossley 2000) into how the education system works to exclude the majority of poor children and adults from excellent tuition, and of how this exclusion is compounded by cultural and racial oppression. Eurocentric education is stratifying and racist. It suppresses knowledge, distorts learning and persuades Europe and its diaspora of their putative superiority. The experience of education in the era of decolonisation indicate that socialisation in neo-colonial ideas of race is still hegemonic (see Ladson-Billings 1998; Singley 2002). Understanding how this works will help comparative educators to carry out critical and dialogic research and teaching to explore how education can be changed to promote social justice.

References

Aronowitz, Stanley, and Henry Giroux. 1985. *Education Under Siege: The Conservative, Liberal and Radical Debate Over Schooling*. Cambridge, MA: Bergin and Garvey.

Arnove, Robert. 1994. *Education as Contested Terrain. Nicaragua, 1979–1993*. Boulder, CO: Westview Press.

The Australian. 2002. Don't Close the Lid on Black History. 14 December: 20.

Bray, Mark, and R. Murray Thomas. 1995. Levels of Comparison in Educational Studies: Different Insights from Different Literatures and the Value of Multilevel Analysis. *Harvard Educational Review* 65(3): 472–490.

Broadfoot, Patricia. 1999. Stones From Other Hills May Serve to Polish the Jade of This One: Towards a Neo-Comparative "Learnology" of Education. *Compare* 29(3): 217–231.

Carnoy, Martin, and Joel Samoff. 1990. *Education and Social Transition in the Third World*. Princeton: Princeton Univ. Press.

Christie, Michael. 2000. Galtha: The Application of Aboriginal Philosophy to School Learning. *New Horizons in Education* 103 (November): 3–19.

Churchill, Ward. 1995. White Studies: The Intellectual Experience of U.S. Higher Education. In: *Beyond Comfort Zones in Multiculturalism: Confronting the Politics of Privilege*, ed. by Sandra Jackson and Jose Solis, 17–35. Westport, CT: Bergin and Garvey.

Crossley, Michael. 2000. Bridging Cultures and Traditions in the Reconceptualisation of Comparative Education. *Comparative Education* 36(3): 319–332.

Evans, Hayacinth. 2001. *Inside Jamaican Schools*. Kingston: University of the West Indies Press.

Fox, Christine. 2003. The Question of Identity From a Comparative Education Perspective. In: *Comparative Education: The Dialectic of the Global and the Local*, ed. by Robert Arnove and Carlos Torres, 133–145. Lanham, MD: Rowman and Littlefield Inc.

Hall, Stuart. 1996. When was the Postcolonial? Thinking at the Limit. In: *The PostColonial in Question*, ed. by Lidia Curti and Iain Chambers, 242–260. London: Routledge.

Hage, Ghassan. 1998. *White Nation. Fantasies of White Supremacy in a Multicultural Society*. Annandale: Pluto Press Australia.

Hickling-Hudson, Anne. 1988. Towards Communication Praxis: Reflections on the Pedagogy of Paulo Freire and Educational Change in Grenada. *Journal of Education* 170(2): 9–38.

———. 1989. Education in the Grenada Revolution, 1979–1983. *Compare* 19(2): 95–114.

———. 1995. Literacy and Literacies in Grenada: A Study of Adult Education in the Revolution and After, Ph.D. dissertation, University of Queensland.

———. 2000a. Caribbean Experiments in Education for Social Justice: The Case of Grenada. In: *Social Justice and Third World Education*, ed. by Timothy Scrase, 133–162. New York: Garland.

———. 2000b. The Cuban University and Educational Outreach: Cuba's Contribution to Postcolonial Development. In: *Local Knowledge and Wisdom in Higher Education*, ed. by Robert Teasdale and Zane Ma Rhea, 187–208. London: Pergamon.

———. 2003. Beyond Schooling: Adult Education in Postcolonial Societies. In: *Comparative Education: The Dialectic of the Global and the Local*, ed. by Robert Arnove and Carlos Torres, 229–251. Lanham, MD: Rowman and Littlefield Inc.

———. 2004a. Towards Caribbean 'Knowledge Societies': Dismantling Neo-Colonial Barriers in the Age of Globalisation. *Compare* 34(3): 293–300.

———. 2004b. Educating Teachers for Cultural Diversity and Social Justice. In: *Planning For Diversity: Education in Multi-Ethnic and Multicultural Societies*, ed. by Gudrun Hernes and Michaela Martin, 270–307. Paris: International Institute for Education Planning.

———, and Roberta Ahlquist. 2003. Contesting the Curriculum in the Schooling of Indigenous Children in Australia and the USA: From Eurocentrism to Culturally Powerful Pedagogies. *Comparative Education Review* 47(1): 64–89.

———, Julie Matthews, and Annette Woods. 2004. Education, Postcolonialism and Disruptions. In: *Disrupting Preconceptions; Postcolonialism and Education*, ed. by Anne Hickling-Hudson, Julie Matthews and Annette Woods, 1–16. Flaxton, Australia: Post Pressed.

Jules, Vena. 2002. Survivors of the Experience: The First Three Years of Schooling in Trinidad and Tobago. In: *Children's Rights: Caribbean Realities*, ed. by Barrow Christine, 148–170. Kingston, Jamaica: Ian Randle.

Keeffe, Kevin. 1992. *From the Centre to the City. Aboriginal Education, Culture and Power*. Canberra: Aboriginal Studies Press.

Kincheloe Joe, Shirley Steinberg, Nelson Rodriguez, and Ronald Chennault (eds.) 1998. *White Reign: Deploying Whiteness in America*. New York: St. Martin's Press.

King Ruby, Hope, and Michael Morrissey. 1990. *Images in Print Bias and Prejudice in Caribbean Text Books*. Mona, Jamaica: Institute of Social and Economic Research, University of the West Indies.

Ladson-Billings, Gloria. 1998. From Soweto to the South Bronx: African Americans and Colonial Education in the United States. In: *Sociology of Education: Emerging*

Perspectives, ed. by Carlos Torres and Theodore R. Mitchell, 247–264. New York: SUNY Press.

Masemann, Vandra. 1990. Ways of Knowing: Implications for Comparative Education. *Comparative Education Review* 34(4): 463–473.

McCarthy, Cameron, Michael Giardina, Susan Harewood, and Jin-Kyung Park. 2003. Contesting Culture: Identity and Curriculum Dilemmas in the Age of Globalization, Postcolonialism and Multiplicity. *Harvard Educational Review* 73(3): 449–465.

McKay, Belinda (ed.). 1999. *Unmasking Whiteness: Race Relations and Reconciliation*. Nathan, Brisbane: Griffith University.

Mies, Maria, and Vandana Shiva. 1993. *Ecofeminism*. London: Zed Press.

Mikaere, Ani. 2001. Racism in Contemporary Aotearoa: A Pakeha Problem. In: *Indigenous Peoples, Racism and the United Nations*, ed. by Martin Nakata, 131–152. Altona, Australia: Common Ground Publishing.

Morgan, Douglas. 2003. Appropriation, Appreciation, Accommodation: Indigenous Wisdoms and Knowledges in Higher Education. *International Review of Education* 49(1–2): 35–49.

Mundimbe, Valentin Y. 1988. *The Invention of Africa. Philosophy and the Order of Knowledge*. Gnosis: Indiana University Press.

Nettleford, Rex. 1978. *Caribbean Cultural Identity: The Case of Jamaica. An Essay in Cultural Dynamics*. New York: William Morrow.

Ninnes, Peter, and Gregory Burnett. 2004. Postcolonial Theory in and for Comparative Education. In: *Re-Imagining Comparative Education. Postfoundational Ideas and Applications for Critical Times*, ed. by Peter Ninnes and Sonia Mehta, 181–200. New York: RoutledgeFalmer.

Omi, Michael, and Howard Winant. 1986. *Racial Formation in the United States*. London: Routledge.

Ramsaran, Dave. 2002. Globalisation and Children's Rights in the English-speaking Caribbean. In: *Children's Rights: Caribbean Realities*, ed. by Christine Barrow, 171–188. Kingston: Ian Randle Press.

Said, Edward. 1994. *Culture and Imperialism*. New York: Vintage Books.

Samms-Vaughan, Maureen. 2002. The Caribbean Child's Right to Education. Educational Provision Socio-Economic and Family Factors and School Achievement. In: *Children's Rights: Caribbean Realities*, ed. by Christine Barrow, 132–147. Kingston: Ian Randle Press.

Searle, Chris. 1984. *Words Unchained. Language and Revolution in Grenada*. London: Zed Books.

Singley, Bernestine. 2002. *When Race Becomes Real. Black and White Writers Confront their Personal Histories*. Chicago: Lawrence Hill Books.

Stromquist, Nelly. 2002. Globalization, the I and the Other. *Current Issues in Comparative Education 4(2)*, http://www.tc.columbia.edu/cice/edintro42.htm, accessed 9 September 2004.

Tikly, Leon. 2001. Post-colonialism and Comparative Education Research. In: *Doing Comparative Education Research: Issues and Problems*, ed. by Keith Watson, 245–264. Oxford: Symposium Books.

White, Sarah. 2002. Thinking Race, Thinking Development. *Third World Quarterly* 23(3): 407–419.

Weatherford, Jack. 1988. *Indian Givers. How the Indians of the Americas Transformed the World.* New York: Fawcett Columbine.

Willinksky, John. 1998. *Learning to Divide the World: Education at Empire's End.* Minneapolis: University of Minnesota Press.

The Author

Anne Hickling-Hudson teaches international and intercultural studies in education at the Queensland University of Technology, Brisbane. As the immediate past President of the World Council of Comparative Education (2001–2004), she coordinated the council representing comparative education societies from over thirty countries and led the organisation of the 12th World Congress of Comparative Education. Her research interests focus on race relations and policy analyses of education, and on intercultural and postcolonial approaches in comparative and international pedagogy.

Contact address: School of Cultural and Language Studies in Education, Queensland University of Technology, Kelvin Grove, Queensland, 4059 Australia. E-mail: a.hudson@qut.edu.au.

AUTHOR INDEX

SUBJECT INDEX